MY WAR

Long Range Reconnaissance in the Highlands of VIETNAM

By

David L. Bristol

xulon
PRESS

Copyright © 2015 by David L. Bristol

My War
Long Range Reconnaissance in the Highlands of Vietnam
by David L. Bristol

Printed in the United States of America.

Edited by Xulon Press

ISBN 9781498428866

www.xulonpress.com

Table of Contents

Introduction

MY WAR: Long Range Reconnaissance in the Highlands of Vietnam

I lost my student draft deferment in the spring of 1968 and joined the Army. After a failed attempt at flight school, I was assigned to the infantry. That is how my journey started.

After my training I was assigned to K Company 75th Infantry (Ranger) in the Central Highlands of Vietnam. I served my tour and returned home to school and family and tried to forget the war. I was blessed with a great family and success in my career. In the summer of 2004, I was diagnosed with PTSD and my oldest son asked me to write about my experiences. What follows is the result.

What you read is what I remember. I have made a sincere effort to be accurate, but the work is not intended to be a history. Some of my recollections match well with historical documents while some do not. I know that others will have different recollections of the events.

Finally, what you read is written for four reasons. I want to try to answer the questions that Derek had about the war. I want to honor the men who served in K Company. Writing seems to be a healing thing for me. Finally, I hope that readers may find a way to listen to the stories of those they love, and that some of the Veterans will be able to share some of the stories that they have held inside for so long.

Dedication

This book is dedicated to all of the men who served with the 4th Infantry Division LRRPs, Brigade LRRPs and K Company 75th Infantry Rangers, and to all who love them. God bless you all.

Acknowledgments

There are many people to thank for making this work possible. First, thank you to the Lord for his protection physically, mentally, and spiritually during those months in Vietnam. To my son, Derek, who first asked me to "write down a few things" about Vietnam. To Paige, Mandy and Brian, who sort of piled on, making it hard not to continue. To my late wife, Ethel, who dealt with most of my difficulties and saw few of the results of her love and support. To my parents, who suffered while I was in Vietnam, and were so strong in their support after I came home. To my wife, Janet, whose strength, faith, and encouragement were needed in some very difficult times. To Chaplain Stanley Millard and his wife for the early grounding in my Christian faith. To Gary Dolan, Dr. Ted Okey and Ken Harton for editing help. To the men of the 4th Infantry Division and Brigade LRRPs and the men of K Company 75th Infantry Rangers, thank you for your service and for teaching me so many lessons about courage, loyalty, and sacrifice. And finally, to the men of these units who did not come home, and to the families who dealt with that loss, thank you, and God bless you all.

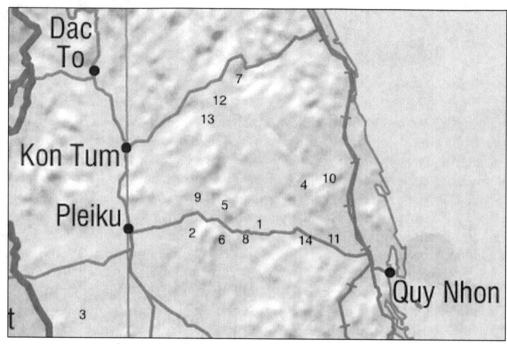

IMPORTANT LOCATIONS IN THE AREA OF OPERATION
(CIA PUBLIC DOMAIN MAP)

1. An Khe and Camp Radcliffe
2. Red Shorts Mission
3. LZ (Landing Zone) X-Ray and Chu Pong Massif
4. LZ Hardtimes and the Vinh Thanh Valley
5. Mang Yang Pass and French graves
6. Running the Gun line Mission
7. POW rescue mission
8. Schuller and LZ Action
9. LZ Blackhawk
10. LZ Snipe
11. QL (Highway) 19
12. Water falls
13. LZ Hooper
14. An Khe Pass (The Hair Pin)

CHAPTER 1

Why?

————————— ❖ —————————

I n any tough situation, humans seem to want to know why things happen the way they do. Seldom are we able to answer that question. I have come to believe that much of my military experience had a purpose. I was not content at home. I was not sure why. I thought I wanted to be recognized, respected, and well thought of. I was self-centered. I had no real confidence in myself. I was able to accomplish some good things, but they did not seem to satisfy me.

I started school and wrestled at Mesa Junior College, but it was not enough. So, to make a long story short, I quit school and soon found myself in the Army. I failed at flight school and ended up in Advanced Infantry Training in Fort Gordon, Georgia. On a cold day in February, we were offered a choice of going to a church meeting or some other outdoor activity. In February, in Georgia, in an ice storm, you should take the warmer choice, and I did. I really thought I was just going there to stay warm.

The evangelist's name was Larry McGill and I accepted Christ that day. I recall walking back to our barracks that night, thinking, "I wonder if this is another of my false starts? Will this really last?" I also remember feeling a huge burden lift from my soul. Over the next three months, I was taught more of the Truth. Chaplain Millard was my teacher in NCO school, and then I went to Ranger school.

Looking back on the whole series of events, I can see a reason for all of it. The day I accepted Christ in that Quonset hut at Camp Crockett was the single most important day of my life. What happened there changed me. It changed my life path and my future. It affected how I acted in Vietnam, it formed me for my later career in education, and it probably saved me from many errors and sins that might well have crippled me forever. I am not sure that would have ever happened had I stayed in school. I was far too focused on what others thought of me to make that kind of change.

Whatever the reason, there is no doubt in my mind that those years were the second most critical years of my life, in terms of forming me into who I am today. Only the influence of my parents was greater. It was there, in their home that I learned of the gospel and of the saving grace of Jesus. What they gave me was the key to my recognizing what Larry McGill had to say.

I would like to be able to say that from that day on I was the model of Christian virtue. I can't. I would like to say that I never failed. I can't. What I can say without any reservation is that that decision to accept the gift of grace offered so freely has made my life much more than it would have been had I never accepted the invitation that day. Perhaps a war was the only way to get my attention! Maybe that is the answer to the question: Why?

CHAPTER 2

Untold stories.

———————◆———————

Make no mistake about this: I am proud of the men who served in the 4th Infantry Division LRRPs (Long Range Reconnaissance Patrol) and Rangers. We were, and still are, a remarkable group of men. We did some unbelievable things, suffered in unimaginable ways, and sacrificed more than even we recognized. We were good men, but not perfect men. We, like all men in all situations, failed at times. I was one of those men.

Those who were in Vietnam with me will recognize that there are stories that I have not told, events that I have not talked about, and things that I did that I have not mentioned here. There are many reasons for that. At a reunion, one of our most respected NCOs said, "Some things are best left in Vietnam." He is a wise man and I have left some things there for that reason. Some stories are not mine to tell, some are too painful to tell. There are some that do not need to be told to accomplish the purpose of this work.

Some stories have been told in other books by far better writers than I. There are many books about the men who served in the LRRP/Ranger units of Vietnam. The Internet is full of documentary information, videos, and stories. Some are very good and some are very specific to K Company. Several authors from the unit have published great short stories on the web. There is a good Facebook site where you can, with an invitation, read the musings of my unit buddies.

Some things that I did in Vietnam are far too personal, far too painful for me to share in so public a forum. I am not trying to create a persona that did not exist in Vietnam. I know not to BS my K Company brothers. They are not a group that would take that lightly, nor would they be slow to call the bluff.

I have not told some stories because I have the same respect for them. I have some things that I would like to forget. I cannot cross that line with others.

Finally, there are things that are mixed up in my memory. I have discovered several missions that I thought were my own and were not. There is a mixing of missions that I heard about, read about, or talked about. I know for sure that I have forgotten some things. My recall is flawed, fragmentary, and full of contradictions.

I am not writing a history. What I have attempted to do here is to provide a small window into the life of those who served in the 4th ID LRRP and Ranger units. I have selected those things that I recall, those things that I think may be of interest, and those things that I can write without causing undue embarrassment to me or to my fellow soldiers. I was certainly not perfect, not without fault nor failure. Some things that do not appear here fall into the category of "best left in Vietnam."

CHAPTER 3

Training for My War

❖

I had no intention of becoming an infantryman, let alone a Ranger, when I joined the Army. I joined in June of 1968 to fly helicopters. I don't remember much about that time. I had convinced myself that I had failed at school, failed at wrestling, and that I wanted to fly in the military. I did have an interest in flying and I had flown a few times as a kid. I enjoyed those times, and that seemed better than going in as an infantry soldier. What is clear to me now is that I wanted to be good at something. Why I failed at flying is still not completely clear to me, but I did. The Army had kept their end of the guaranteed training deal and could now do as they pleased with me! Here is how it happened.

BASIC TRAINING PHOTO

Basic Training

I took my basic training at Fort Polk, Louisiana. It was a hot, miserable time, but I did have some positive experiences there. I liked the physical challenge, I thrived on the structure, and I was able to do the training very well. It was nice to be good at something. Most memories of basic training have long since gone away, but four things come to mind about Fort Polk. First, we were located right across the street from the Brig and there was always noise, lights, and alarms at the place. Our Drill Sergeants used it to great effect. Second, we lived in old World War II vintage barracks that seemed pretty outdated to us at the time. We had to polish the floors and stand fireguard. Why those things remain and other seemingly more important things didn't is not clear. The third thing I recall about Polk was the violent thunderstorms. There were several of these storms and the lightning was unreal. At some point during the training, another company had some guys hit by lightning. I don't think anyone was killed, but it made for some uneasy days in the eight weeks I was there. The fourth thing was being left on guard duty at a golf course all night. Apparently they just forgot I was there. After I finished Basic Training my next assignment was flight school and I went straight to Fort Walters, Texas for flight training.

Flight School

What a shock! The barracks were new, very nice, clean, cool, and pretty much state of the art. The level of pressure on the Warrant Officer Candidates (WOC) was by orders of magnitude greater than Basic Training. Again, I seemed to fit in and even enjoyed the training. The ground school or preflight phase was very focused on the academics and on officer training. When we started to fly, some of the pressure was dropped, at least in the barracks. I did well in the academics and was among the first ten in my class to solo. I remember well the tradition of throwing the pilot candidates into the swimming pool after the first solo. I had a flight instructor, a huge man with red hair, who wore a spectacular handlebar moustache and would beat on my helmet if I messed up. He was a great pilot and most guys thought he was among the best, but I feared his tirades.

Something happened about halfway through the first phase and I failed a flight test. It was not a big deal, it happened and, like everyone, I was given a second chance. On my flight out to the training field, I entered the landing pattern from the wrong direction. I realized the error and managed to get it right the second time. The damage was done and I was shaken. I had to try to gather myself for the check ride and I failed again. Now I was in real trouble. I was called into the commander's office and told that I was close to "washing out" and "get your shit together or you will be gone". He gave me a weekend pass to relax and gather myself.

I took my third check ride the following Monday. I failed again! I was depressed and requested a hearing to reverse my dismissal. As I sat there and talked to the board of combat pilots, I knew I was never going to fly for the Army.

I managed to make it home on leave, but most of that time was a blur of emotion and disappointment.

Advanced Infantry Training

In the emotional time after flight school, I apparently volunteered for airborne training. I do not recall doing that. My next duty station was Fort Gordon, GA. I was shipped to a place called Camp Crockett for AIT (Advanced Infantry Training). Crockett was a training camp for airborne volunteers and a very primitive place. The barracks, if you could call them that, were Quonset huts with no insulation, no showers, or toilets! A pair of small kerosene-burning stoves provided the heat. These were supposed to work like an old-fashioned weed burner, heating the fuel to a vapor and then burning a hot, clean flame. They never worked right, required constant cleaning, and produced as much soot as heat. We cleaned the stovepipes by scooping dirt into the pipe and sliding it around inside. We would awaken each morning to a cold barracks and soot around our noses and mouths.

Toilets were a row of "port-a-potties" at the end of each row of barracks. They were frequent targets of sabotage. Someone apparently stole some C-4 plastic explosive and a detonator from training and blew one of them up. In 2010 I read some Internet posts recalling this or a similar incident. These toilets were quite a distance from the barracks, making access an ordeal in the cold. The showers were located at Leightner Pond, a considerable distance from the camp. It seemed like a long ways to walk, and lots of guys did not go there. It was at least a half-mile from the camp, maybe further. Once there, you were treated to a shower house located at the base of the dam that formed the lake. There was a heater of some sort for the water, but it never could keep up with the demand and the water was cold. The shower house itself was unheated. I think the water came directly from the lake. You could get clean, but you smelled like pond water afterwards. I doubt that we went more than once a week. It was a cold and miserable place to be sure.

Very little of the specifics of the training that we did there stand out in my mind. I do not recall the training cadre, any of the ranges, or even the mess halls. There was a chapel in the area, and that is where I became a Christian.

This was the only place I ever had anything stolen from me while in the Army. I lost a class ring and some other things while I was there. I learned later that this camp was an experiment of mixing some of the "good" kids with some of the "bad" kids. To what purpose, I do not know. I have heard stories of attacks, racial tensions and riots, and even rapes, but I don't remember those at all. I do know I was glad to get out of the place. It was closed soon after I left.

19

Near the end of this training, we were told about the Non-Commissioned Officer School and several of us volunteered. I was off to Fort Benning, Georgia the day we graduated.

NCO School

When I arrived at Fort Benning, I was taken directly to the Chapel Hill area and assigned to a company. I am sure that everyone thought I was totally nuts when I saw the barracks and was glad to be in such palatial accommodations. They were old WWII barracks that were well past their prime, but compared to Camp Crockett they were heaven. This was a whole new ball game in terms of the men who were there. They were a motivated and capable group. Every one of us knew where we were going and it kept us in sharp focus. The training was very good. Map reading, navigation, radio procedures, leadership, and much more kept us busy and going strong.

The instructors were almost all combat veterans who knew what we would face and took that to heart. It was rare that you did not see a CIB (Combat Infantryman's Badge) on the chest of an instructor, and it made an impression. It was during this time that I began to realize that I had found something that I could be good at, and it changed my outlook on life. I had dealt with some other issues and found a spiritual mentor while in NCO School. Chaplain Stanley Millard was a rock in my early Christian life. He and his wife, Dorothy, mentored many of us during that time. I was now free to pursue some goals and I did so with great intensity and confidence.

It was impossible to be in the Army at the time and not know about the Rangers, and the newly formed 75th Infantry. Every time you marched, there was a cadence call that started, "I wanna be an Airborne Ranger." You saw Ranger Tabs on cadre. The Ranger Training School was at Fort Benning. Some time in the course of NCO school we were given the opportunity to volunteer for this prestigious infantry school. It fit right into the sense of wanting to be something special. I knew I was going to Vietnam, and I wanted to go very well trained. I applied and was accepted. I was excited and way over-confident in myself, but off I went to become an Army Ranger.

Ranger School

I came to the Ranger training company and was immediately told that we would have to wait a few days for the class to form. We were assigned barracks and given a pass. The last words they said to us were, "Don't forget, in three days you will be in the toughest training the Army has to offer; don't screw around too much."

I had no intention of doing that, nor did my friend, Larry Bergman. We actually stayed in the area, working out and running, confident that we were more than ready for whatever they thought it took to make you a Ranger. We were soon to get a very rude introduction to reality.

The first week was almost all physical training. We ran and ran and ran. We went through confidence courses, which were a series of diabolical ladders, mud holes, and obstacles designed to reduce you to a pile of pulp, physically. The emotional pressure started immediately and never let up. Classes lasted late into the night. Sleep was a thing of the past, food might or might not be available, and we trained no matter what the weather. It became clear very quickly that the releases we had signed at the beginning of Ranger School were not just a formality. They were real.

Each of us was assigned a Ranger Buddy. It was a pairing specifically to help each man complete the course. At the beginning of the class, all rank was stripped from uniforms. It did not matter if you were an E-5 sergeant or an officer. You were now a Ranger candidate. After the first day, I recall thinking that it "It can't get any worse than today. I can make it." Every day for the next sixty days, I was wrong about the first part, but somehow managed to be right about the second. I cannot do justice to what it was like to go through Ranger School. The training was very good; the TAC officers were all Rangers and all combat veterans. They knew the path we would walk and they knew what it took to be a Ranger. They were very good at teaching the skills and they were not going to put a Ranger Tab on someone who did not measure up. The attrition rate was very high. I don't know the numbers, but I believe that less than one-third of those who started the class actually finished.

Parts of the school are indelibly etched in my memory. Much of it is lost in a haze of sleep deprivation. The Darby Queen, the ultimate physical challenge, was not as difficult for me as it was for my Ranger Buddy. I was small, and most of the course was suited to my strengths. My buddy was an officer who had played college football. He was a big man and the climbing and heights really got to him. Yet he made it and we went to the first patrolling phase together.

This part of the school taught basic patrolling technique and it was pretty much a twenty-four hour a day thing. If everything went as planned, you got one meal and two or three hours of sleep. It seldom went as planned and so you seldom slept or ate. At the end of this phase, we were all pulled into a single location and told that we would be trucked to Victory Pond the next day for the Darby Queen events. As was the case many times, that was just a ruse to see if we could adapt.

At some point in the middle of the night we were rousted out of our tents and told to pack up and be ready for a long forced march. I don't know how long it was, but I am sure it was at least ten miles. They had a truck follow the formation. If it caught you, they gave you a ride right out of Ranger School.

We left in the dark, carrying everything we had on our backs. I was doing okay, but my buddy was struggling. He was a powerful man who held his own at most everything else. He was not an endurance athlete and the truck was getting closer. I took some of his load and his rifle, hoping that it would be enough to allow him to get to the finish. He rallied and we made it with time to spare. He would return the favor later in the jungle phase, when he pulled my waterlogged rucksack and me out of the Chattahoochee River. I would have been gator bait for sure had he not been strong enough to pull me up the bank.

One of the most enduring images of Ranger School happened at the end of this march. As we finished, we could smell a hot breakfast in front of us. We were told we should go eat. That was a most welcome order. I found a place to drop my pack, and as I looked toward the chow line, I saw guys going through the line with their packs on. I was shocked that anyone could be that dumb. I slipped off the pack, looked at my Ranger Buddy, and stood up, sort of. I fell over and tried again to stand, with the same result. I had so accustomed myself to the load we carried that I could not walk without the load on my back. I slipped it back on and joined my "dumb" colleagues in the chow line.

The next part of training was near Dahlonega, Georgia. The mountain phase was difficult due to the steep terrain. The patrolling was relentless. The mountaineering training was good and rappelling was actually a nice break from the rest of the work. This area was good preparation for the mountains of the Highlands of Vietnam.

We were soon off to Eglin Air Force Base in Florida for the jungle phase. By this time we had little reserve, physically or emotionally. I recall most of this time very much like I recall the last few months of Vietnam: bits and pieces, detached and scattered, apparently real, but strangely out of focus. You had to pass a specific number of patrols and you had to pass a certain percent of your patrols to qualify as a Ranger and receive the Ranger Tab. Only those who have successfully completed the school can wear it. I was close to getting the required number while in the mountains and had only one or two to go when we got to Florida. I passed the first assignment that I was given and I knew that I was probably going to make it. I specifically remember thinking, "I can relax a bit." It nearly cost me my coveted Ranger Tab.

I was rotated back into the platoon to be a patrolling member for some other Ranger to lead. I dozed off during his briefing and a TAC officer saw me. He let us go about two hours into the patrol and then had the platoon Sergeant get "killed." Guess who he picked as the replacement. I had no idea what was going on and failed the patrol. It was a brutal lesson and I never forgot it. I got another short patrol a bit later and passed it.

The other event of the Florida phase that will never go away was being in the field when Hurricane Camille hit the coastline. We spent the night on the ground in ninety miles per hour winds and torrential rain. Finding any land that was not covered with water was difficult, and when we did, there were usually several types of snakes on the high ground. I do not know what happened after that night, although I suspect we just went right on with training.

Hunger was a given. I ate whatever I could find. Grubs and leaves supplemented the hit and miss C-rations, but at this point in the school, no one was going to worry about that. We were too close. I was in the middle of my last patrol, and was moving my platoon toward some objective when I fell and cut my thumb on a piece of brush. It was a perfect spear and it went right into the bottom of my thumb and deep into the meaty part of my hand. I was immediately declared Wounded in Action and someone else got the patrol. The TAC officer was concerned enough to have me sent to the aid station to have my hand cared for. I remember getting there and being given something to eat while they took care of the wound. It was getting late and they suggested that I stay the night and rejoin the patrol the next morning. I could sleep, eat, and go back later. I started to say yes, and then realized that I might never be able to go back the next day. I resisted their efforts to change my mind and returned to the platoon. The TAC looked at me, asked me if I was "Okay," and said, "You passed that last patrol. Go to the CP" (command post). Nothing else was ever said. I knew then that I had probably earned my Tab, but I did not relax this time.

We were soon pulled from the field and returned to some tin barracks. We were allowed to clean up and they had a big barbeque for us. I think everyone who was still in the class got a Ranger Tab. We graduated the next day and were given some time off. My Ranger Buddy and I shook hands and we never saw each other again. He limped off on a very sore leg and I left with an infected hand. But I had that Tab, I was a Ranger, I had done something special, and I knew it would affect me the rest of my life. It was at graduation that I first heard, "Once a Ranger, Always a Ranger."

Jump School

Jump School, unlike my previous training, was actually fun. We ran everywhere we went, and the physical training was not easy, but nothing really bothered most of us. I enjoyed the drop towers. These tall towers were used to pull trainees up about 300 feet and release them to experience the feel of a jump and a real parachute landing. The actual jumping was as much of a thrill as you would expect. Food was plentiful and we left there in great shape physically and brimming with confidence. I was soon on my way home on leave with orders for Vietnam in hand. I would soon get to see if my training was of any value!

In Vietnam

I arrived in Pleiku and was assigned to K Company. My Ranger training would be tested while serving as a LRRP, and I was pleased with the assignment. The men who had already served there would add much to the tried and true methods we would need. In K Company, much of our Standard Operating Procedure could be traced to the men who served earlier in the original LRRP units. These men created the tools that we used.

It is amazing now to look back and recall the often nameless, but dedicated and selfless men who worked so hard to train us. From basic training to Vietnam, each gave me something to help me get my men and myself home. I believe that some of my attraction to teaching was the result of the dedication of these men. Thank you, gentlemen, wherever you are.

CHAPTER 4

SSG Rick Williams

I met Rick Williams on my third day in Vietnam. As a boy, I watched my dad work on the farm and wondered if I would ever be able to measure up to him. I had the same feeling when I met Rick Williams. Rick was a soft-spoken, quiet man. He was a little older than most of the guys. He had a college degree in agronomy. I was assigned to Rick's team, and he knew I would probably take over his team when he went home, and he took great pains to train me.

From the moment he met me on the "Golf Course" as the Heliport at An Khe was called, he drilled me about map reading. "If you get lost, you probably get killed," was his rationale. Subtlety apparently was not one of his gifts. He was a fanatic about planning and had a two-page checklist that he used with every team member before every mission. He spent hours teaching me how to pre-plot artillery and how to get it in very close if needed. Later in my tour, on the <u>Red Shorts Mission, Chapter 20</u>, Rick's attention to detail would pay dividends.

Rick knew that you could live longer without food than you could without water and ammunition. He taught me to carry more of the latter and less of the former. He seldom carried M-16 ammunition on more than one mission. He used this as an opportunity to get extra weapons practice, and we fired nearly every round in practice after every mission.

He made me practice with the radio shackle codes until I could do the process fairly quickly. These codes, on a small card, were used to encrypt messages to be sent over the radio. They were slow at best, but Rick insisted that I get as fast as possible. Every team member had to be able to read the maps during a mission. Rally points were memorized, as were escape and evasion routes. Rick was a pain about these details of a mission, but I am convinced that his attention to detail saved lives.

Every pack, or "ruck" was loaded the same way every time out so that team members knew where everything was. First aid materials in each pack were in the upper right hand pouch. Frags (fragmentation grenades) on the web belt, right front, and spoons taped down with one wrap of green tape. Extra batteries for the two radios were in the top of the back pouch on the team leader's pack and on the assistant team leader's pack. In a firefight or other emergency, everyone knew where everything was and could get to it quickly. This attention to detail was the reason Rick had his list.

Radios received even more special attention from Rick. They were the only way to get help. They were carried a certain way. The radios were packed on the ruck so that everything but the radio could be dumped in an emergency. They were used only when needed. Before leaving on a mission they were checked and rechecked, cleaned and re-cleaned, covered with green tape. Handsets were covered with plastic if wet weather was a threat. More than once he refused to carry a PRC-25 radio, and returned it to the supply room when it failed to meet his standards. "If you can't talk to the choppers, or artillery, they can't help you." It did not take long to develop the same obsession with this critical communication tool. His list extended beyond just mission preparation as well.

He had similar ideas about how teams should conduct themselves in the bush. He was one of the team leaders who never allowed smoking in the field. He did not allow books to be carried, and only limited heating of food and water. He constantly looked for ways to camouflage everything we carried. He taped any metal with the ubiquitous green tape to prevent shining and to dampen any noise. He taped everything that might move and rattle. He made use of the soft bladder type canteens because they were quieter. One of the first things I had to do for Rick was to jump up and down with my pack on to see if it made too much noise.

He was the first to teach me to wash mission uniforms in Vietnamese soap or not to use soap at all. He said that the detergent made us smell different and that the North Vietnamese Army or Viet Cong (NVA or VC) might smell us. I considered this to be excessive, even for Rick, until I saw him detect an NVA soldier by smell alone. Heated meals were often prohibited for this reason. Rick used a system of hand signals that I used with my teams later. We could go for days without speaking if needed. He used squelch to answer radio calls without making a sound. This was not uncommon, but Rick did it all the time. The PRC –25 radios always broadcast a slight bit of static. When the handset was keyed, this squelch stopped, indicating that the operator had responded.

In the field, Rick was all business. He was respectful of my Ranger Tab, but not awed by it. He told me, "Be quiet, pay attention and do what you are told," on my first mission. He started teaching before we went out the first time. Night locations were selected with great care. Eat early, move, and then stop to listen for someone following you. Just before dark, move into the night location, doubling back on your trail so that anyone following would have to walk in front of you. Claymores (defensive anti-personnel mines) were placed at the last possible moment to prevent detection. The detonators were all shunted, safety on, and everyone knew where they were. If preparation was important, safety was an obsession.

Missions were always important to Rick. He understood that what we did was critical to the safety of soldiers other than ourselves. He never took short-cuts with the information we found. He took care of the team, but accomplished the mission as well. He believed the good LRRP mission meant, "Get in, do what you have to do and get out without anyone ever knowing you were there." As a result, creature comforts were not high on his priority list. The casualties of this philosophy were many. He never allowed his teams to make a tent from the poncho. We called these "hoochs".

You spent more time awake than asleep. You carried all your trash. If the mission was especially dangerous, you might carry your bodily waste until it could be disposed of safely. You covered your trail, always, no matter what. The only concession I ever saw him make for comfort was a bladder canteen that he used as a pillow.

Rick taught me to have good procedures and plans, to think things through but to be flexible. Both of these skills would save my teams and me in the months to come. He was a master teacher, the best at teaching these skills that I ever met. The fact that I remember very little about him except what he taught me about LRRP missions speaks volumes about the man. I know little about this gifted soldier except that his professionalism and dedication saved many lives. I suspect that it was indicative of a very intelligent man with a kind, compassionate heart who hated the war.

I am not sure when I last saw Rick, and I have not been able to make contact with him after he left 'Nam. It is probably because he does not want to be found, and I understand that. It is one of the greatest disappointments of my life that I have not been able to thank him personally. Until I can say it in person, this will have to do. Thank you, Rick! Thank you for what you did for us and for your service. You saved many lives. Welcome home, Brother.

In 2013, I made contact with several men who knew Rick during NCO school and two who served with him in K Company. I discovered that others shared my assessment of him as one of the best soldiers and LRRPs we ever knew. He graduated first in his NCO class and that explained the rank of E-6. He had not gone to Ranger School, but we all agreed that he was as good as anyone we had ever worked with. Our experience with Rick after Vietnam also matched up. No one had heard from him after he left K Company. All of this is consistent with my summation of Rick as a quiet, intelligent, kind soldier. I would also bet that most of the people who know him now have no idea that he was a LRRP or so respected as a soldier.

CHAPTER 5

The World According to John Wayne

A mericans have a well-developed sense of what is acceptable in a fight. That code carried over into my team's experience in Vietnam. One mission in early November, probably my second as a team leader, revealed one of these idiosyncrasies in a vivid way. Highway 19 or, QL 19 as it was called, was the only ground route from to Pleiku. There was a fuel pipeline that ran along the road to supply petroleum products to units further inland. Both the road and the pipeline were critical security concerns for the 4th Infantry Division. Our teams were often tasked with recon missions along the road. We would check out the areas one or two clicks (1,000-2,000 meters) from the road. These missions were often considered "soft" because larger NVA units did not often operate close to the road. Contacts were fairly common, however, because small Viet Cong units did operate near the road. They mined the road and blew up bridges and the pipeline at night. I hated these missions for several reasons. They were close to American units and that was dangerous if they saw you. I was concerned about the close proximity to many friendly Montagnards, the indigenous people in the area, and breaking contact was hampered by the proximity of both.

On this mission, we had movement for several nights. We needed to locate the people who were in the AO (Area of Operation) and determine what they were doing. Movement in this area was tricky because of the many open areas and the resulting lack of concealment. As we moved around in the scrub trees and grass, my point man was trying to skirt a clearing when he stopped and froze in a ready position. This caused all of the team to do the same. Carefully, slowly, I turned my head and looked over Bob's shoulder. Three men squatted around a small fire in front of a hooch, the typical grass hut, about thirty meters in front of us. At first I thought they were Montagnard woodcutters. They would wander into these areas at great risk to their lives. That thought was soon dispelled when I saw three weapons, one near each man.

Bob's first thought was to back out and avoid contact. Before that could happen, one of the VC saw Bob and instinctively reached for his weapon. Bob fired and apparently killed or wounded all three men. We immediately heard movement and voices, and we were forced to leave the area. We had stumbled onto a fairly large unit hidden in small bunkers. What followed was a nasty and dangerous running contact. This contact is detailed in Chapter 6, Running the Gun Line. Using artillery as cover, we moved to our extraction point, one of the firebases in the area and were pulled from the AO.

We returned to An Khe, where Bob supervised weapons cleaning and repacking while I debriefed at the brigade operations center. We cleaned up and went to the mess hall for a hot meal. There was the normal nervous chatter and bravado common after a contact mission. Bob withdrew from the discussion and I found him outside our barracks, alone and disturbed. He, like most Americans, struggled with the fact that he had killed someone. It was not easy for most of us and few ever really got used to it. This contact was different, more difficult than normal.

Deep in the mind and soul of Americans is the idea of a fair fight. Countless westerns and popular culture taught us that you never shoot a man in the back. Two of the VC killed that day had their backs to us when they died. Bob felt some deep betrayal of a "code of honor," no matter how silly it seemed to others. We talked long about this. His actions may well have saved the team from harm. His actions were proper in every way, and most LRRPs thought he had shown extraordinary courage and restraint in trying to back out of the situation.

In a few days, we were back in the bush, pulling more missions, and he had no choice but to put the mission behind him and move on. We talked about this mission many times later and he said it helped. Little did I know that our roles would soon be reversed.

CHAPTER 6

Running the Gun Line

————————◆————————

Despite the myth of being viscous and aggressive killers, most LRRP teams avoided contact if at all possible. There were several reasons for this. The most obvious one is that you didn't want to start a fight against a bigger unit, and with four men, a K Company team was almost always going to be in a fight with a bigger unit. A firefight meant you had been discovered, and that usually meant any information you had gained was going to be worthless very soon. Finally, a contact always meant your primary element of security, being undetected, was gone. You were no longer in control of the situation and the carefully orchestrated security of the team was no longer possible. For most team leaders, the worst situation to manage was a running firefight. A contact that required you to move, and fight as you moved, presented a myriad of difficulties. The chaotic nature of this contact has created very different memories for Bob and I.

These contacts were rare for me. I had only two, but they were memorable. In the last chapter I described a mission that led us into a running contact. Bob's first and best instinct was to back out of the area and try to avoid detection. When that failed, we had to break contact. Bob recalls bunkers in the area, I do not, but there were a substantial number of VC or NVA in the area, and they started to chase us. Enemy in this area were almost always VC and in groups of four to eight men. This group of soldiers behaved more like NVA, particularly in the aggressive way they pursued us. In breaking contact, the first thing a team did was a rapid fire drill. This was simply each team member in order firing a full magazine on full automatic, turning and running past the rest of the team while re-loading. The next man in line would do the same and each in turn would fire, run, and repeat this until some separation had been achieved. This sounds relatively simple, but to do it well, and safely, required considerable practice. In this situation, the open nature of the terrain made this tactic much less effective. We ran four or five of these cycles before we were able to find any real cover.

The second line of defense was the artillery. We always had pre-plots as we moved. These were locations that we marked on a map and sent to the supporting artillery batteries before we needed them. If a team made contact, the first rounds were called on a pre-plot. From this first round, usually a smoke round for safety, the TL (team leader) could adjust the HE (high explosive) rounds to the target as needed. Under the best of conditions, this was a tricky business. The big guns, like any gun, did not shoot in the same spot each time. Variations in the charges and heat in the tubes changed even the very accurate 105 mm guns point of impact. The slope of the terrain, wind, and even temperature could cause the impact points to change. Most of the time a team was sitting still, and adjusting the artillery was still somewhat tricky. Bringing it in close was difficult and dangerous. A running contact added further to the challenge.

When a team adjusted artillery, they used their own location as a point of reference. They would give a compass heading or direction and a distance from their location to the target. The artillery computed all of the required data to hit that spot. So the TL had to move or adjust the impact point by telling the guns to shoot right or left, further away or closer. "Right fifty, add fifty" from the TL to the guns meant shoot fifty meters right and fifty meters farther than your last shots. The team's adjustments were made on their line of sight to the target. These references were converted by the artillery to adjustments based on the gun line, a line from the guns to the target location. It worked well and all of our teams were skilled in its use. A running contact changed the rules.

The team's point of reference was always changing in a running contact. As the team moved, the distance and direction to the target changed. Of course, the targets were moving as well. In this situation, accurate adjustment became almost impossible. On this mission, we used a technique that Rick Williams had told me about, but cautioned me that it was dangerous and not to use it if I could help it. We were being pursued hard and I needed to get the rounds in close without hitting the team. We changed our direction of movement and "ran the gun line." This meant that we were running directly toward the guns and they were firing over our heads. The advantage to me was that I only had to adjust distance on the guns. As a team moved toward the guns, the TL had to keep track of the distance moved and "drop" the rounds an equal amount. If you were moving away, you only had to "add." This technique removed most, if not all of the left/right adjusting. That was no small thing for a TL who was trying to keep track of the team's location, to avoid areas too difficult or unsafe to navigate, coordinate arty, (artillery) gunships, extraction choppers, and to be sure that he knew where the "bad guys" were.

The danger was that the least predictable part of any artillery shot was the add-drop or the distance that the round would travel. This meant that any round-fired short was likely to fall on the team! This technique also required that a team know where the guns were, something that was usually not the case. In addition to that, the terrain had to allow you to move on that line, again very unlikely in the Highlands. On this mission we were in terrain that allowed it and we knew the guns were at LZ Schuler, an artillery fire support base in the area.

We had attracted the attention of a larger group of VC or NVA who were not at all interested in letting us go peacefully. They persisted in chasing us. I had an Air force FAC (Forward Air Controller) plane in the air that knew where we were and he could see the enemy soldiers who were following us. They were too close for us to get choppers in for extraction, which required the artillery to stop shooting while the choppers came into the area. Some of the NVA seemed to be trying to get in front of us as well. My solution to this dilemma was to use two batteries of 105s, one shooting pre plots in front of us as we ran, and the other adjusting behind us. The tactic worked and we were able to create some space between the team and the pursuing enemy soldiers. When we did get gunships on station, most of the enthusiasm for chasing our LRRP team seemed to fade away. When I recalled this mission later, I thought we had run about 600 meters. Bob White remembers it as much longer than that. Looking back, he was probably right. It was closer to 2,000 meters. To put that in perspective, we would often move less than that distance in three to four days.

I would have had at least three other people talking to me on my radio. I had artillery, the FAC, and my Zero (Platoon leaders call sign) talking to me. There might have been gunships and a command and control ship in the area. I was busy with them, and probably never was aware of the distance we traveled or the true ferocity of the contact. Bob would have been choosing the path we took, directing the point man or walking point himself. He would have been concerned with keeping the team's organic firepower working effectively. This probably accounts for his recall of bunkers and my failure to do so. It also accounts for a huge difference in our recall of the mission. He was face-to-face with all of the terrain problems. For me they were a line on the map, a compass heading that kept us on the gun line. He had to move around obstacles and possible ambush locations, see good paths, and avoid bad ones. He had to find the safe way through and keep an eye out for any threat. I never really worried about the artillery rounds that were hitting, because I knew if we were still moving, they were not too close. I was already adjusting for the next battery when those rounds hit. Bob and the other team members had no such comfort. They lived with each round passing over our heads, wondering if this was the short round that would get us! Other than the sound of a Huey, few other sounds evoke more emotion in LRRPS than the sound of artillery rounds passing overhead. Each team member would have known exactly where the rounds were and the threat they posed.

The physical battering the team was taking was astounding. Our packs would have been between sixty and eighty pounds, depending on the time we had been on the ground. We were literally running with these loads. The temperature was high, and this was the dry season, so we would have had water in the rucksacks. Everything in Vietnam seemed to have been designed to make movement difficult. The open nature of the area would seem to make movement easier, and it did to some degree. There were fewer vines and thorns, but you were running through elephant grass. It was like running through razor blades. The need to stay in some concealment meant that you ran from one stand of small trees, to a clump of bamboo, to a depression, to another group of trees. The effect was that you ran 200 meters to gain 100.

As we moved toward QL 19, we were climbing a ridgeline between the road and us. There was little if any time to stop and drink, so if you drank it was from your quart canteens as you moved. None of us would have had more than two canteens outside of our packs. That water would soon be gone. Dirt and smoke from the artillery and our own guns and grenades would have covered us all. I recall giving some of my ammo to someone on the team. This would have meant that we were expending a lot of rounds as we ran. We might also have been using grenades as we ran, adding to the noise, dirt, and danger of the contact.

As we finally crested the ridgeline and stopped to rest under the cover of the Cobra gunships, everyone was totally spent. The FAC or gunships reported movement behind us, so we needed to keep moving ourselves. After a quick check to see if everyone was present and okay, a weapons check, and a drink of water, we were off again, this time running down the ridge.

Running downhill has its own challenges, and falling with a heavy pack was the worst. When you fell, and you did fall, the pack would hit you in the head or neck, and pin you to the ground. Getting up was an excruciating exercise. It was like falling out of a car with your hands tied to your side. You protected your rifle and your radio handset before you protected yourself. As anyone who has backpacked will tell you, downhill is usually harder on your legs than going uphill. Torn uniforms exposed your flesh to the grass; the steep ground and the increased speed rewarded you with its own special kind of road rash.

I remember seeing Bob with blood all over his face and thinking he was hit! He was simply cut and battered by the constant collisions with brush, trees, and vines. I think my recollection is accurate, with many details missing from the narrative. I do know that we were all nearly spent at this point in the mission, nearing the limit of what we could do.

As we approached the edge of the tree line at the bottom on the ridge, a new and potentially more deadly issue confronted the team. We were now going to have to approach an American firebase. These link-ups were so dangerous that the topic was a specific class in Ranger school. A team would stop and contact the unit, or firebase, to let them know you were coming toward them. The challenge was to be sure that everyone got the word. It would take only one man on the perimeter that did not know you were coming to unleash the defensive firepower of the American unit. While the NVA could bring an astounding amount of fire onto a target, it was nothing compared to what a fixed American base could do. After seeing this firepower from the inside of several base camps, we had no desire to experience it from the outside.

Since we still had to be concerned about being pursued, we could not spend too much time coordinating the link-up. We also needed to go quickly because we had 200-300 meters of cleared area to travel through. Along the roads and around the firebases, American units cleared the area of all useful cover. They were defoliated and bull dozed, leaving very little concealment and almost no cover. The situation could allow the pursuers to snipe at us from the relative safety of the trees. I would have been the one to announce the team's location and probably have thrown a smoke grenade out to positively locate the team for the firebase. The team then moved into the open and started to sprint toward the road and safety. As soon as we cleared the wood line, the artillery or gunships began working the hillside behind us.

We made it to the firebase and collapsed. How long we were there, I can't say. We rested and drank water, getting water from the base supply rather than our own. The ironic thing about this situation was that the adrenaline that had been pumping through the team members' bodies would not let them rest long. Debriefing the mission was a top priority, so we would have gone back as soon as we could have done so.

Any specific memory of the rest of this mission is gone, but the end of every mission was always pretty much the same. The TL debriefed the mission with someone in the Brigade TOC (Tactical Operations Center); the ATL and the rest of the team would have been cleaning weapons and equipment. Once they were clean, they would have turned them in to the supply/ weapons rooms. Still running on adrenaline, there would have been a lot of nervous and macho talk about the mission. Each team member would begin to look for the opportunity to clean up and to eat. It would not be until the next day that we felt the full effect of the physical punishment we had endured.

My mind's eye sees us moving fast and with the artillery really close, but there is not any VC/NVA in the picture. Bob remembers this as the second most difficult contact that we had together. I remember the concern I had for him afterward much more vividly. For me it was a contact mission that we survived and learned from. I never really saw it as anything more important than that.

Bob, however, recalls several things about the mission. The nature of the contact and the KIAs clearly are central to the story, but he decided on that mission that he wanted to stay on my team. For him the mission was the instant that he and I became a team. He said in e-mail many years later, "I saw you come into your own as a team leader." What was for one man a defining moment was for the other just a contact that we survived and soon pushed to the back of his mind. Bob and I were to pull many more missions together. We believe that we might have pulled as many missions together as anyone else in the company at that time. While Bob can point to a time when he decided to be on my team, I can't remember a time when I ever thought it would be any other way.

CHAPTER 7

Just Like Us

———————◆———————

After the <u>Running the Gun Line, Chapter 6</u> mission, Bob and I found our roles in a contact reversed. Our team, Romeo 5 was assigned a mission to monitor a trail and village for enemy activity. We found a safe location where we could see the village and the trails leading into and out of the surrounding valley. We watched and moved to a new night location, watched and moved again. We saw small groups of men, armed and moving with military bearing, come and go for several days. They moved up and down the trails past our location. It was clear that they were using the village as a base or staging area. We were ordered to ambush some of the men as they moved past us.

This was what we called a hasty ambush, meaning that you did it with whatever weapons you had and you planned it on the spot. These improvised ambushes were always dangerous, but not uncommon, and these orders were no different than those of any other day. We selected a site that gave us plenty of space to maneuver, if needed, and allowed us to see about forty meters of trail. This was critical to prevent the team from hitting the point, a small lead element, of a larger unit. This mistake was often fatal to the LRRP teams.

When all was ready, we waited. Soon, a small group of armed men appeared on the trail. When the ambush was sprung, three of the men fell mortally wounded. Several others managed to escape in the brief firefight that followed. Our job was to gather information and intelligence about the enemy. Because some VC/NVA had escaped the ambush, we knew we had little time to search the dead. We grabbed weapons and the small packs each man carried and checked the uniform pockets. While my team gathered the material, I coordinated the team's extraction.

When the team returned to the base camp at An Khe, we had a chance to look at the captured materials. One of the packs we took was larger than the others. We opened it and discovered that it held papers and official looking forms. This story would end here, but for the contents of a small pouch on the side of the pack.

Ambushes of this type usually required specific targeting. Each team member had a specific "target" in the group to be ambushed. The man with the larger pack was my target that day. I knew that I had killed him. The pouch contained some personal items. There were several papers, probably letters, and a picture of a woman and child. It seemed clear what the picture was. It told us two things. First, the man was almost certainly NVA cadre working with the VC, and secondly he had a family. The reality of this soaked in and I realized the awful work that we were doing. As we tried to process this, one of my team members said, "My God, Dave, he is just a poor dumb SOB like us!" He was young, scared, and far from home. He was doing the things that his country's leaders said were needed. Just like us!

This mission left no doubt in my mind that we were killing human beings, not gooks, and I never forgot it. I went to my platoon leader, Lt. Martin, and asked him to assign ambush missions to other teams. Romeo 5 would take any deep penetration mission, any LRRP mission, no matter how difficult or dangerous. We were good at that, well trained for them, and other teams wanted the Hawkeye (a planned ambush) missions anyway. He agreed and we got some pretty nasty missions as a result. The strategy did not keep us from contact or from inflicting casualties, but it somehow seemed to be a better option. As I watched some of the Hawkeye teams operate over the next several months, I had no doubt that we had made the right decision.

CHAPTER 8

Lost Missions

———————◆———————

"You have undoubtedly forgotten some events, and that is probably a good thing." These words were spoken in a session with my VA psychiatrist. He was not particularly concerned about it, and I accepted it as good advice at the time. I still think it is good advice, but part of me wants to know everything I can about my time there.

With the availability of the Internet, it has become easy to talk to guys who served with me. These discussions inevitably begin with the question of, "Do you remember?" Often I do not. There are many reasons why that might be. I may not have been on those missions or my recall is inaccurate. It is possible that I have just forgotten an inconsequential mission and someone else has a better memory. There are some, however, that do not seem to fit these patterns at all. There are missions that I cannot place, have no memories of and are clearly missions that I was on, and should probably remember.

It should be said that the memories of any mission vary greatly from team member to team member. This, as discussed elsewhere, is sometimes due to the differing roles and focus of the men involved. I can point out many such situations. That does not seem to be the case with lost missions. Sometimes, my memory can be jogged and I can begin to rebuild some of the mission, place it in some kind of time line and often place it geographically.

There are times when none of the mission ever seems to reemerge from my brain. There are some memories that are disconnected from any mission or event. Bits and Pieces, Chapter 9 is about some of those. I know that I have somehow mixed missions of other teams with some of my own, morphing them into a very real memory, but an inaccurate one. For many years, I was sure that my team captured a large pack with gold leaf and documents. I know now that it was another team. There have been other times when I have ascribed some event to another team or soldier, only to find that I was the one involved. I once attended a writer's workshop with some students. The instructor insisted that everyone in the room write a short story, so I did. I thought that story was about another team — it was not. Several years later, a good friend reminded me that this was my team. This is all pretty common with the guys I have talked with, but it does not explain how whole missions, with significant events involved, just disappear.

There are two clearly lost missions that I am aware of. Two of them involve the area around LZ English. Both seem to be missing in my recall. Bob White remembers three missions in this area, and I can place only one. The other two are blanks. Bob recalls one mission with a huge crater in the AO and a long discussion about what might have caused it. I have tried to place this mission and I cannot. There was another mission in the same area, where Bob remembers a mission where we saw three rivers meeting and emptying into the sea. Again, this is a complete void in my own recall. I can find only one mission that even remotely fits these two, and I am pretty sure that they are not one and the same.

I kept track of my missions on what I called a mission stick. It was a short piece of bamboo about eight inches long that I cut a notch into for every mission. If the mission involved a contact, I cut a circle around the stick. I had two of them when I left Vietnam. When I returned to Fort Lewis, My duffel bag had been opened and ransacked. One of the sticks was gone. I think the one I have was from the second half of my tour, and the first half was lost. This is interesting, because as I have tried to sort out the missing missions listed above, I find a fairly large blank space in the missions from those first few months at. There are some other missing details from that time, and that might be an indication that I have a whole section of missing missions. Both Bob and I remember something about a mission where we fired artillery and the rounds were much different than we had ever experienced. We both think we were told that it was naval gunfire, we both think it was early in my tour, and we both have told the story many times. The issue that I have is that there is no connection in my mind with these two missing missions. The possibility of one of us not being on either mission is very small, as neither of us can remember the other missing a mission while we worked together. We have slightly different versions of Christmas 1969, and we have changed our minds on several details of this mission over the years. I have written about leaving Bob in the field once when I cut my hand, but we were clearly both on that mission and we know where we were when it happened. That is not one of these lost missions.

It is no great problem that I cannot remember these memories. It does make trying to sort out some of the difficulties I have had with my time in Vietnam frustrating. There is something in me that needs to know about everything, and another part of me that wonders if that is wise.

CHAPTER 9

Bits and pieces

——————◆——————

Some missions stand out because of some event or some important consequence. Others seem to have faded away, lost in the haze of time. One of the most maddening things I experience is the recall of small and detached events from my war. They are some of the clearest memories that I have, but they often lack any specific context.

One such memory is walking out of an AO on the Mang Yang Pass. I don't recall who was with me, if I was the team leader, or why we walked out. I only remember being told to get out of the area quickly and walking, almost running down a trail toward the road. We ran into a small group of Montagnards who were storing rice in a small hooch. I can't remember anything else. I have no idea what the reason for leaving the area might have been. If there was a "never ever do that" for LRRPs, it was to walk on a trail. The threat of staying must have been enormous to cause us to put ourselves at that kind of risk. This episode is the basis for one of the two recurring dreams I have had about Vietnam. It is the only one based on an actual event.

While returning from a road security mission, we were coming into one of the firebases along QL 19. It was probably LZ Schuler and the grass was waist high. The areas around these firebases and the road were defoliated and Rome plowed to remove any cover and provide good fields of fire for the defense of the installation. For some reason, the artillery on the firebase fired over our heads. The rounds apparently went out at a fairly flat trajectory. I saw a line of color approaching in the grass. It was moving rapidly toward us. It looked like the wind blowing on a grain field, when you see the deep green and then the gray-green as the wind bends the grain over. Before I realized what was happening, I was knocked flat. There is no recollection of getting to the fire-base, or of a second shockwave, only that snippet of seeing the color and getting knocked off my feet. This may have been the end of the "Running the Gun Line" mission.

There was a "LOACH" (Light Observation Helicopter) pilot named Mahoney who often took team leaders on VR flights. I recall two events with him. On one VR (Visual Recon) we had several team leaders on board that day. Mahoney liked to do some pretty fancy maneuvers in his chopper, and this day he put us into a zero gravity mode. As he did this, one of the team leader's maps floated out of the door and into the countryside below. We were forced to report the loss for obvious security reasons. What exactly happened is lost forever, but I suspect someone paid dearly. My map, as always, was tied to my fatigue jacket with a bootlace.

Mahoney also liked to bomb things from his LOACH and would let team leaders fly his helicopter briefly while he threw white phosphorous grenades out the door. On a VR, I was in the front seat with Mahoney and another TL was in the back. I don't know who it was, although I suspect they remember it well. Mahoney saw a "target of opportunity" on the return flight and made one of his high G turns, lined up for his bombing run, and said to me, "You have the air craft." I had some idea of what to do, having an unsuccessful stint in flight school and several unauthorized lessons from Mahoney. I took the controls and kept the aircraft on track while the pilot hung out the door. Over the intercom, I hear the TL in back scream, "Who's flying this thing? Who the hell is flying this thing?" as Mahoney chucks white phosphorous grenades out the side of the aircraft.

One evening at Pleiku, we were watching the aircraft land on the strip behind the K Company area. As we watched, one of the twin engine Cessna spotter planes came in for a landing. As we watched, we could see that about three feet of one of the wing tips was missing. The landing was pretty fast and a bit wild, but the plane did land with no further damage. The pilot taxied to a revetment and shut down. After exiting the aircraft and talking to some ground crew guys, he walked away and left the flight line. All in a day's work.

"Hover holes" were tiny openings in the jungle just large enough for a Huey to hover down into them. They were bad news, but in the area northeast of An Khe, they were often the only LZ available. My team was in an area where we could see well and we were watching another team being inserted into one of the hover holes. I think it was Gary Shellenbarger's team. The team got into contact. We could follow the fight on the radio and we could see the smoke from the firing of weapons filtering up through the trees. It was eerily disturbing to hear the contact, see the Huey go in to extract them, and never once see the team.

On a similar ridgeline we watched a team being inserted into an LZ on top of another hill. On the final approach, the Huey apparently lost power and suddenly dropped hard onto the LZ. The team on board exited the chopper and the aircraft flew out. We saw the Huey later on the Golf Course (heliport at An Khe) with its skids bent nearly flat. Why that picture remains in my mind is a mystery. In 2013, someone posted a photo of a Huey with the skids bent and folded under. I believe this was the helicopter I recall.

There were two unique structures that I have pictures of in my mind at An Khe and Pleiku. At Camp Enari, there was a large four-sided monument made of concrete, painted white and adorned with the 4th ID patch. Where it was located on the post has long since left my memory, but the image is clear. I thought I had a picture of it, but could never find it. When the book Reflections came out, there was the monument. It was just as I remembered it. The other was a chapel at An Khe. It was sort of an "A" frame building with large beams forming the structure of the roof and walls. The sidewall was short, perhaps four feet, and made of stone. There was a steeple on the roof and the beams were extended into steel fasteners and then into round concrete anchors. There was a cross on the steeple. I have been told that K Co had a memorial service there, and that I attended. I do not have any remembrance of the inside of the place, and only tiny snippets of the memorial. It is frustrating, because that should have been something that remained.

At the reunion in 2005, I won a picture in a drawing. The picture is of an M-16, a hat and a pair of boots, arranged in the traditional posture for a military memorial service. The rifle is standing vertically, its muzzle down, the boots placed on each side, and the hat is resting on the butt. This photo is from a G Company 75th Inf. memorial, but when I saw it the first time, it brought a similar image to my conscious memory. I know I saw the same thing while with K Company. When it happened, where it happened, or for whom, I do not know. The picture that I won is in black and white; the picture in my mind is in color. I wonder at the importance of that moment and my inability to place a name with the event. Later research would seem to indicate that I am recalling the memorial for Jim Doss, but I still do not know for sure.

My team was in the steep and heavily forested mountains, probably north of An Khe. Our extraction was complicated by the lack of any acceptable LZ in the area. I think we must have been concerned about contact because we would not have attempted the extraction in such abnormal fashion. We found a small opening on the side of a very steep slope and the extraction was to be by rope ladder. The pilots hovered over the opening, the extraction officer, who I think was Lt. Davis, rolled the ladder out of the door.

To use these ladders, one person had to hold the bottom down to make the ladder tight, while the other team members climbed up into the ship. My ATL tried to tell me to tie our packs onto the bottom rung to hold it tight as we climbed. I did not do this for some reason and as my point man started up first and it soon became evident that he was not going to make it all the way up. We decided quickly that our best option was to just get everyone on the ladder and go out that way. Each man climbed up as far as possible and hooked their legs through the ladder. I was the last man on and just sat down on the ground, ran my leg into one of the rungs and the pilots took off. We found a suitable LZ a few minutes later, landed and got on the chopper in a more normal way. I later met one of the pilots who remembered a similar extraction. He recalled the team being in contact and throwing grenades as they left the LZ. My most vivid memories of this are of my point man telling me he could climb no further and of me sitting down on the ground to get on the ladder.

I was on a mission with Roger Crunk. We were to be extracted and there were several Cobra gunships flying around the LZ as we waited for the slick to pull us out. The pilots would roll in on our team and then pull up and make another run. Each time they came closer and closer to actually flying right over the team. I looked up to see the business end of a Cobra. The mini gun and rocket tubes were clearly visible and obviously loaded. Roger apparently saw the same thing and asked the pilots, "Are you sure you have those things on safe?" I laughed out loud at the absurdity of the situation. We were laughing, but one of the things we feared immensely was the possibility of getting strafed by our own guns. Gallows humor was a good way to deal with the situation.

There is a picture in my mind that is totally without context. I have no idea when or where this happened, who I was with, or what we were doing. We had moved into a night location, and it was getting dark. We were all on alert when suddenly several American jets flew directly over our location. They were no more than 400 feet above us. Four LRRPs, straining to hear even the slightest sound are suddenly hammered with the deafening roar of jet engines. The result was that we all had more adrenaline on board than was really needed, and found it difficult to relax and sleep that night.

I vividly recall this event, but again without any context, or time frame. This must have happened somewhere near the Mang Yang Pass, because that is about the only place where there were huge open areas like we were in. We had to move across one of these open patches of elephant grass. Apparently, we could not go around the area to stay in the cover and concealment afforded by the jungle. There was usually good concealment from the ground due to the height of the grass; concealment from the air was a different matter. I avoided these areas if at all possible because of the potential problems of re-entering a tree line, but also because of the possibility of being seen by America aircraft.

LRRP teams feared being seen and fired on by choppers. The fear was well founded for several reasons: we wore dark uniforms and traveled in small groups like the VC, and could easily be mistaken for them. We almost always worked in free fire zones, meaning that the rules of engagement were basically fire at will. To be seen from the air could be very dangerous. As we moved across this open area, a slick flew over and saw us. Banking hard, the ship pulled around and appeared to be ready to open fire. We went to ground and did nothing to threaten the Huey. I frantically grabbed the signal panel from my ruck and began flashing it at the aircraft. It took only one more pass to convince the pilot that we were friendly. It was no more than thirty seconds, I suppose. It seemed a lot longer, looking up at the front end of the door gunner's M-60.

Rumors, legends, and just plain fabrications abounded in Vietnam. What I am about to recall may well have been the latter. This may have been part of the mix of strange happenings on LZ Hooper. There was a story about a female company commander in the North Vietnamese Army. She was rumored to be very good, very aggressive, and very much a soldier. That is the total of what remains in my mind of this story. It is pretty vivid, but totally without any supporting evidence. It was not unheard of for women to be seen with NVA units, and it was fairly common for them to be part of the VC. I suppose it was inevitable that this story was told.

Many years after I returned home, I started to recall some missions that I had forgotten or just stashed away. Two, or possibly three of those missions were in an area near the coast. Bob White and I started to talk about these, and it became clear that I had many holes in my recall. The first totally unconnected memory involves naval gunfire. In my mind's eye, I can see my team in tall elephant grass on a steep ridgeline overlooking a small valley. We see soldiers moving about in the valley and are directed to fire artillery on them. I call a fire mission and the results are both spectacular and unexpected. The shells are devastating as they impact the ground, and horrifyingly noisy as they pass over our hiding place. When I asked about the guns, the reply was something to the effect of, "Courtesy of the *USS Missouri*." I know that cannot be what actually happened, because the *Missouri* was not anywhere near the coast of Vietnam during my tour. What really happened? Who really fired the shells? Was it really naval guns? I cannot answer any of these with certainty. In the process of researching this mystery, I found a few naval ships listed as on duty in the South China Sea that might have been the source of the fire, but I have never found anything that confirmed my memory.

Another disconnected event is probably related to the last one. I have a memory of being on LZ English, a large firebase very near the coast on the far eastern edge of the 4th Infantry Division's Area of Operations. I remember eating fresh crab with some pilots and spending the night there. I am not sure why I was there or who was with me. I do not remember any staged missions from there, but after forty-plus years, a conversation with several other K Company Rangers leads me to think that in fact, I did stage at least three missions out of the place. As the stories are told, vague pictures seem to begin to reappear in my mind. Like an old fashioned photo being developed under a red light, the image seems to make some sense, but then it never quite becomes clear, remaining frustratingly, tantalizingly, and bafflingly clouded. After some visits with other members of K Company, there is still no clarity as to when or why I was on LZ English.

For many years, I had told a story of getting a bullet in my radio during a firefight. I believed it was an accurate account of a mission with Bob White on his birthday. We were recounting the mission and he said that it was his radio, not mine. I took exception to his version and he to mine. As we tried to figure out what had actually happened, Bob asked if I remembered the can of C-ration beans that had been hit. As soon as he said that, I knew he was right and that I was wrong. It had been his radio that was hit, not mine. The image of that can of pork and beans, spilled in his ruck, was all it took to bring the memory back.

This story illustrates perhaps the most interesting thing about some of these tales. I have memories that I thought were things that happened to other teams and team leaders. I had told some of these stories as just that for many years, only to discover that they happened to me. Sometimes it goes the other way. I have read many books about the LRRPs and Rangers, and one thing I know for sure is that there are some things that happened to many of us that were far more common than any of us suspected at the time. These bits and pieces may well be part of the common experience we share that somehow has been stored away, waiting for a reason to return to our consciousness.

In, <u>Contact, Chapter 51</u>, I wrote a fictionalized account of being extracted from an LZ that was booby-trapped. In the story, the LZ was covered with many small explosives. When I wrote this account, I had intentionally fictionalized the events, knowing that this was a fairly common thing. When I asked Bob White to read the stories, he reminded me of the actual events forming the basis of this story. He did pull us off the primary LZ and we did return to the primary LZ for extraction. The booby trap was not a series of small explosives, but a single large artillery round, triggered by a tripwire on the LZ. We discovered it and placed C-4 to blow up the shell. When we set it off, the explosion was far bigger than we expected and both of us were stunned. We apparently thought it was funny, because we both laughed. A few minutes later on the bird, we both realized that had we landed on that LZ as planned, we would all have been killed. Laughing at this kind of thing was not uncommon then, and even today when we talk, we find ourselves laughing at things that are really not at all funny.

CHAPTER 10

Flora and Fauna

Jungle warfare is a pretty unique experience for anyone, but for a kid from the high desert of Colorado, it was doubly so. I had spent a considerable amount of time hauling critters out of a stock pond and I thought I had seen some pretty nasty bugs. I had hunted the mountains of Colorado and thought I had seen some steep hills and thick brush. I was wrong on both counts.

14FT 7 IN PYTHON.
L TO R. T.H.E.DOG, DON MELANSON, GARY JOYCE, GUY SEJOURNE, TEX ATKINSON.

The first thing I realized about the bugs in the Highlands was that they were all bigger, much bigger, than those at home. The trees in the mountains could be huge as well. These large trees had buttress-type roots. Some were so big that you could stand behind them and have total cover. The trees were perhaps 150 feet tall and would block out the sky for long distances. Smaller trees, brush, and bamboo would fill in any spot where the sun could get through. They became a nearly impenetrable tangle of brush and vines.

There were many large clearings in the area of the Mang Yang Pass. They could be miles long and were covered with tall and dense elephant grass. This grass was often more than ten feet tall and would fill any opening in the trees. It offered good concealment for our teams and was used frequently. It was, however, very nasty stuff to move in. The blades were much like corn leaves and any bare skin in contact with the grass was likely to be cut. When it was dry, it was noisy and like walking through razors. Any cut it made was soon infected. It made good night locations for the teams because nothing could move in it without making a lot of noise. I used it often, but developed a real love-hate relationship with the stuff.

MANG YANG PASS AND FRENCH GRAVES IN ONE OF THE HUGE CLEARINGS IN THE AREA.

Bamboo was the same way. It grew incredibly fast, so it usually had new growth that offered concealment and some cover as well. It grew near streams, along the tree lines, and in smaller clearings, offering a good place for a NL (night location), or to just hide and observe. The leaves shed constantly, leaving a thick layer of debris that was quite comfortable compared to some areas. It offered the same alarm system that elephant grass did. Like the grass, there was a dark side to bamboo as well. The litter under the bamboo was comfortable, but home for thousands of small, aggressive land leaches. These nasty little beasts soon exploited any bare skin. Anyone serving as a blood donor soon had oozing black wounds and infections. The possibility of a bamboo viper sharing our bamboo patch made all of us very nervous.

The infamous "wait a minute vine" was one of the Highlands' very special challenges. These vines seemed to grow everywhere. They came in all sizes. Some as small as a man's finger, many as big as his forearm. They made a tangle of vines that defied movement, but it was the spiny hooks on the vines that created the worst problems for us. These spines were shaped like the thorns on a rose bush, but could be as much as an inch long. They were very densely packed onto the vine. They were very sharp and would penetrate clothing, packs, or even boots. Human flesh was no match for the spines. Movement through them was something to be avoided if possible, but often it was unavoidable. When you tangled with one vine, you had to "wait a minute" while you untangled yourself. Often while you worked your way out of one, another grabbed you. Frustration could lead to a rip in your clothing, or worse. Falling was also an invitation to cuts or puncture wounds. You learned quickly not to grab at these vines if you fell.

BOB WHITE AND A "WAIT A MINUTE VINE" ON THE RIGHT.

There were just as many unique animals in the Highlands. There were birds, but except the small wild chickens, I saw few. These birds looked like the fighting cocks seen in the US and South America. They loved the elephant grass and would flush only when you were very close. They made a lot of noise and

51

left me shaking on the ground a number of times. There were at least two kinds of deer in the mountains. I saw two of the larger kind, both hanging from a Huey skid, destined for a barbeque. They looked like the spotted fallow deer in Europe. The other was a smaller animal about the size of a medium-sized dog. My one and only experience with them was when one ran full speed through my team while we were stopped and listening. It happened so fast that none of us fired at it. It was into our perimeter and out again before we could react.

The official position was that there were no tigers in Vietnam. We were told that they were extinct. They were not. I saw one. There is a story about a 4th ID LRRP killed by a tiger that I could not confirm until 2013. Apparently a tiger grabbed one of the LRRPS in a night location and killed him. There are pictures of a team with a tiger that they killed, and we had one walk around a night location for several nights. We were on a radio relay mission and could not move, so we got close together and everyone stayed awake at night. We could smell this cat before we heard him, and that only added to the terror of the encounter.

There were monkeys and some type of smaller ape-like creature there as well. They were noisy, smelly, and rude creatures. Stories about them abound. They include incidents of feces being thrown at teams, urinating on teams, stealing things, and just making a lot of noise when they saw a human. Some teams tried to set up near them, because if they let you do that, no one was going to get close. Sergeant Grimes had a small monkey that he kept on a leash made with bootlaces and a repelling rope. He was cute but mean, and would bite if you got too close.

Another wonder of the highlands was the trees. There were many different kinds of trees, and they varied in size from small to very large. Where the very tallest trees did not block out the sun, smaller trees, thick brush and bamboo grew into dense thickets. These areas were nearly impossible to move through at all, let alone quietly. They were a huge difficulty to our missions, and at the same time a place we sought out for night locations. The trick was to find one of these places that offered the security of the dense vegetation and yet allowed a team to move out of the dense stuff and to exit in case of an emergency.

There were places where three different levels existed in the jungle. The lowest level was brush, then a layer of smaller trees and finally a third canopy of very tall trees. More often than not, the presence of this third layer of tall trees did not allow the undergrowth to get really thick. This could be a problem for a Ranger team, because concealment was not as good as in the thicker brush. Movement was much easier in these areas, but the one thing that made it most dangerous was the lack of landing zones. They were rare, and almost universally small. We called them hover holes and hated them almost as much as the pilots hated them.

Some of these trees were huge. I recall seeing some that were probably eight to ten feet in diameter, and they all had huge buttress roots, extending several more feet outward. I used these trees and the roots for night locations several times. I think they were a type of banyan tree, but I never really knew for sure. I saw several different flowering trees but never knew what they were either.

Insects were terrible in Vietnam, at least for me. They were all big. Mosquitoes were big, aggressive, and carried malaria. Centipedes looked familiar, but were thirty inches long and had stingers as long as your fingers. Millipedes, while apparently harmless, made enough noise at night to worry an unsuspecting Ranger. Leaches were everywhere, and we took great pleasure in squirting insect repellent on them. It looked like the Wicked Witch of the West melting. Several ant or perhaps wingless wasp species caused problems for us. There were flying bees and wasps as well. My point man bumped into a large leafy nest and was soon fighting hundreds of some kind of a wasp. True Ranger that he was, he screamed silently while we got them off of him. The dry season added ticks to the mix of things that wanted to feed on your blood. My team woke up one morning to find 200-300 ticks on each man. Some had fastened themselves across the eyelids, making it impossible to open the eye.

The worst of the lot, however, were the rats. They did not always show up on missions, but when they did, they were most unpleasant. They were scavengers and they wanted food. It was important to keep anything they might think was food stored away. Even that might not help. We usually ate late in the day and then moved to our NL shortly before dark. This was a security measure, making it difficult for VC or NVA to find us. It helped with rats as well. Any food spilled during a meal was sure to be found by the rats. Moving away from where you ate made you a bit less likely to be invaded. These rats were, like everything else, big. Fortunately, I never had any close encounters with these animals, but several team members did.

Another animal of legend was the bamboo viper, commonly called the two-step snake. Stories abound about the deadly two-step snake. I was always aware of the possibility of these snakes, as we often used bamboo as a night location. The risk/reward equation always favored using bamboo as concealment. I think I may have seen one of these snakes on a mission. We had stopped for a rest, and I looked up to see a small green snake in the bamboo about two feet from my face. I don't have any idea what we did, but I suspect we just moved on quietly. There were pythons of some type, and I saw one on a mission somewhere near LZ Hardtimes. Again, I doubt we stayed there very long.

No story about the strange critters in the Highlands could be complete with out the " Re-up bird" and the "F——- you lizard". The term for re-enlisting in the army was "re-up." "Re-up" was not a popular phrase in Vietnam, to say the least. The "F-word" was used liberally in 'Nam, and it was used as virtually any part of speech. The most common use was as a negative response.

Imagine the pure joy, and the universal sense of vindication when a GI first heard the call of the "Re-up" bird followed by the croaking reply of the "F —— you" lizard! Yes, they both existed and yes they both sounded a lot like their names imply. Regrettably, I never heard them both in close sequence.

There were many other kinds of birds and animals in the highlands, according to later reading, but I saw very few. Perhaps we were not looking for them, as we were certainly distracted. I suspect we never saw them because we had come to accept them as no threat. I have often wondered about what other kinds of things we just did not see because they posed no threat.

CHAPTER 11

Developing a Sixth Sense

To survive, LRRP teams had to be very good at small unit patrolling skills. They could read maps and a compass, move quietly, and communicate without speaking, and they could use artillery, gunships and personal weapons with deadly effectiveness. The teams became very adept at gathering information and they could interpret that information quickly and accurately. The everyday skills of a LRRP team became second nature to most of the young men in K Company, or any LRRP unit.

This was to be expected, because they were well trained and highly motivated. What was not as obviously expected was the "sixth sense" that many developed. There were times when someone would seem to know something that they really should not or could not know. Good team leaders never assumed that a mission would be easy, but there were times when you just knew a mission was going to be bad. Perhaps, after a while, you started to think like the VC or NVA, and could predict what they might do. Maybe it was a super-heightened awareness that made this possible. Whatever the reason, team leaders often knew after the VR flight that they were in for a bad time. The team members developed this ability also.

Bob White had a highly reliable ability to sense trouble. He didn't always pick up on danger, but when he did, it was a good idea to listen. Several times, Bob sensed that there was something wrong and stopped the team. On one occasion, we had no indication that there was anyone or anything in the AO, but he stopped us and we listened for a few minutes. In a very short time, we heard voices and other sounds indicating that there were NVA in the area. We eventually did get into contact and were extracted, but we did not walk into an enemy unit. The NVA were probably in bunkers. Walking into them could have been a death sentence for the team.

I learned the wisdom of paying attention to Bob's premonitions on a very memorable mission. We were to be inserted in an AO that was remote even by our standards. There were very few landing zones that were suitable for even one ship. I had chosen a likely LZ as our primary insertion point, and we were getting close to the insertion when Bob yelled across the chopper for me, indicating that we should change the insertion to our secondary LZ. I was not sure what he had seen, or if he had seen anything, but I changed our insertion point and we were soon on the ground without incident. Any details of the mission, except for the extraction, are long since gone from my mind.

Landing zones in most of the highlands were limited, and especially so in this area. We had to check out the primary LZ, and because of that, would use it for our extraction. It soon became apparent that Bob's concerns had been warranted. As soon as we approached the area, we encountered booby traps and lots of them. The entire LZ was peppered with explosives and punji sticks, but more deadly than these was an artillery shell buried on the LZ and rigged with trip wires!

Had we landed on this spot, it was certain that some or all of us would have been hurt. They could have caused significant damage to the helicopters as well. Like most of these events, I never really knew why it happened. Bob could not have seen these booby traps from the air, and he had no more information about the secondary LZ than he had about the first one. He had no concerns about the area until we were nearly committed to inserting as planned. We managed to clear the site of booby traps and were successfully extracted, saved again by a premonition.

David Siglow, my point man, demonstrated a variation of this on another mission. We were moving in an area where we had not found anything that indicated an enemy presence. We were operating in very thick and heavy double canopy jungle. The sides of the hills were steep, making movement dangerous and difficult. Following a predetermined route was nearly impossible. Siglow had been walking point as usual. After battling this for hours and becoming more and more frustrated, we took a break. Fatigue could make you careless and that could get you killed. We rested and then started to move again. After a short distance, perhaps twenty-five meters, Siglow stopped. He did not indicate any specific threat, but just stopped. We were close to each other due to the dense foliage, so I moved up and asked what was happening. He was not sure, but something was wrong. After a few minutes we started to move again, and just as quickly we stopped again. This time Siglow was still not sure what was happening, but he was very sure we should not move any further. I trusted him, so we stopped.

After a few minutes, Siglow whispered to me, "Spider webs, no spider webs." He was suddenly aware that he had been breaking spider webs as we moved, and now he was not feeling them on his face. He was just as convinced that there was some sinister reason for this, so we did the prudent thing and got very still and very quiet. This tactic was something I called "laying dog," and was used to great effect by teams in the Highlands.

After a few minutes, we started to hear sounds, voices, and then a signal shot. We were close to some enemy camp or group of men. We listened, made notes of what we could glean from the situation, and backed out of the area. After finding a suitable night location, we listened and watched. We were able to determine a sizable unit was in the Area of Operation We moved away from the area in the morning and were extracted without incident. I don't recall the exploitation of the target. Exploitation was the Army language for what happened to a target after we found it. But I am sure that David's actions prevented us from walking into a bigger unit that might have been in bunkers. This was a feared event for a Ranger team, because it usually ended badly for the team.

Why the webs were broken, or even if that was what had alerted David, we never knew. Did an NVA soldier break them cutting a firing lane? That didn't seem likely, because we would have seen that type of damage to the vegetation. Did some animal break them? Maybe. Did the spiders just not like the brush right there? Who knows? Divine intervention can't be ruled out, but for what ever reason, Siglow's sixth sense told him to stop. We stopped without knowing why, and I believe that we probably are alive because we did.

Bob did this several times after he took his own team. On one of his early missions as a TL, he was leaving for the Golf Course and I was packing up my team for a mission later that day. I probably said something about being careful and we will see you in four or five days. Bob's response was something to the effect that he "would be back sooner than that, probably today" His team made contact on the LZ immediately after the insertion and was pulled out within a few minutes. I have a tape of Bob and me laughing about this mission.

Stories of similar events are fairly common among LRRPS. There are several things that may explain what was happening. Clearly, as you learned the terrain, the enemy, and their tactics, you could and should be able to anticipate their behavior. The better you got, the more likely it was to happen. The men in these teams became so totally attuned to their surroundings that I think many were aware of things on a subconscious level. Siglow's spider webs were an example. Bob's stopping the team may well have been the result of his hearing or seeing something that he was not even aware of. While I believe that there were some of all of these involved, I also think that there were times when there was no earthly reason for us to "know," and yet we did know and survived because of that. I believe that there was divine intervention at times.

CHAPTER 12

An Unlikely Warrior

❖

Bob White was in so many ways an enigma to me. He was an unlikely warrior. He was in Christopherson's words "a walking contradiction." He was a very good LRRP, a good assistant team leader (ATL) and TL. Make no mistake; he carried his weight and then some. He walked point, the most dangerous and demanding assignment on the team. He was more than proficient with his weapons and all the tools of the trade, and he was a fighter when he had to be.

I came to trust him as only close brothers at arms can trust. He proved worthy of that trust over and over again. He bore the physical, mental and emotional burdens of our missions as well as anyone, and often better than many of us did. He could be tough if needed, and it often was needed. He dealt with the discomfort of our missions with stoicism. He knew how to provide information and help to a sometimes-arrogant TL. In short, he was a good soldier.

But Bob was more than that. The contradiction, at least in my mind, was that he was not a warrior in the sense that we often think of them. There were men in K Company who by nature seemed to enjoy the thrill of the fight. Some seemed immune to the fear of losing a teammate. Some outwardly relished the power given to them, and a few apparently enjoyed using the power to kill. Some were athletes who saw the brutal physical challenges as another way to prove themselves. Some never questioned what we did and they just did it. Bob was not any of these men.

Bob was not a great athlete, nor was he a thrill seeker. He was more concerned with losing a team member than he was about being hurt himself. While he was an outdoorsman, he did not embrace the discomfort of the bush. He learned early that we were involved in an awful task that sometimes ended in

59

the death of another human being. He never learned to live with that burden lightly. Bob was married and wanted nothing more than to get home to Cathy. He carried that burden while many of the rest of us did not.

I believe he was in many ways ill suited to be a LRRP. Even as we all hardened to the task, Bob seemed to carry more of the burden of knowing the cost to us and to our enemies. Someone said that "courage is not being unafraid; it is being afraid and acting anyway." I think that applied to all of us, but especially to Bob. He was not a LRRP by nature; he was a LRRP by choice. He placed himself among those special men who did this job, and by the force of his will and character became a true warrior.

BOB WHITE, RT., AND LT. TOM MARTIN, MY PLATOON LEADER.

His incredible sense of humor was one tool he used to deal with the situation we were in. He kept his humanity with great effort. To someone seeing him in his camouflage fatigues, he probably looked like the rest of us. To those who knew him, he was anything but the stereotypical LRRP. He was an ordinary man, thrust into an extraordinary war against his will, but he was by choice a LRRP and he became an extraordinary soldier. By an act of his will, he excelled and kept his humanity. By an act of his will, he did the job of being a LRRP. His strength of character was what made him a LRRP. I don't think it was ever easy for him, but he was a Ranger.

CHAPTER 13

A Gentle Warrior

T he war and the Central Highlands of Vietnam could and did harden men quickly. The physical punishment of a LRRP mission was vicious, to be sure, but the numbing psychological beating was even worse. It affected some of us by making us mean, some angry and cynical. Some became fatalistic and started to shut down emotionally. "It don't mean nothin'" became the mantra of many, indicating that they just did not care anymore. I found myself feeling all of these at one time or another. At times, it seemed to many of us that we were watching our old self become someone new and we wondered, "Who the hell is this guy?" The stresses of the war changed men. You could see it in every pair of eyes; hear it in every voice. There were some who were not changed as much as the rest of us. Wayne Mitsch was one of those soldiers.

SGT WAYNE MITSCH, A GREAT SOLDIER WITH A BIG HEART.

Wayne was subject to the same strains as the rest of us. He did exactly what we all did, and he did it well, but he had something that most of us valued. I don't think I understood what it was at the time, but I do now. It was more than his ability to be involved in a difficult situation and deal with strength, firmness and without losing his cool. It seemed that no matter how nasty the situation got, Wayne managed to retain his humanity.

In his book Achilles in Vietnam, Jonathan Shay talks about men who seemed to have this ability and makes the point that they were highly valued by those around them. When I read this for the first time, I wrote in the margin, "Wayne

Mitsch!" Wayne was in all ways a soldier and LRRP. He was subjected to all of the brutality of the war and the missions we were tasked with. He did all that was required of him and more, and yet he seemed to have the ability to keep his humanity, his soul, from the damage many of us suffered. At one of the reunions, I was talking to Wayne's wife, Fran, about this part of the book. She listened, smiled, and told me that someone in her church had once described Wayne as a "quiet, gentle and very strong man."

At another reunion, there was a man who was very determined to talk about the political situation at the time and had made a bit of a pest of himself. Several of us had had enough and were about to unload on the guy when Wayne stepped in and stopped the confrontation from happening. This would have been forgotten except that later that evening, I found Wayne in the hotel bar, talking politics with the same guy he had reprimanded earlier in the day! Wayne has never been mistaken for a weak man, but he has always been able to maintain the kindness and gentleness that made him special to us. As Shay stated, "Such men are highly valued in combat units," to which I can only add, "And they still are!"

CHAPTER 14

Capt'n Crunch

R oger Crunk was known as "Capt'n Crunch," "Charlie-Charlie," or just plain "Charlie." He was a big, strong, good-looking redhead who fit the stereotype of a Ranger in so many ways. He was good with all the weapons, but was known for his use of the M-60. He reveled in that. An outdoorsman, he was more at home in the field than most of us. The brutal physical demands of the Highlands seemed to bother him less than others. While some of us struggled under the loads, he sought out the additional weight of the M-60 and its ammo. He offered to carry extra weight for a smaller team member. His big smile, easy laugh, and sense of humor made him a valued friend. Paired with Bob White, they provided a welcome respite from the serious side of the war.

ROGER CRUNK ON INJURY PROFILE AFTER BURNING HIS HAND ON THE M-60 DURING A FIREFIGHT

He had a number of voices that he used to entertain us. I have a tape of him reading from a book titled <u>Reading for Rhetoric</u> in an English accent. The fact that I can recall the name of the book highlights the bizarre nature of the situation. I would be willing to bet that fully one half of all the tapes I sent home from Vietnam were of Roger Crunk engaged in some form of idiocy.

I think Roger and I shared the desire to be really good at something, and he was really good at this business of being a LRRP. He was a ready student and quick learner. He was a leader from the start. His concern for the guys on his team and in the company was as evident then as it is today. He knew everyone and they all knew him. He seemed to be everyone's friend, but more importantly he was universally respected. He had a swagger, cockiness, and a confidence that just seemed to be natural. There were others who tried to be that way and it came across as arrogant and self-serving. Confident as he was, he was very willing to take advice and to learn from others. He was probably as good as anyone at all four of the jobs on our teams. He had walked point, been an ATL and TL, and carried the machinegun as a team member. He simply seemed to be made for the task.

Confidence could lead to recklessness. While I saw this in myself and some other team leaders, I never saw it in Roger. Guys wanted to be on his team because they understood who he was and they trusted him. His confidence led him to make good decisions and make them quickly. He was in every sense of the term a true Ranger.

In the capricious nature of war, that didn't keep everyone safe. In August of 1970, I received a tape from Bob telling me that Roger had been badly wounded. As clearly as I can recall anything from those years, I recall being ill, physically ill at the news. I could not talk; I only sat in horrified silence and imagined this strapping young Ranger in a hospital bed somewhere. (Or worse.) We eventually made contact again and Roger came to Colorado to visit. He met and married my sister! Brothers in arms became brothers-in-law!

We have both had our battles with our "'Nam demons," but Roger has borne the additional burden of the physical injuries and the loss of a team member. He overcame the physical challenges and soon went to work doing hard physical labor in a cinder block plant, seemingly unaffected by the damage to his body. But 'Nam does not release you easily. There were many more challenges to overcome, but those are his stories to tell. I have watched and marveled at his battle to heal. We have shared many long talks, some anger and some tears, but he has always "continued the mission." Today, I see much of the same big handsome country kid that I knew in 1969 and '70. He doesn't seek out the physical punishment he once reveled in, (none of us do!) but the care and concern for his fellow LRRP/Rangers is still there. He still knows everyone and they still know him. We still go to him for a smile, a laugh, or for help. His confidence, not as brash as it once was, is still there and trusted by most of us as much or more now as ever.

CHAPTER 15

Shooting the Moon

◆

When road security missions were assigned to K Company teams, they often fired artillery at targets near the road at night. The NVA did not often operate near the road, but the VC did. They would carry explosives to the road at night and attempt to crater the road, blow up bridges or sever the pipeline. They apparently needed light to do this, because it was very common to see lights near the road or on the surrounding high ground.

The American units in the area and the LRRP teams who worked the area knew where most of the trails were, and had a large number of artillery pre-plots on all of them. Teams could bring fire onto a trail quickly and accurately, if needed. On a mission in this area, we were tasked with two things. First, we were to check out a cave in the side of a big ridge near the road. There was a strong point near this cave. A strong point was just a cleared parking spot for a tank. The area was cleared to create a good field of vision so that the tanks could see and shoot at anything in the area. This cave was visible from the road and from the strong point. The tank would, from time to time, fire high explosive rounds into this cave. I later read on the 69th Armor web site that firing at this cave was a favorite pastime. We were justifiably nervous about this part of the mission, but managed to get to the cave without incident. We verified that the VC were not using it, and continued the rest of our mission.

We then started the rest of our assigned mission, watching for sappers attacking the road. Sometime during the night, we saw lights on some high ground in front of us. The timing was about right for an attack and there was a trail on that ridgeline, so I called up a fire mission. The first rounds seemed to be right on target, but the lights did not go out. Usually things went dark

65

quickly and stayed dark if artillery was anywhere close to the lights. This time nothing happened. I fired again with the same negative results. The lights still flickered along the top of the ridge. I adjusted my artillery, fired again and still the lights remained! What was this? Could it be a larger unit preparing to hit one of the firebases in the area? Both LZ Schuler and LZ Action were close and could be targets, and there was a pump station nearby. Were they after that? Were the lights just a distraction? Were they trying to find us? What could this possibly be?

As we watched for a few more minutes, the mystery solved itself as the moon rose above the treetops on the ridge. The rising moon had shown through the spaces at the bottom of the trees and appeared to be small flickering lights. There was only one acceptable way out of this mess. That was to adjust the artillery one more time, fire a battery of artillery at the moon, report the lights out, congratulate the guns on a good job, and act like it was all in a night's work! That is what we did. I have sheepishly confided this story to only a few close friends, until now.

Chapter 16

Navigation

❖

"Ranger, Ranger, where ya been? Out in the jungle, lost again!" So go the words to a common marching cadence used by some of the LRRPS from Vietnam. There were many things that could go wrong on a LRRP mission, but few could cause more anxiety than not knowing where you were. Getting lost was not as hard to do as you might think. There were a multitude of ways it could happen, and I doubt that anyone made it a whole tour without ever needing some significant help figuring out where they were. Many things could cause a team to get lost, but whatever the cause, it was a very dangerous thing to have happen. It was as embarrassing as it was dangerous. Typical of the gallows humor of K Company, someone who got lost would be the target of much good-natured abuse.

Knowing where you were was critical for obvious reasons. Close artillery and gunship support required that you know where you were within five to ten meters. Extraction also required that you know where you were, or be close enough for the pilots to see your smoke grenade. The procedure for firing artillery required the guns to fire a smoke round or marking round before any high explosive rounds, to be sure that the projectiles would not fall too close. If you were 200 or 300 meters from where you thought you were, you were not lost in the strictest sense of the word, but you were certainly in some danger if you needed artillery support quickly. It was also important to accurately locate anything that was found, since incorrectly locating something like a bunker complex could have dire consequences to any unit sent to investigate. Errors of just twenty or thirty meters might prove fatal.

On most missions, teams were assigned an area about 2,000 meters square. This is not a particularly large area, and it would seem that getting lost might be hard to do. It was not. One of the common problems was the maps themselves. They were typically fairly accurate, but the scale often was not large enough to show every significant terrain feature. This could cause a team to become confused quickly. Most of the time this could be overcome by carefully accounting for the direction and distance moved. All teams used this technique, called dead reckoning, and it worked well. The problem was that the terrain often made following a compass heading impossible.

There were places that simply prevented movement, and you had to avoid them. Areas of extremely thick jungle could be impassable. Small but very steep areas might not show on the map, but a team might be forced to move around them. Moving on steep hillsides made dead reckoning impossible. The more times a team changed direction or had to move on steep ground, the more likely it was that errors would occur. After several hours of fighting any or all of these, a team could easily be several hundred meters from where they thought they were. Anything that required the team to move very fast, like a contact, made keeping track of their location difficult.

Ironically, the same problem could be caused by exactly the opposite terrain situation. If a team was assigned an AO that was heavily forested and relatively flat, dead reckoning was often the only way to navigate. Doing this depended on having an accurate starting point. Insertion points such as clearings might or might not be accurately located on the map. Manmade landing zones or bomb craters, for example, were not on the maps at all, so the starting point for dead reckoning was only as good as the team leader's initial plot. If that plot was incorrect by even a few meters, several small errors in the heading and distance could easily have a team's location off significantly.

Teams had several ways of getting an accurate fix on their location. If the AO had open areas that allowed a TL to see other identifiable terrain features, the method of triangulation could be used. This method was simply finding a known terrain feature some distance from the team and shooting the azimuth or compass heading to it. This was used to find the direction from the feature to the team's location, called the back azimuth, and that line was drawn on the map. This was done a second time with another known location, usually some type of high ground, and the point where the lines intersected was the team's location. It was very accurate and easy to do if the terrain allowed it. Teams went to great lengths to do this, sometimes climbing steep hills or even trees to be able to see. This was the method of choice because it did not attract attention to the team. It could be very difficult to do if two terrain features could not be seen or accurately identified.

Another method was using artillery. The method was simple and accurate. A team would fire a smoke round at a known position, often a pre-plot. The distance and direction to the smoke round would tell the team where they were. The round had to be relatively close to be heard and located with any degree of accuracy. That was not as easily accomplished, as it might seem. The terrain and jungle could distort the sound, leading to a false direction, distance, or both. The major problem with this was that the NVA and VC could hear the round as well, alerting them to the possibility of a LRRP team in the area. Sometimes this would compromise the team. If the artillery was the less accurate 175 mm gun, there could also be significant errors introduced.

Aircraft could be used to find a team. The team would find an area where a signal mirror or panel could be seen from the air, and an aircraft follow the team's instructions to fly over the team and see the signal. Once they saw it, they would report the location. As opposed to artillery, this was a very accurate way to get a fix on the team's location. However, it had all of the same problems. It was more likely to compromise the team, because the pilot usually had to make several passes and corrections to find the team. It drew attention to the area. It also presented significant danger to the aircraft.

A far less common but potentially deadly error was insertion into the wrong LZ. This happened for several reasons. It was often difficult to tell exactly where you were when the choppers were flying at lower than normal altitudes. This might be due to weather or the tactical situation. It might also be the result of an attempt to disguise the insertion point. Pilots, team leaders, and insertion officers could miss the LZ. This was especially true in the area around the Mang Yang Pass, where there were many landing zones. When a team was inserted more than 500 meters from the anticipated location, any contact could become unmanageable very quickly. A team leader who was trying to locate his team and get artillery on target at the same time was in a nearly impossible situation.

Another danger was the practice of harassing and interdiction fire. This was artillery fire that targeted likely areas of NVA or VC activity, usually at night. It was often used in free fire zones, and no American unit was supposed to be in that area. There was never any marking round, only the high explosive rounds. Not being where you were supposed to be might mean you were in one of these target areas. It was standard practice for team leaders to check the insertion location with the insertion aircraft as soon as they were on the ground. When a bad insertion did happen, it rarely went undiscovered by the aircrews or insertion personal. If it did go undetected, the team usually became aware of a problem quickly and the error corrected. The longer a bad insertion went undiscovered, the more dangerous it became.

During the time I was in K Company, there was only one time when I was really lost. There were a few other times when I was "temporarily unsure of my exact location." It happened on a mission in April or May of 1970. I had a new team with a fairly new ATL, and two brand new LRRPs. We were assigned an AO well north of An Khe. The insertion was bumped several times, and was executed very late in the day. The selected LZ was on top of a ridge and there were several very similar clearings in the area. I undoubtedly contributed to the problems by changing the LZ just before we left the Golf Course. The pilots had probably already flown a long time that day, and I suspect they also made a map reading error. Neither the insertion officer nor I realized the error.

We were inserted nearly 1,200 meters from the intended LZ. We were not even in the assigned AO. We had good communications and we could not move too far from the LZ because of impending darkness. I saw nothing that indicated we were not exactly where we should be, probably because it was late and I was concerned about finding a good night location. I did not realize we were in the wrong place until after dark. By then, it was too late to do anything.

I saw lights in a valley and decided to fire artillery at them. I had a pre-plot in that direction and we would adjust the fire mission from that. It was far enough away from us that there was no need to fire a smoke round. I had my new ATL fire the mission for practice. He called the first battery and we waited for the rounds to hit in the valley in front of us. The artillery called out the splash, telling us that the rounds were about to hit. We saw nothing but heard rounds impacting in the wrong direction and very far from our location. This was strange, but I assumed the ATL or the guns had made an error. That was very rare, but it could happen. It was not until it happened a second time that I realized that something was very wrong. I don't recall the details of distance or direction, but after a few more artillery rounds fired, it was apparent that we were nowhere near where we should be.

When my ATL reported this, it did not take long for the TOC to get a better location for us. He gave them an azimuth to the sounds of the artillery and they were able to find a probable location for us. It was an uneventful, but very nervous night. After we were sure we were not in immediate danger, we moved to an area where we could triangulate our position. We were not only a very long ways from where we were supposed to be, but we were also a long way from the position that the TOC had plotted. Our azimuth to the sounds during the night had been inaccurate. Sounds in the highlands were often hard to locate, as they are in any mountainous area. Had there been any problem during the night, we would have been in real trouble. The rest of the mission was apparently uneventful, but the potential for disaster that night was huge. Fortunately, there was no other problem that caused the error to become any more serious.

Any team that made contact and was forced to escape and evade could very easily lose track of where they were. Dead reckoning was very difficult to do if you were moving rapidly. Counting steps was out of the question. Most team leaders, myself included, spent a considerable amount of time plotting rally points and memorizing the area they were to operate in. This allowed us to move quickly and still know to some degree where we were. This worked for a short time, but it was difficult to do for longer times or over greater distances. If a team could stop, often the first thing the TL did was to locate the team. In contacts there was one advantage. The air support usually was on station very quickly, and once they had located a team, navigation often became comparatively simple. The team would just tell the ships which direction they were moving and the gunships could adjust accordingly.

In the opposite way, the helicopters always had a better view of the terrain and could give the teams a heading and distance to move. This was especially true when teams had to move to an unplanned LZ. Pilots had a bird's eye view of the situation. They could locate the team, the LZ, the best route, and the enemy activity. A single radio call from a slick could solve all the navigation issues a team had. A simple sentence, "Romeo 5, Blackjack 34, Your secondary LZ at 060 degrees, 250 meters, stay on the west side of the ridgeline, Gamblers are on the bad guys to the East," told the TL exactly which way to go, how far he had to go, how to get there, what the enemy situation was, and where his help was.

Each mission had its own navigational challenges, and the art of using a compass and map could mystify all of us at times. The skills were simple; the application was critical, and the execution was anything but easy. Most of us managed to keep track of things well, and most of the time errors caused nothing more that harassment and chagrin.

CHAPTER 17

Weapons of War

❖

Much could be written, and indeed has been written about the weapons carried by American infantrymen in Vietnam. A simple search on the Internet will give you all the technical data about most of these weapons. I will make no attempt to reproduce that data here. There was always controversy about some weapons. There was always someone who wanted some exotic weapon. There were a significant number of modifications to standard issue weapons, but for the most part we carried what we were issued.

The most basic weapon of any infantryman is his rifle. We carried the later model M-16 and the folding stock Car-15 model. These were all Colt manufactured rifles. By the time I was in country, most of the problems with the M-16 had been resolved or mitigated to a great extent. The problematic jamming had been reduced significantly with the issue of cleaning equipment and chrome plating the chamber. The open ended flash suppressors had been replaced with the closed type. The weapon's advantages were that the rifle and ammunition were light, a high rate of fire, and very light recoil. The first two were very important to LRRP teams because of the normal weight of their loads.

The down side of the M-16 was also threefold. It had to be kept clean, much cleaner than the AK-47 or the older American M-14. Field maintenance was critical, and failure to keep the rifle clean and lubricated would cause it to misfire. The lighter ammunition fired a very light bullet at a very high velocity. This prevented the rounds from penetrating heavier cover that the AK-47 rounds could penetrate. The lighter rounds were less stable than the heavier rounds, affecting accuracy if the round hit something like a small branch or twig. This was probably not an issue at very short distances, but it might be at longer ranges. Finally, the rifle was made of aluminum alloy and many believed it to be more susceptible to damage than the M-14 when hit by a bullet or shrapnel. The Car–15 was just a shorter version of the M-16. It had a folding stock and a shortened barrel. In my experience, the performance was not different from the M-16 in any significant way. It was lighter, shorter, and easier to carry in the bush.

There were some AK-47s in the company armory. There were stories of guys carrying them, but I never saw that. Most of us knew the distinctive sound of an AK-47 and would shoot at the sound in a firefight. I never wanted to be on the receiving end of an M-16. I certainly did not want to invite that with the sound of an AK-47. There were also stories of Swedish K, and old Thompson submachine guns. I never saw any of these used, but I know that some of the early LRRPs did carry them at times.

The M-16 was not often modified, but the Car-15 was. There were several that had acquired a front handgrip. Taking an extra rear grip and fastening it to the front hand guard of the Car-15 accomplished this. This modification had some merit, apparently, as the modern versions of the M-16 have this feature. There was a cottage industry of sorts in the magazines for the M-16 and the Car-15. Some were pretty low tech, simply taping two magazines together. This arrangement placed the two magazines side by side with the feed end in opposite directions. It did speed up a magazine change, but as with all the attempts to modify, it brought about jamming concerns. We had access to a very few thirty round magazines. These were functional and used if available.

Some small telescopic sights were used. They had limited usefulness at short range and most of our contacts were close. One of the most popular modifications was a silencer/flash-suppressor that fit on either M-16 or Car-15. They were effective and simple to use and maintain. They were not common. Hawkeye or ambush teams used them more extensively than did the recon teams.

The M-60 was usually carried on ambush missions, but rarely on recon missions. It was, in my opinion, the best of the American weapons and probably better than anything the NVA had. It was a very reliable weapon. It had a good reliability record and was easy to maintain in the field. It was used by everyone, from the Infantry to the door gunners on the helicopters. It was versatile, tough, and deadly.

For the LRRP teams, it was often too heavy to carry. It took a strong man to carry the M-60 and the normal load for a LRRP mission. Consequently, they were carried on ambush missions that were usually shorter and required less movement. Ammunition was heavy and hard to carry. LRRPS did not carry M-60 ammo in the can because of the weight and noise. This made it harder to keep clean. Carried this way, it could still be noisy and difficult to camouflage. It was, nonetheless, a welcome addition to any fight. It had very real physical and psychological effects on anyone attacking a team. It had an unmistakable sound and often led enemy units to believe they had attacked a larger unit. I have read accounts of NVA soldiers that indicate that they truly feared this weapon.

RAY ALLEN AND LOWELL TIDLINE WITH A CAR-15, (FRONT)
AN M-16 CENTER AND AN M-60 REAR.

The M-79 grenade launcher was a rather strange piece of weaponry. It looked for the all the world like a homemade shotgun. The barrel looked like a piece of two-inch pipe, and the stock looked like someone had put it on upside down. It was a single shot weapon that fired a high explosive round, a shotgun round, and later in the war a flachette round. There was a newer model that mounted under the barrel of the M-16. The older models were more common in K Company. Most teams that carried an M-79 carried it as an additional weapon. Whoever carried the M-79 also carried an M-16. It was not heavy, very simple, totally reliable, and effective. The HE round was of little use in a very close fight. They needed a specific distance, arm them, and explode. For attacking bunkers, discouraging snipers, or in fights over a distance of fifteen meters, it was a good weapon.

Conversely, the shotgun rounds fired 00 buck shot and were devastating in close fights. They were limited by the single shot capability. This type of ammunition was applied to Cobra gunship. Here, the weapon was automatic, and not as limited by the weight of the ammo. Mounted on the front end of a Cobra gunship and paired with a mini-gun, it was a formidable weapon.

We sometimes carried the LAW, or Light Anti-tank Weapon. This was a rocket-powered explosive charge, sealed in a disposable tube. It was fired once and discarded. It was a reliable weapon that could be used on vehicles, light armor, or bunkers. These were not common targets for LRRP/ Ranger teams, thus their use was limited. They were brutally effective against snipers, and were sometimes carried for that reason. I carried a LAW twice during my tour, and did not fire it either time.

Our hand grenades were the newer baseball type grenades. I trained with both the old pineapple type and the round grenades. I much preferred the new type. They were easy to throw accurately, and comparatively light to carry. The spoons were durable and the grenades were dependable, effective, and relatively safe. They had a short delay in the fuse that made it safer to throw them. The design to the grenade made the pattern of shrapnel pretty much spherical. The interior of the shell was filled with serrated wire that separated into thousands of tiny pieces on detonation.

Without any doubt, the most brutally effective weapon we carried was the Claymore mine. As described elsewhere, it was a horrific weapon that killed and maimed anyone or anything unfortunate enough to be in front of it when detonated. The sound of the mine detonating was deafening, and the amount of dirt, smoke, and debris it created had its own shock factor. It was the hundreds of quarter-inch steel balls blasted forward from the curved mine that did the awful work. Placed correctly in an ambush, and detonated at the proper time, they created a wall of steel pellets that was not survivable.

Most weapons of the NVA and VC compared favorably to American weapons. The AK-47 was a very dependable and easy to maintain weapon. It had a lower rate of fire than the M-16, it was heavier, and so was the ammo. Ammunition was heavier than that of the M-16, but the AK had more magazine options. It was a much simpler and older weapon, and therefore did not suffer the growing pains of the M-16. I would not have traded the M-16 or Car-15 for the AK, but some would have done so. The SKS, an older semi- automatic weapon was similar to the American M-1 Carbine in some ways, but it was a vastly inferior to the AK-47. It had a slower rate of fire; it was less reliable and not as durable. It was commonly carried by VC, and was a prized trophy, because it could be legally taken home.

The M-60 was better than the NVA counterpart, the Chinese made RPD. They were both air cooled, fired very similar rounds, and weighed about the same. The M-60 had a higher sustained rate of fire; it could sustain 200 rounds per minute, the RPD only 150. The M-60 was belt fed and could be fired without stopping to reload. The NVA gun used a cylindrical magazine with a 100 round capacity and a long curved magazine that held thirty rounds. I never fired the RPD, but the feeling among most Americans was that the M-60 was superior in three areas. It had a slightly higher rate of fire, it was easier to clear and maintain, and it was less likely to miss-fire. Like the AK–47, the M-60 was used so many places and in so many applications that all of the bugs had been pretty well worked out. The M-60 was used for many years after the Vietnam War, signifying its effectiveness. For me, the sound of an M-60 was the third most identifiable sound of the war. The thump of a Huey and the crack of an AK were number one and two. The M-60 was the only American weapon that I heard from the business end. I do not recall ever hearing an M-16 fired at me in Vietnam, but on any contact mission or hot extraction, the door gunner's M-60s often shot over us, giving us the audio signature that was usually reserved for NVA or VC weapons.

The American LAW (Light Anti-tank Weapon) was the only weapon of this type that we ever carried. There were other recoilless rifles in the inventory, but they were far too heavy for us to use. The RPG (rocket propelled grenade) that the NVA used was a superior weapon, at least in the kind of fighting we did. The LAW was lighter, carried a much better warhead for piercing armor, and was easy to use. The RPG was close in all areas and had the advantage of being a reusable weapon. Once fired, a new round was placed in the tube, and it could be fired again. In any kind of firefight that I was ever in, the RPG would have been the weapon I would have preferred. In fairness, these weapons are not really comparable at all. The LAW was an anti-armor weapon to be used on tanks and light armor. The RPG was a primary infantry weapon, and as such had considerable advantage over the LAW in that setting. The fact that the RPG, essentially unchanged, is still in use around the world today, speaks to the effectiveness of the design.

There was no NVA weapon comparable to the claymore mine that I know of. As mentioned earlier, it was a horrific weapon, capable of crippling a unit ten times the size of a LRRP team. The VC made attempts to make similar types of mines using anything they could find. I saw an improvised claymore type made out of an American combat helmet. The helmet or "steel pot" as it was called was filled with all manner of metal. There were C-ration cans, M-60 ammo links, and M-16 brass in the helmet. It was then filled with a layer of some kind of explosive. This may have been C-4 found by the VC, or perhaps some other kind salvaged from a bomb. It would have been far less effective than a claymore, but dangerous nonetheless.

In many ways, our best weapons were the artillery and the helicopter gunships that we used. They all allowed Americans to do something that apparently no other military has ever been able to do very well. We could get these guns and aircraft in very close to our locations and use them effectively. The artillery was our second choice for in close support. It was somewhat difficult to fire accurately and there was a limit to how close it could be used. All kinds of things affected the guns and rounds, introducing some changes in where rounds would land. The two primary advantages of artillery were that it was available almost immediately and it could keep firing nearly indefinitely. If the mission was in range of these big guns, it took only a few minutes at most to get them to fire. I once fired artillery all night long. The comparison of NVA or VC artillery is difficult for me to do. I don't think I was ever on the receiving end of enemy artillery in the bush. In base camp, we did get shelled with mortars and rockets. I have been told that the NVA guns had considerably greater range than American artillery, but this was never an issue for me.

Helicopters were far better at getting really close. They could put rockets within ten meters, mini-gun fire even closer. They could not always get to a team quickly. In bad weather, they might not be able to get to a team at all. They were limited in how long they could remain with the team. Because of this, teams used them almost exclusively to break contact and provide covering fire during a hot extraction. Artillery was not available during the actual extraction, but gunship and door gunners could bring great close support.

THE COBRA GUN SHIP OR "SNAKE" A LRRP'S BEST FRIEND.

The communications equipment that we had was good for the time. We carried the PRC-25 AM radio. It was about twelve inches wide, fifteen inches high and three inches thick. It was a fairly rugged piece of equipment, light, and dependable by the standards of the day. I recall that it weighed about eight pounds. It used batteries that were prone to fail after a few days. The handsets were susceptible to getting wet, which caused them to fail. The tuning to various frequencies was done manually with knobs. They were sensitive to weather and could be very inconsistent about the range they offered. By today's standards they were big, heavy, temperamental, and short on range. By the standards of the day, they were the best available. I cannot compare the PRC-25 to the radios of the NVA, simply because I never actually had the opportunity to see the NVA radios. The NVA did not use as many radios as the Americans did, nor did they use them like the Americans did. The PRC–25 was equipped to communicate with other infantry units, helicopters, artillery and other aircraft. It was used as a command and control radio. The NVA, as far as I know, used their radios only at the higher levels of command.

There were times when teams took new technology into the field for testing and evaluation. The new Starlight Scope was one such tool. It was the first version of the night vision equipment used today. They were about fifteen inches long and weighed five pounds. They had a three-inch objective lens and required several D batteries. They used these at an incredible rate. They had a very high-pitched hum when in use. They were still classified when we used them. They were of limited use to LRRPs, but they were very effective at letting you see at night.

We also tested small seismic devices that were used to monitor trails. They recorded any small shock waves on the ground and sent an alert to the team. They were simple and effective. A small probe was pushed into the ground and a head set received the signal if they picked up a vibration. Again, they were good tools, but of limited use to us. The biggest issue we had with them was that they were too sensitive and went off constantly. One team, using this device, detected a tiger approaching their ambush site and retreated to the safety of a tree. My good friend and Ranger school colleague, Larry Bergman, had an engineering degree and was often tasked with field-testing these new weapons.

For the men of the 4th Infantry Division LRRP and K Company 75th Infantry, these were our weapons, our tools of the trade. They were for the most part good, dependable tools that served us well. They had issues, to be sure, they were difficult at times, impossible at others, but without them we would have been lost. I recall discussing the M-16 with my dad. He had carried an old Springfield 1903 bolt-action rifle in WWII. He could hardly fathom the firepower of the new Colt. When I said the M-60 was heavy, he pointed out that the machine guns he had trained with were three times as heavy. I have experienced the same thing as I see the new weapons of today's army. A radio that fits in your hand, a starlight scope that fits on your helmet, and a machine gun that weighs less than half that of an M-60. We never dreamed of these kinds of weapons, but used the ones we had to great effect.

CHAPTER 18

Sapper attack

❖

In mid-November of 1969, the 4th Inf. Division started to move much of the division's resources in one of several steps toward the coast and eventually to leave the country. All of K Company would be moved as well. My platoon had been there almost all of the time, but the rest of the company was scattered around the highlands. This concentrating of the troops and equipment had several effects. First, it made the perimeter a very busy place. Where once we could literally see footpaths through the wire, a strong perimeter provided tighter security. On the other side of the coin, there was now a wealth of targets to be had inside the wire, inviting the sapper attacks that came. Sappers were well-trained soldiers who specialized in working their way through the perimeter defenses of American units and blowing up equipment, material and buildings.

There was not much to be concerned about in the company area most of the time. We had access to weapons if we ever needed them, but I don't think I ever drew weapons except for a mission or reactionary force until the night of this attack. The men in K Company, much to the consternation of everyone else, did not stand any perimeter guard duty at An Khe or Pleiku. We were pretty much without duty assignments when we were on stand down. We were scheduled to go out the next day, and I recall packing during the late afternoon. Our web gear was packed and loaded with ammo and grenades.

My first hint that all was not well was an explosion from the direction of the Golf Course. It was not uncommon to hear things at night, but this was not normal. It was clearly not outgoing mortars or artillery fire. There had been sporadic gunfire from the perimeter called the "green line." It soon became apparent that something bigger than normal had happened when several more explosions shook the Golf Course. The glow of a fairly large fire could be seen from the direction of the heliport.

In the company area, I heard several Rangers shouting that there were "dinks in the wire." That meant that enemy soldiers had penetrated the perimeter and that they were probably responsible for the explosions and fires that we had observed. That information caused concern for those Rangers in the area. If the VC or NVA had indeed breached the wire and were on the Golf Course, we were in some danger.

If we were given orders to get our weapons, the specifics of the order are long gone. We must have gone to the weapons room, because my next memory is of crouching in one of the small infiltration bunkers scattered throughout the company area. The number of explosions continued to grow and it was now apparent that the helicopters were being targeted. Some pilots apparently had managed to get their machines up and there were some gunships flying and firing over the perimeter. There was increased gunfire from the big towers on the perimeter. There must have been some warning sirens sounding, but I do not remember them. If the attack included mortars or rockets, they were not apparent to me during the attack.

There seemed to be a lot of confusion on the perimeter. Shots would be fired in one area and then in another. There were some vehicles moving around on the road between our area and the perimeter. Some of the guys who were in the company that night recall a warning that someone had seen an enemy soldier inside our company area. That added to the concern and confusion. None of us had radios, and without the proper frequencies, they would have been of no value. I am sure that our senior NCOs and officers were checking on the guys in these bunkers, and that had to be very dangerous. Adding to the issues at hand was the way these infiltration bunkers were made. They were shallow dugouts with pieces of corrugated steel at the front. They looked like the bands used to fasten corrugated steel culverts together, and they might have been just that. They had some sand bags in the front as well. They faced outward toward the wire, which made perfect sense if the attackers were trying to get into Camp Radcliffe, the sprawling base camp at An Khe. In this case, however, it was very likely that we would encounter sappers coming in and going back out as well. This exposed the backside of these bunkers, adding to the stress of the situation. I found myself in one of these bunkers with my point man, and neither of us knew what was going on, so we decided to just stay put and see what happened.

I think we were in the bunker for about two hours. After some time, we could hear equipment on the Golf Course, trying to fight the fires. Some time later in the night, we returned to the barracks. We were to be inserted the next day and so we were among the first from K Company to see the carnage on the Golf Course.

Between many of the steel revetments, designed to protect the choppers from artillery or rocket rounds, were the smoldering wrecks of much of the 4th Division's aviation assets. I clearly remember seeing the outline of an observation helicopter burned into the ground. Most of the machine was now a shadow of white powder on the ground. Arranged precisely within the outline were the steel parts that had not burned. The engine, rotor heads, and a few frame members were all that remained. I saw a slick, the Huey helicopter, with the entire top burned off. The lower third of the machine appeared to be un-damaged, but the upper two-thirds was gone. The sappers had placed an explosive charge in or under the helicopters, rupturing the fuel cells and igniting the fires that destroyed the machines totally.

A HUEY DESTROYED IN THE SAPPER ATTACK AT AN KHE.

Nothing of the mission we were assigned the next day seems to have been remarkable enough to recall, except that there were many team leaders like me trying to get out of the base camp and back to the bush. However, the next few weeks were more uncomfortable than usual for us. The attack had significantly reduced the choppers available to insert or extract teams. Several team leaders tell of missions where a VR was not possible. I don't remember ever doing that, but I have no doubt that it happened. While LRRPs were not usually anxious to get into the bush, and generally were glad to hear that insertions had been cancelled, after one night in the big base camp under attack, most of us were relieved to get the heck out of there.

I don't think anyone in the company was hurt, I don't know of anyone who fired a weapon or really was ever in imminent danger. It was the confusion and not knowing what was going on that bothered me the most. There was no control over the situation at all. It seemed to be pretty much the opposite of what we faced in the bush. There we had some control; we had some feeling of comfort with the threats. We sought out opportunities to get out of Radcliffe for a while after that attack. I wrote home about this incident and my parents saved a clipping from the local paper about the attack. Reading the article, dated November 16, 1969, many years later, triggered a flood of emotion in me. It was the fear that I felt over the lack of control that returned as I read the story. The story itself seemed true, but strangely detached. It seemed to be a piece of historical fiction that I was reading, that somehow was related to what I experienced that night.

Like much of the war, I have come to accept that what I recall, what I know happened, and what I feel is often not as neatly tied together as one might expect.

Years later, after talking to others who were there, it seems that my memory of this attack was flawed. I now know that what I recall was actually an attack in May of 1970, not the attack on November 16, 1969. Three things now seem to point to that. First, there were no infiltration bunkers in the platoon area, north of the Golf Course, where I was in November. There were bunkers in the company area, south of the Golf Course, after the whole company moved to An Khe. This seems to eliminate the November attack, and points to the later one.

Second, Bob White thinks that we were out in the bush during the first attack. His confidence in that fits well with the rest of the information. Third, the Division did not move until well after the November attack. The attacks were very similar and it is not at all surprising that they could be confused. Whether I recall the early or the later attack does nothing to change the emotional reaction I have to the article. It still gives me the chills when I think about being in the bunker, and not knowing what was going on.

CHAPTER 19

Peace on Earth

In many ways, it was just another day in the bush. There was nothing particularly worth remembering, no contact, or any real excitement. I don't recall where we were or much of anything else about this mission. It would have been just one of many forgotten nights in Vietnam, except that it was Christmas Eve.

I think there was supposed to be some sort of Christmas truce, but it apparently never got to us, at least in time for a pre-Christmas extraction. I recall one of my teammates being very offended about being out on this of all nights. We probably ate as we usually did, part of a C-ration and tepid water from a plastic canteen. We might have heated the "C-rats" and water for hot coffee, if I thought it was safe. I probably didn't. We slept as we always did, on the ground, wrapped in a poncho liner. We would have placed our claymore mines out in a defensive perimeter. Our weapons were checked and ready to fire. Artillery preplots had been registered around the night location, ready to bring a firestorm of explosives and hot shrapnel onto anyone attempting to find us. Just before and after last light, all four men were on full alert. The team was ready, willing, and very able to unleash an incredibly violent response to any threat. After that, guard was one hour on and three hours off for the rest of the night. The situation reports to our command center had started for the night.

Our night location, chosen for defensive purposes, would have offered no concession to the date. The bush was a harsh and unforgiving place, and we could not afford to make any special consideration, not even for Christmas. December 24, 1969, was totally devoid of any of the trappings of Christmas. There were no parties, no special food, unless someone packed an extra can of peaches or fruit cocktail, or maybe an extra pound cake. There was no eggnog, no punch, no lights, no gifts, no carols, no tree, and no family. We had tried to salvage some of Christmas at Camp Radcliffe, but there was none of that here, not in the field. Sometime during the early part of the night, when situation reports were being called, someone acknowledged the day.

Zero called, "Romeo 5- sit rep?" and Romeo 5 replied in a whisper "Negative and green."

"Romeo 6- sit rep?" and the reply, again whispered, "Negative and green."

"Romeo 11- sit rep?" "Romeo 11- negative and green and Merry Christmas!"

Whoever was manning the radio in base camp replied, "Merry Christmas," and played a short part of *Silent Night* on the radio net. A few more short bits of Christmas music and some unauthorized radio chatter followed between sit reps for the next hour. Then it was back to the usual business of night security for LRRPS at war.

What I recall about that Christmas has colored every Christmas since. The words of *Silent Night* were in stark contrast to the situation we found ourselves in. There was not any Peace on Earth, not here to be sure! I was concerned only with defending my team and myself. I certainly felt no good will toward the NVA, the VC, or anyone involved in putting me out on this mission. And yet, there was a very real feeling of gratitude for the birth of the Savior! The reality of the war, being involved in it, living it, made Christmas important to me. It was more than a holiday. I remember a real and deeply defining moment of gratitude. There was peace, real peace, not on Earth, but in my soul. It was there, in between the reminders of the war. It was there despite lying on the ground, cradling an M-16 in my arms. It was there despite the possibility of killing or being killed.

For many years after, I have struggled with the commercialism and the seemingly shallow nature of Christmas in America. In some ways, I have longed for that moment when all of the wrappings and trappings were gone, and briefly I felt Christmas anyway. I have sought moments like those when, lacking the "stuff' of the holiday season, I knew the Spirit of Christmas was there with me.

That Christmas day was in 1969. Some of the hurt is still there, some of the anger still occasionally bubbles to the top. I still struggle with Christmas, perhaps for reasons even beyond that day. I wonder why I am still here to celebrate the holidays and others are not. I still struggle with the way Christmas happens, but I count it a blessing to have known a Christmas with nothing, absolutely nothing, but Christ's birth to celebrate.

CHAPTER 20

Red Shorts Mission

T he Red Shorts mission was assigned on the 27th of January 1970. In spite of a new year, it was the Vietnam equivalent of a World War II SNAFU. If it could go wrong, it did go wrong on this mission. It was a well-planned mission, it was a well-supplied mission, it was a well-manned mission, and nothing went as expected. The area near Fire Base St. George was infamous for several reasons, but specifically lots of VC and extremely poor communications. My team and Rick Noble's team were assigned an ambush mission in the area while the entire company was working out of Pleiku. There was an armored unit in the area, and while they found plenty evidence that the VC were in the AO, they had not been able to make any substantial contact with them. The VC wisely decided that they did not want to tangle with American armor.

The solution to the problem, at least according to the higher command, was to put a heavy LRRP team in and ambush the enemy. This was a Hawkeye mission that I tried to avoid. We were the ones chosen to do the task. The basic plan was to insert the two teams together and have them work as one. This was somewhat rare for us, but not something that caused any major issues. The two teams knew and trusted each other, so it was just a matter of doing the planning and then executing the mission. Or so we thought.

The plan started with the insertion of the teams on the morning log birds. Logistics birds flew supplies and men into these units once or twice a day, and so they would attract little attention. Our plan was to take advantage of this and get into the area without doing anything that might indicate that a Ranger team was there. Once on the ground, the teams were to quickly get into an armored personal carrier and go to the site chosen for the ambush. Once there, we would dismount and set up our ambush, do our thing, and be extracted. A simple plan, that was not so simple in the execution.

We carefully coordinated the plan with the armored commanders and loaded up to be flown to the area. We landed as planned and moved quickly to the APC to load up. The door was not open, so we got down in the grass, and I started a common check. The other TL was doing the same. I had no contact with our Zero at all. I quickly changed to the tanks frequency or in our slang "push" to contact them, and found that they apparently had changed their radios to another unknown frequency. Before anyone realized what was happening, the tank unit throttled up the engines and moved out, leaving us alone and a very long way from the assigned ambush area! Coordination with the tanks had failed at some point. We had been on the ground less than three minutes, and most of the plan was now compromised. It does not take long for things to go wrong in a war. Both teams tried to establish some communication, without any success. To make matters worse, no one expected us to call in until we left the tracks. That meant no one would be concerned about not hearing from us for an hour or so. We found ourselves alone and without communication. The only good news was that we were well prepared to fight if we had to.

Rick and I knew that we had to find an area that had some radio signal. There was little concealment or cover in the area, and the risk of being seen was high. It was only a matter of time until we were discovered. Our assigned ambush site was a considerable distance from the insertion point. I cannot remember how far it was, but it was much further than we normally moved. Any attempt at mounting an extraction depended totally on the radio, so we had no choice but to move. Seeing a slight rise, we moved toward it, checking for commo as we went. After a short move, we still had not found any radio contact, and the tracks were still not answering our calls. Again we located an area that looked like it might offer some help with the radios and moved. Again, the move produced no results. We found another small hill and settled in for another commo check.

Before I could try the radio, someone alerted the team to movement in the area. I moved to the spot and looked across an open area to see an apparently unarmed man running at full speed along a path about 200 meters from us. It was unusual to see someone in the open like this. It was also strange to see them un-armed, but the most striking thing about this man was his uniform. The man we saw running across the open terrain was wearing nothing but very bright, very red shorts. On most other missions, we might have spent some time considering the meaning of the sight, but on this day, being unable to contact our support units put the puzzle into the back of our minds.

We continued to move until our own radio people in Pleiku contacted the tanks and figured out what had happened. They quickly sent some airborne relay to find us. With this relay in place, we now could communicate with our artillery, if needed. The tanks were now well away from the area and were not coming back. Except for an extraction, we were left with no option but walking to the ambush site or establishing a new one. We were concerned about the possibility of having been seen by the red shorts guy, but the radio contact made it feasible for us to try to move toward the assigned area. As we moved, we seemed to get a stronger signal on our own radio net, and K Company had a team near the Mang Yang pass that could relay for us. Perhaps we would be able to do our assigned mission after all.

Had this been a recon mission with four men, we would almost certainly have been extracted. Undetected movement here was nearly impossible. We had probably been detected at this point in the mission. A four-man team would have been in extreme danger.

I do not know how far we moved or how long it took. I know that as we moved, we saw more and more indication that we were indeed in an area with a significant amount of VC activity. Our radios were still not functioning well, but communications were getting better. We were in an area that might offer a suitable ambush location and provided more cover than before, and since movement was not difficult, we pressed on.

Some time late in the day, we started to look for a night location. None of the artillery pre-plots we had registered for the ambush site were close enough to be of any use to us, so we needed new ones. This revealed another unwelcome surprise. The guns we were counting on could not reach us, so we would have to use another firebase. That firebase was LZ Black Hawk, with 175mm guns. These huge guns were very powerful, but they were not especially accurate. Bringing these rounds close was very dangerous. For many years, I believed that the guns were at maximum range and that was part of our concern about the accuracy. As I was able to research this mission, the guns were probably about six to ten miles away, well within their twenty-mile range. Ironically, I learned from an artillery guy that these guns sometimes had problems at the shorter ranges. He said this might be because, at short distances, the gun tube had to be raised to a very high angle and that could interfere with the long gun tube's stability. I don't know if that was the case or not. In any case, our concern about staying in the field started to rise dramatically!

Just as we found what looked like a suitable night location, we lost radio contact again. We decided to move up another small hill and soon had better commo. As we moved, it became apparent that we would have to spend the night in an area that offered little in the way of cover to maintain our contact with the radio relay team.

The normal procedure for our teams was to stop late in the day, eat, and then move into a night location just before it started to get dark. On this evening our movement was stopped prematurely by two problems. If we moved one way we lost our radio relay team, when we moved the other way, we ran into what appeared to be the opening of some sort of tunnel or bunker. We had no choice; we stayed where we had the ability to use our radio. We set up a defensive perimeter, taking some comfort in the fact that we had plenty of firepower if we needed it. We would have been carrying extra claymore mines, an M-60 machine gun, extra grenades, and ammo for this type of ambush. Our packs might have been lighter than normal because we would not have had food or water for a full five days, as was normal. We found a depression on the side on a small finger of slightly higher ground. This offered minimal cover, and allowed us to watch the tunnel at the same time. By using our long whip antenna, we had reasonably reliable radio contact with our relay team. We registered our new pre-plots and settled in for the night.

About an hour after last light, we got another nasty surprise: we could not get helicopters to our location for some reason. I have always thought that it was due to weather, but others on the mission thought it had something to do with another unit in contact. For whatever reason, a night extraction was apparently ruled out. Night extractions were avoided unless the team had absolutely no other option. With the Blackjack slicks unavailable, we did not have even that option. More critical to us, however, was the lack of gunship support if we did get into contact. The gunships, call sign Gambler, were the very best close support we had in a fight. The mini guns on these ships, mostly Cobras, could be brought to within a few meters of a team and would usually end any attack very quickly. The after action report for this mission asserts that we had gunships early in the evening, but no mention is made of them later. This may account for later differences in our recall about the availability of air support. The possibility that our friend in the red shorts had seen us was now a huge concern.

After the full alert at last light, we placed half of the men on watch, and were just about to allow the remaining men to sleep when we started to hear and see movement in front of us. It was not long before we all knew that we were being probed. They did not know exactly where we were, and I don't think they knew exactly what we were. Both worked in our favor. For some time they just moved around the area, searching for us. Our somewhat unconventional defensive location may have confused them. We were not where they expected us to be. Inevitably, they got too close and we had to begin a defense of the position.

Our first response was to fire single rounds from our M-16s at targets we could see. This lessened our exposure and risk of giving away our exact location. They soon realized that we were able to see enough to shoot accurately and tried to approach by walking behind a water buffalo. Bob White stopped this tactic with his M-79 grenade launcher. At the time we were not sure exactly what was happening, but Bob's "blooper" seemed to stop whatever it was. We needed to use the artillery, but I was also very concerned about an errant round falling too close.

The decision was soon made for us when we started to get more and more movement all around us. It was clear that they now knew about where we were. I called artillery, while Rick Noble ran the defense of the perimeter. My first rounds were a long way off, because the guns were concerned about accuracy. My adjustments had to go through the relay, slowing the process even further. I was able to get the big shells in close enough to cause the bad guys to reconsider the situation for a while. I do not know how close to troops the 175s could be used, but we called them close enough to drop dirt and debris on our position. I do know that the HE rounds from that gun weighed 174 pounds. Bringing the rounds close was scary even with the very accurate 105mm guns, but it was absolutely terrifying with these guns. We were so close that the artillery Fire Direction Center nearly refused our request. That did nothing to make us feel safer. I was able to convince them that it was far safer than not firing them. We continued this terrifying game of cat and well-armed mouse for several hours. At some point during the night, the VC decided to try one last time to overrun us.

For the first time on the mission I got a pleasant surprise. I was told that there was an air force flare ship, call sign "Spooky," that could get to us. This plane was an old AC-47 or DC-3, a World War II vintage plane that could drop large parachute flares and illuminate the area around our team for long periods of time. Good for us, not so good for the VC. During the night, the clouds had obscured the sky, making it nearly impossible to see anyone moving in front of our perimeter. I hammered the area with artillery and then Spooky made a pass, dropping a flare. The flare lit up the area around us, revealing several targets and allowing us to fire our personal weapons accurately. When the flare went out, we used artillery again. The flare ship made another drop, exposing the VC to our small arms fire. This pattern continued, and then some time during the early morning the probing stopped, and by first light the VC had vanished.

After we were sure that we were not going to be ambushed ourselves, we did a sweep of the area around our perimeter. There was plenty of evidence that we had indeed had a sizable unit looking for us during the night. It was also apparent that we had inflicted considerable punishment on that unit. There were blood trails, discarded bandages, and other signs of wounded men in the area. We found shell casings and damaged equipment and one dead buffalo, but little else. This was no surprise to us, nor would it have surprised most infantrymen in Vietnam. The VC and NVA were very good at leaving a battlefield without leaving any bodies. It seemed to be a surprise to some of our higher-level commanders.

We were later accused of faking this contact because we could not produce any bodies. This led to a heated exchange between a battalion commander and me. After searching the area, checking on the tunnel, and doing our normal intelligence gathering, we were to meet the tanks and be extracted. Extraction by tank was not normal for us, but then nothing on this mission was normal, so why start now? The extraction had its own adventure, and that story is in The Spider Hole, Chapter 21. I had forgotten about many of the details of this mission, and several questions remain unanswered. One question that baffles most of us is that Spooky had mini guns on board and we could have used them instead of the artillery. For some reason we did not, and I do not know why. What changed to require the use of the 175mm guns from LZ Blackhawk? Again, none of us can remember. Most of the questions are focused on the guy in the red shorts. I have often thought of the man, running unarmed through an open field in a combat zone. What was he doing? Did he know we were there? Why was he unarmed? Did he have a story about us to tell years later? If he did, what was it? Mostly I have wondered what caused him to be wearing red shorts. It is one of the most bizarre moments that I can recall in Vietnam. I have no explanation, none at all.

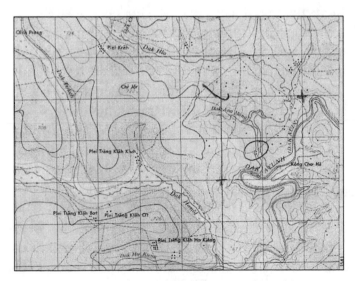

A copy of the map and overlay of this mission. Two crosses define the corners of the AO. The circle is the ambush area and the "j" shaped line is the route we traveled. Source: After action reports.

CHAPTER 21

The Spider Hole

———————— ⬥ ————————

S pider holes were small holes in the ground with a little lid made of woven grass or vines. The VC would dig these holes in strategic locations and hide in them. They would pop up, shoot someone or something, and then disappear back under ground, often unseen. They were nearly impossible to see and so were a real danger to all infantrymen. I considered them a greater threat than snipers because there were many more of them in the area where we worked. On the Red Shorts mission, I had a personal encounter with a spider hole.

We had been dropped off to ambush an area and we had lost commo and been in contact off and on all night. After a harrowing night on the ground, armored vehicles arrived in the morning to extract us. A short ride on the tanks ended when shots were fired at a tank from a spider hole. That abruptly ended the ride on the tanks, and all of the LRRPs with me decided to walk out. We decided that walking was better than riding if the VC were willing to shoot at tanks. As we moved, we always had a team member walking drag. The last guy in line looks backwards and covers the six (back side) of the rest of the team.

As we walked out, I walked past a spider hole and did not see it. I had no idea it was there. As I passed the hole and moved a short distance past it, the occupant of the hole slowly pushed up the lid and raised his weapon, intent on shooting me in the back. Bob White, walking drag, turned in time to see the lid move and fired on the man, killing him. The unexpected shots caused an immediate reaction among the LRRPs and armor crews. Every LRRP was on the ground and looking for the threat. Bob let us know what had happened and we continued our walk out of the area.

I know that this happened. Bob recalls it in vivid detail. This is the kind of incident one would expect to be indelibly etched in my mind. It is not. I have a very vague picture of some event in my mind. I cannot place it on this mission, I cannot say that I would have remembered it without Bob's reminder, and I do not have the emotional reaction to the story that one would normally attribute to such an event. This was an honest to goodness "you saved my life" moment! There is no other way to characterize this event. But I do not have any detailed recall of that happening at all.

Why would that be? There are several things that come to mind. Both Bob and I remember this mission as the worst mission we ever had together. We were without commo and had shaky artillery support. We were probed all night long by a sizable group of VC or NVA. They were persistent in their attempts to find us and were willing to lose people to do it. We had limited helicopter support. We did get a "Spooky" flare ship to help keep them away. I fired artillery all night long. They were 175 mm guns from LZ Blackhawk and not dependably accurate, adding to the stress of the night. As we rode out, we were shot at again. I was pretty well spent and it is possible that I just had reached my limit and emotionally blocked it out. I never saw this event either, it all happened behind me and was over before I knew what happened.

After we got back to Pleiku, I was debriefing and someone challenged my honesty about the contact. They accused us of faking a contact and said a contact like that should have produced a big body count. I was instantly livid and responded with something to the effect that I had eight live bodies going in and I had eight live bodies coming out. That was all the counting I had time for and that was all I did. This certainly added to the emotional turmoil I was in.

This story shows how deeply distorted the thinking of men in combat can become. It shows the perverse nature of combat and its effects on the minds of men. I know it happened. I know Bob White saved my life that day, and I am grateful beyond measure. There is little head knowledge, but my heart seems somehow to know it happened. I cannot tell this story or hear it told without a deep uneasy feeling. It is a feeling of dread, or awe, or maybe both. My dad once told me that "We should be thankful for God's miracles in our lives, whether we are aware of them or not." I have come to believe that this may well be one of those miracles, almost unknown to me, but real, very real.

CHAPTER 22

War is (funny as) Hell

⸎

The names in this piece have not been changed to protect the innocent or anyone else. Not that anyone was innocent! War is neither fun nor glamorous. It is not often what the popular media presents it to be, but sometimes it was funny. Here are a few of those stories.

When the 4th Infantry Division was leaving Vietnam, all of K Company was moved to An Khe. To make room for the extra Rangers, many old unused barracks in the company area were pressed into use. These old buildings provided two of the funny stories of my war. One evening I had gone into one of the old barracks to visit. Bob, Roger, and others were visiting, laughing, and messing around with a tape recorder. They were, as usual, usurping my tape to my folks and filling it with their special brand of silliness. It was cheaper than beer and really very effective as a stress reliever. On this tape you can hear music, guys singing, hollering for more beer and generally being rowdy. If you listen carefully you can hear the wind blowing. Suddenly, there is a horrible crash. The tape records total silence for ten seconds or so until someone says softly, "What was that?" Another few seconds of silence and someone else says, "That was the TV antenna." You hear a few nervous, relieved giggles as we realize that we are not dead and have not been mortared. Then the place erupts in laughter.

The old barracks had a TV antenna on a pole that broke in the wind. The metal antenna fell directly onto the tin roof of the building. With no ceiling or insulation above us, it was loud and very much like the shattering sound of an incoming mortar. I have the incident preserved on CD. It is a treasure.

The same building provided this story. Late in my tour, we got a new 1st Sergeant, named Richards. He was a small, wiry man. He was rumored to have three stars on his CIB. The Combat Infantry Badge signifies having been in combat in a war, a star lets you know that the soldier has been on more than one. It seems unlikely that he had a three star CIB, but in any case you knew you were in the presence of a very rare and very real soldier. His position as 1st Sergeant was enough to cause fear in our hearts.

Top was known to have a drink from time to time, and on this evening he had indulged his desire well. He came to visit us for a while and probably share another round or two. All permanent structures at Camp Radcliffe had blast walls around the outside. These were short walls of sand bags to protect you from shrapnel during attacks. These old buildings had blast trenches for protection. During an attack, you just hopped in and you were relatively safe.

On this night, Top was either leaving or going out to pee. In either case, he forgot about the trenches. They were long neglected and full of water and who knows what else. He walked head long into this foul brew. We all heard the slosh and then the unmistakable, full-throated roar of a 1st Sergeant wronged. The air was blue as Top vented his wrath. It took a minute, but someone must have helped him out. I recall that there was not a sound from any of us until we were sure Top was well out of earshot, for to be caught laughing at Top was not something any of us wanted to do. Men who faced the best the NVA had to offer in tiny four-man teams were afraid to even smile at Top Richards for weeks.

Bob White, my long-time ATL had, and still does have, a way of making just about anything funny, sometimes without meaning to. On a mission into the notorious mountains northeast of An Khe, we were forced to "E and E" (escape and evade) during a contact. The extraction LZ was tiny, steep, and exposed, so we had to get close to the downhill side for extraction. This position minimized the exposure of the chopper and the team. To get to this position we had to cross an open and exposed area. The first two across made it safely, but when Bob and I tried, we drew fire from the ridgeline above us.

Time gets warped in these moments. What happened takes longer to tell than it actually took to do. The twenty or thirty meters we had to cover could not have taken more than a few seconds. We had packs on, but we were also very motivated. Bob, bent over and sprinting hard, was the first to draw fire. I was running for my life behind him. As we gained speed and straightened up, I saw puffs of dust in front of Bob and between us. I knew they were bullets hitting the ground. What I saw next was Bob jumping over the puffs of dirt. I realized instantly what he was doing and started to laugh. When we made it to cover, I was still laughing. I don't know what the team thought, but when my mind replays the sight of Bob jumping bullets, I laugh.

After the entire company was moved to Camp Radcliffe at An Khe, it took some time for several of our needed services to catch up. We had plenty of food and ammo for missions, but some other things just didn't get done right away. One of these was the shower facility. There was a nice shower building and an elevated tank to run the showers. It was primitive and old, but it worked, if we had water in the tank. That was an issue for a while. LRRPs and Rangers were and still are to some extent a very practical group. We prided ourselves on the art of field expediency, making due, improvising and getting what we needed. That sometimes led to some less than regulation solutions to problems. We were out of water one day and it started to rain very heavily. Water was soon pouring off the tin roof of every building in the company area. It was not long until half a dozen or more Rangers had solved the problem of no water for showers. Field expedience and a total lack of modesty of any sort placed these men on the blast wall and under the torrent of water coming off the roof. Soap in hand, and totally naked, they scrubbed off. I doubt this would have happened in any other company area on the post, but as far as I know, nothing was ever said. This incident is recalled broadly and with some pride. We remember some very strange things.

During the Cambodian invasion, one of the brigades from the 4th ID was rotated back to the base camp at An Khe. Some landed on the airstrip at the airfield and were unloading from a C-130. I am not sure why I was at the field, but I was there and witnessed an event that remains in my mind for several reasons. As the men walked down the ramp at the back of the plane, it was apparent that this was a combat unit and that they had been in a fight. They were filthy. Faces, hands, and uniforms were covered in red dirt. Most had the telltale signs of weapons smoke on them as well. Uniforms were not only dirty, but most were ripped and torn. More than one young grunt got off the plane with some part of his fatigues missing. Some had only a flak jacket and pants on. Many had legs torn off their pants or arms off the shirts. Several guys had lost some strategic hind parts of the uniform, and since underwear was optional for many grunts, the level of exposure was high. A significant number had minor wounds bandaged, and their uniforms showed blood through the fabric. It was a pretty un-funny sight in fact, until the last several men marched down the ramp.

A group of six or seven older men, probably officers and senior NCOs, exited the plane wearing nothing but OD green underwear and "steel pot" combat helmets. One was a chaplain and the others carried weapons. They walked out of the plane with their white bellies and legs flashing in the sun. All of them had on battered boots. Each of the men still had his load bearing equipment on, and that only made the absurdity of the situation worse. The entire group of men, tired and battered as they were, could not stifle a laugh as these men walked to the front of the formation, took command, and marched them off to wherever they were going. They marched off, with their rear ends hanging out and their leadership nearly naked.

The men in their underwear had probably given their uniforms and other gear to men who remained in Cambodia. None of them were in any mood to be laughed at, even though they were laughing at each other. There was a small group of ARVN soldiers at the airport that day and they started to laugh at the Americans. But for the quick thinking of the leadership and a chaplain who placed himself between the two groups, there would have been a firefight right then and there. Etched indelibly in my mind is the picture of these professional soldiers, very much "out of uniform," but also very professionally exercising their authority. I had witnessed an act of courage and sacrifice to be sure, but it is one forever colored by the bizarre picture left in my mind's eye.

One of the best parts of doing this writing has been the tendency for discussion to bring some lost memories to mind. This is one such story. I still have only a vague picture of this, but even if not totally true, it is worth telling. I had gone out to pull my claymore mine in after a night in the bush. I apparently had to do my morning duty, and while squatting with my pants down, realized we were very close to a trail and I saw an enemy soldier. I apparently fired at him, and ran to the night location with my backside still flapping in the breeze. Someone fired at me, and Bob bravely grabbed me and pulled me behind a tree, still in a state of semi-nudity. While he recalls this all clearly, I do not.

While the potential for some really funny and off-color writing exists, I will end this story with this: Apparently I decided not to tell the story and used combat stress as a means of conveniently forgetting it. The only other possibility is that Bob just got me to write a story that he will point out was a total farce, and we will both enjoy the trickery.

CHAPTER 23

The Company Mission: POW Rescue

N othing could have grabbed our attention more completely than the words "American Prisoners of War." There was a mixture of fear and excitement in our minds as we listened to that first briefing. It was a totally unique mission in every way. Nothing about this mission fit the way we normally operated. It seemed, to some of us, nothing more than a trap. All the warning signs seemed to be there, but if there was even the slightest chance that there were Americans being held, we knew we were going.

GLEN KLUIE AND I ON THE COMPANY MISSION, THE ONLY TIME I DID NOT
CARRY MY OWN RADIO. (COURTESY OF KC CRUNK)

I am not going to try to write a history of this mission. That has been done, in the cited book <u>Reflections</u>. I will not chronicle the whole mission, because I do not know about the whole mission. My recall of the mission is very limited. Like much of the rest of my time in K Company, there is a frustrating discontinuity in what I recall. The years have stripped away details, my specific task limited my perspective, and there was a great deal that I never knew about this mission until thirty years after the fact. Security was a high priority, limiting information even further.

In February 1970, units of the 4th Infantry Division captured a Vietnamese soldier. This man apparently indicated to intelligence personal that he was an escaped POW and that he was held with American POWs. As one might imagine, that caused quite a stir. K Company was assigned the mission of assaulting the camp and rescuing the POWs held there. How and why we were given this mission remained a mystery to most of us for many years.

This mission was the absolute antithesis of everything we normally did. It was to be a company-size mission! We normally worked in four-man teams, and occasionally eight-man teams, but never larger. We were reconnaissance and ambush, hit and run, sneak and peek, not assault troops. This was an assault mission. We did everything we could to keep from being seen or heard, but this mission was going to be big and noisy. We knew our four-man teams better than we knew our own brothers, but we were going to be working with many men who had never been to the field together. Team leaders, who operated with near total autonomy as LRRPs, now became squad leaders, under a platoon sergeant, who was under a platoon leader, commanded by the company commander. While we trusted these men in the roles they filled in the Ranger Company, we did not know them at all in this situation. It was not mistrust, but it was the unknown that bothered us.

Below the company commander and his staff, none of us knew much about the plan. It was developed by our leadership and approved by the Division. Each of us got just as much information as we needed, and no more. We practiced the mission inside the wire at An Khe. There was a detailed sand table model of the compound and the surrounding area. We all spent a great deal of time on this model.

The only really clear memory of this portion of the training happened at this table. I expressed some doubt about my ability to do the job assigned to me. Top Keller looked at me and then said, "You are a Ranger, you wouldn't be here if you couldn't do this!" I quickly diverted my attention back to the plan.

My team was part of the point element, Rick Noble's team with some added men was the actual point, and Lt. Martin was the point commander. This focused me on two parts of the mission. First, we were responsible for leading the assault unit to the camp. Our primary responsibility was the route and movement to the objective. Exiting the compound and moving to the extraction was our second task. I had this part of the map memorized. I knew it inside out, upside down and backward. We were all very paranoid about the possibility of this being a trap. We tried to anticipate all kinds of contingencies. The first concern was getting hit on the LZ; the second was getting ambushed on the way from the LZ to the camp. We tried to anticipate everything and work through the best responses. The rest of the company made up the assault group, and another platoon served as a blocking unit. They planned and practiced their part just as we did.

The mission was staged out of LZ Hard Times. The choppers flew the company into the assault LZ, dropping us in reverse of our order of march. This meant that the lead group was the last to go in. As we came into the LZ, there was red smoke on the ground. That normally signified that the LZ was hot and troops were in contact. I remember yelling across the cabin of the Huey, "LZ is hot," and thinking that we had been right about this being a trap.

The next thing that I remember is realizing that the LZ was not flat and that I was going to be pretty high up when I left the skids. I had no choice, my guys on the other side of the aircraft were already out, and those on my side had to go as well. It seemed like I fell forever. I have no idea what happened during the next few minutes.

The next picture in my mind is of moving forward to begin the movement to the camp. Rick and his team were moving with us, and I knew that the red smoke had been an accident. We were not in contact. We knew exactly where to go, and that was a huge relief. Again, there is a blank in the sequence of events, before another vivid event appears. We were forced to move in some low ground that narrowed into a small ravine. As we moved, the point group saw pungi sticks on the banks, indicating that we might be in danger of being ambushed. Rick stopped the column and I called Lt. Martin to come up to me. We decided to move on quickly. We were close and we needed to get to the compound to prevent harm to any prisoners that might be present.

Looking back, this appears to have been a huge risk, warranted only by the possibility of Americans in the camp. Rick moved out and we followed. Another gap, and another very clear image. Rick's team was right at the point where we were to begin the assault when a man literally walked out of the brush and right into them. They grabbed him and held him down. I recall very clearly the look of absolute terror on the guy's face.

The point element had done its job of getting the assault group to the camp. We were now flank security for the main assault. There are many descriptions of what happened in the assault of the camp. I seem to recall some firing, and Bob White got a bit of shrapnel in his belly from his grenade launcher. Others do not recall firing. I saw no one except K Company guys during this part of the mission. Others remember seeing several people running from the area. I know Bob fired his weapon, because I had to bandage his belly. It was not a dangerous wound, but it was painful. We did not find any Americans, nor did we find any evidence that there had been Americans in the POW compound.

What we saw in the area was not as memorable as what we did not see. There was nothing resembling a real secure fence or cage. That was very apparent to us at the time and made no sense if this was indeed a POW camp. Except for punji sticks there seemed to be no significant attempt to defend the area. That seemed strange at the time.

My next recollection of the day must have been several hours later. We were moving away from the assault area toward the extraction LZ. My team was now on the point and we were picking our way through the rocks and jungle. I can still feel the discomfort at the amount of noise we were making. As quiet as we were, it was loud compared to a four-man team. Some time during the move, we were told to look for an area to set up a perimeter for the night. This task was totally foreign to my experience in Vietnam, but we found a place and it was approved. After we stopped, the other part of K Company, the blocking force, now had to link up with us! This was a very dangerous thing to do, but we accomplished it without mishap.

Security for a large unit bears no resemblance to that of a four-man team. One of the major differences is the use of a LP or listening post. This was simply a two-man position, placed out in front of the main perimeter to listen and warn the larger unit of anything in front of them. For us, being alone like that was pretty normal. However, being in front of an American unit was not. No one wanted to be on an LP.

That frames the other two memorable events of the day. Top told me to set out a LP and to put my best guys out there. Bob had a piece of shrapnel in his belly and was not happy about going out. I sent him anyway, and I regretted it. Later during the evening, I went to the command post for something. I saw the man we had captured, sitting on the ground with his hands tied and a sand bag over his head. Next to him was the man who had brought the tale of American POWs to the Division. I can still see that picture in my mind as clearly as if it happened yesterday. I have no idea why.

It was apparently a quiet night, because the last things that I remember about this mission was the extraction, firing into the tree line as we left, and seeing a beautiful waterfall as we flew back to An Khe. I remember nothing of the night, or the morning. I don't know how far we moved to the LZ, I don't remember moving to the LZ at all. We were among the last to be taken out, and it would seem to have been a very quiet extraction. I have no idea what we did after the mission, other than a day of stand down and a steak fry.

All of us were relieved that there had been no contact and that our fears of a trap were unwarranted. We had done the job well and we were glad it was over. There was also a sense of discontent and even some anger that we had not found the Americans who were supposed to be there. Many of us believed that they were never there at all and the whole thing was a hoax. We all had been keyed to the other possibility, and it was disappointing to have found no one. We soon returned to our normal duties.

After the mission, there was little time for or interest in the mission. Years later, however, it became the center of much of the K Company lore. What we know about it now has raised as many questions as it has answered. I had always thought that what we called the Company Mission was just that, our company alone doing a POW rescue mission. It was not. It was part, albeit the central part, of a much larger operation. That operation, Operation Wayne Stabb II, involved several regular line units and hundreds of infantrymen. I thought that the one man captured at the beginning of the assault was the only one captured. Others in the blocking unit have stated that they captured several others. If there were others captured, where were they that night when I went to the CP? Some also say that they did not link up with the main K Company perimeter. If this is true, there must have been a fourth group involved in the plan.

How did we get the mission? A senior leader told me that when this mission was discussed at the Division level, the General asked for a unit to volunteer. There was a short silence and then, "The Rangers will do it," answered the General's request. I have no reason to doubt that. This also leads me to think that we were not the only ones who thought this might be a trap.

The most intriguing questions concern the American POWs. Did they ever really exist? Did we miss them? Did we act too slowly to get them out? No one has any real answers. Some still think this was a trap and that the size of the rest of the operation caused the NVA to back off. That is quite possible. The Operation Wayne Stabb II documents indicate that the line units in the area were very busy. They found large caches of supplies. It certainly seems reasonable to me that these NVA units decided to avoid a battle with a very large American presence and the reserve units undoubtedly ready to pounce. Some think that the captured man was just trying to secure some preferential treatment. Again, that is possible. I thought this was the case for many years; I am not sure any more. Had we been hit on this mission, this man's life would have been in very real danger. It seems a huge risk to take.

Another theory is that the camp was never a POW camp at all. Based on the lack of walls and a cage, that seems possible. Vietnamese POWs might not have known where they were and feared leaving, but Americans would have tried to escape. That little bit of information, the apparent lack of confinement tools, has led some to believe that there was an American in the camp and that he was there by choice! Bobby Garwood's name has been presented as a possible answer to the puzzle. Garwood was a controversial Marine who was missing in action for several years. His story has many twists and turns, and there were questions about his loyalty. He was accused of desertion, and some reports indicate that he was fighting with the VC or NVA. I did a small amount of research and find it unlikely that he was in South Vietnam at the time. However, so little is known about this man that it cannot be ruled out.

What we all know for sure is that when the call came to go to the aid of an American soldier, we went. We knew it could be a trap. We knew that we would want the same done for us. We went hoping to do something of great value, and to a man we were sorely disappointed that we did not bring someone home.

CHAPTER 24

The Empty Seat

Many Vietnam veterans will tell you that there are triggers that bring memories to mind. Smells, like JP4, the fuel used in helicopters, insect repellant or gun lube can be powerful reminders. Sounds like a chopper overhead or a rifle shot can and do trigger the same powerful emotional memories. Fireworks on the Fourth of July always remind me of the dull thump of mortar rounds leaving the tube. The big white flashing ones sound like the shattering crash of artillery hitting the ground. A date on the calendar may be all it takes to trigger a memory of a bad mission or a casualty. Sometimes these triggers can be from the most unexpected sources. I had been home for four or five years when I had one of these unexpected reminders.

I was teaching and coaching at Westcliffe, Colorado. The head football coach and I were talking and he made the remark that we needed "just one more kid" on the team. Maybe we needed another lineman or linebacker or perhaps a kicker. Coaches make those kinds of statements all the time and I thought nothing of it. The next day in class, I noticed the number of empty desks in my room. My mind began to fill in the gaps. We were short a player, he was not in my class because he was not born, because his dad was killed in 'Nam. I know that this was an irrational thought. Intellectually, I know it makes no sense, but from that day on, I always seemed to notice an empty seat in my classroom. There was that silent reminder that there was loss beyond those who died, beyond those who were missing, beyond those who never healed. There is a loss not seen in the widows and orphans, in the grieving parents and family. There is a loss beyond what those men might have been. It is the loss of those who never were and never will be.

Unlike some of the triggers and associated memories, I believe this one has had positive effects on me. I think it helped to keep me from becoming totally cynical about people and students. My nature is not to remain positive and optimistic, especially with students who were habitually a problem. More than once, that empty seat reminded me of the value of a child and I was less likely to write them off. The trigger reminds me to do all I can do to see that I don't lose another one.

CHAPTER 25

Huey

─────◆─────

It was, and is, the icon of the war. It was not only a visual icon; it was a multi-sensory icon for those who were there. Almost anyone today will be able identify the Huey by sight, but only those who were with it can identify it by sound. The whop- whop-whop of the main rotor is so distinctive that most Vietnam vets can identify a flying Huey, sight unseen. LRRPs had a special love for this machine, because often it was literally our only way into or out of trouble.

The Huey served as a troop carrier, and as armed gunships. Later in the war, the Cobra gunship was used. This was the first helicopter to be designed as a gunship. It was a new airframe, built on the Huey's engine and rotor system. It had a very similar sound. There were other helicopters and they also had unique signatures, but none ever rivaled the UH-1 slick. Almost any K Company Ranger or 4th ID LRRP could tell you, from sound alone, if a Huey was traveling toward them, away from them, climbing, descending, turning or flying level. It was the machine that was most closely tied to our survival, and we learned its character, limits and strengths well.

The slicks that we flew in were of various vintages, some were pretty new, some were old and war weary. They all had some degree of battle damage apparent. The smell inside these birds was always a mixture of JP4, the fuel that they used, sweat, sometimes blood, and usually one or more of the other fluids that might be leaking from the machine at the time. The cargo doors were usually removed to lighten the machine. It was common for the seats in the cabin to be removed as well. We never used the seats; we sat on the floor, with our legs dangling outside the aircraft. The skids became our perch as we approached the landing zones for insertion. I can recall the chipped paint along the seams in the skin of these choppers. It seems strange today, but the sight of that chipped paint was somehow very comforting. I knew the bird was a veteran!

Our familiarity with these machines was not that of a pilot or crew chief, but that of a trusted compatriot. We knew we had to take care of them, because if we did not, they would not be there for us. We could look at an LZ and tell quickly if it was big enough for the bird to land safely. We knew if an LZ was too steep or had obstructions that might prevent a safe landing. We studied the topography around these areas so that we knew what approaches might pose a risk to the choppers. The LZ itself drew our close inspection, and we tried to avoid those with stumps or snags that might prevent the chopper from landing. Booby traps and wires were always a concern. Much of this was training, and we did not want to needlessly risk a chopper or crew, but it was mostly self-preservation.

The better the information we gave the pilots and crew, the safer and quicker an extraction could be made. A well-chosen LZ could allow the birds to get in and on the ground, saving us any time spent climbing into the cabin. Anything that damaged the bird could cause an aborted extraction, leaving us on the ground and looking for another LZ. Worse yet, undetected damage to the machine could cause a crash or forced landing. We tried to select an extraction area that would allow us to load from both sides. This had the advantage of speeding up the loading, and it allowed us to provide some covering fire for the helicopter and crew. We avoided any LZ that was too small to allow a normal approach, since that could also cause a slow extraction.

The Huey was in some ways a fairly fragile machine, but most of the time it was amazingly tough. The majority of the machine was very light aluminum alloy, and bullets passed through with little effect. The main rotor could, and sometimes did, survive hitting branches or brush. These blade strikes were loud, scary and dangerous, but many times they did not down the aircraft. The tail rotor was a different story. The engine and transmission had some light armor, I think, and often survived rifle or even machinegun hits. When forced to use a small LZ, we paid special attention to the area where the tail rotor would be, because a tail rotor failure at a hover would bring the chopper to grief very quickly. Another reason to pay attention to the tail rotor clearance was our own safety. When one of these came apart, a pilot was going to put the machine on the ground. This could be a catastrophic event, shattering the main blades as well as the tail. The air could be full of flying pieces, and there was always the danger of the out-of-control machine landing on us. More directly, if there were any concerns about the tail clearing something, the crew chief or door gunner would be hanging out of the door looking at the rotor. That meant that he was not manning the gun on that side. Those M-60 machine guns were critical to our protection as we boarded the choppers.

A HUEY ON FINAL TO PICK UP RANGERS ON THE POW MISSION.

More often than not, these aircraft took whatever we threw at them in stride. The weight of a fully loaded LRRP team could tax the lift capability of some of them. The altitude and heat sometimes made for some wild rides into or out of an LZ. This resulted in some bent landing skids, holes in the belly, and other damage. I was pulled out of a mission in a Huey that had the Plexiglas chin bubbles broken out. Apparently a branch or something had hit the bottom of the machine in another LZ and smashed them. Pilots would take risks for LRRP and Ranger teams that they might not take for larger units, and that could push the limits of the machines' capability as well.

Hover holes were very small landing zones that forced the pilot to hover into and out of the LZ. This required more power than a normal landing. An insertion into a hover hole was sometimes risky because of the heavy load and the danger of blade strikes. A large unit would rarely use this kind of LZ. We avoided them, but sometimes we were left with no choice. Our insertions and extractions were rarely into areas large enough for more than two or three ships. We went into LZs that were on the sides of hills, on steep ridgelines, or both. The terrain created severe wind currents and made flying conditions very difficult.

The Cobra gunships were a lot more exciting, sexy and deadly. We admired them as well, but for many of us, the old Huey slick was our first love. We called them angels sometimes, we used their call signs sometimes, but mostly they were just called a slick. No fancy nickname, no common terms of endearment, no intimidating persona, just plain old slick. In a fight, it was the bad boys with the guns that we wanted to be there. It was the firepower of the nasty Cobra gunships or "Snakes" that we wanted to protect us. Like a big brother with a reputation for being a real bad ass, we reveled in their power. But the Huey was different. It was not a fighter; it was not the guy with the reputation. The Huey was the big, quiet, brave and homely kid who you knew you could count on. He was not as fast, not as outwardly tough, not as attractive, but you knew he would be there, not watching from afar, but right there with you. And the tougher it got, the more he risked to save you. I think we viewed every slick like we viewed our team members. We knew they were vulnerable, but we knew they would do whatever it took to see that we all got out, at pretty much any cost. I think we came to see them as part of us.

At the reunion in Kansas City in 2010, there was a Huey set up as a static display in the parking lot. This Huey had been in Vietnam. It brought back many emotions as I climbed aboard, dangled my legs over the side and stepped onto the skid. I was not alone. I saw a Ranger, who I knew had been wounded, walk up to the chopper, run his fingers around a hole in the tail boom, kissed his hand and pat the ragged hole.

"Thanks old girl, thanks," he whispered, and walked away, tears in his eyes. He was not the only one!

CHAPTER 26

Air Crews

❖

As much as I loved the Huey, it was just a machine. As much as I marveled at the things it could do, it was just a tool for our war. It was the men who flew and maintained these helicopters that I respect as much as any soldiers I have ever met. I think of them often and thank them when I can, because they were truly brave men. The aircraft was to them much like our M-16, Car-15 or M-60; it was the weapon they had to use.

The slick crews exposed themselves to the most dangerous parts of our missions, insertions and extractions. They did it many times. Some undoubtedly did this more times than most of us. I knew some of the men who flew from my failed stint in flight school, and I knew they were a good group of men. They were in some ways like us, ordinary men who did extraordinary things. They were often not much older than us, sometimes younger. They were very aware that what they did affected us and they took that seriously. We had the same dedication to our missions, knowing that what we did might be critical to someone's survival. They were very well trained and we understood that. They were viewed as a little crazy, so were we. Both groups enjoyed that reputation. Both groups got "special" treatment and many thought of both groups as arrogant and cocky. For the most part, both Rangers and aircrews were volunteers. Huey crews thought we were nuts and we thought the same of them. We all had a somewhat cavalier attitude toward the Army and its idiosyncrasies. It was natural that friendships and respect grew between us.

For me, the respect for aircrews and pilots especially came from three areas. First, they were incredibly skilled at what they did. Pilots could do things with a chopper that I am sure were never imagined by the builders, and certainly not by the higher command. The crew chief and door gunner could use an M-60 machine gun in ways that we would never have believed until we saw it. Their navigational skills saved our butts many times. They could find us, sometimes when we couldn't find ourselves. They knew the limits of the machines they flew and pushed them to the edge and beyond at times.

I watched a crew fly into An Khe with a team on board, drop them off, hover to a fueling station, quickly refuel. When I talked to the returning team leader, he told me that the pilots had risked running out of fuel to bring the team back. Apparently there was not another ship available and this team had some problem requiring a quick extraction. A miscalculation of a few seconds could have been disastrous, but they knew what they were doing.

Secondly, these guys were very mission-oriented, and totally focused on doing what needed to be done to provide support for the guys on the ground. Some folks do not view them as soldiers, but I have no problem calling them that. Just as we dedicated ourselves to taking care of each other on a team, these men were dedicated to taking care of each other in the aircraft. There was no less dedication there than in our company. We tried to do what needed to be done with the least amount of risk, so did they. When called for, we would risk everything to help a fellow soldier, so would they. As we worked together, there was a connection that grew up between us. As a team leader, we most often knew the crew by their call sign, and we identified them that way, our insertion officers and NCOs had a more personal relationship. They worked with the pilots directly, but that relationship spilled over onto us as well. We got to

STEVE HOWARD, "ANIMAL," ONE OF THE GREAT MEN, PILOTS AND CREW WHO FLEW FOR K COMPANY.

know the crews and pilots by nickname, and then there was a real connection. More than once, my LT would get ready to board the chopper and say, "We're in good hands, Animal is flying today." There were many others who seemed to prefer working with us and we came to trust those in a special way. While a few were better known, I do not ever recall being concerned about who was flying, and they never seemed to be concerned about flying for us. Soon, I came to trust that these men in their thin-skinned machines were as trustworthy as any of us.

Thirdly, these were brave men, pure and simple. There is no other way to say it. Anyone who flies a military aircraft has to have some courage, but these guys did something that was unique. Air Force pilots might find themselves down low at times, but these flyers were down low all the time. They put their choppers on the ground time after time, day after day for a year! They flew into areas where the rest of us were flat on the ground, seeking any cover available, and sat there upright with only aluminum and Plexiglas between them and enemy bullets. They would sit there and pick up a team, or wounded, and then fly away with some very grateful cargo. They flew into hot LZs, knowing that they were in huge danger. Don Lail and Brad Stutz left their ship to bring three wounded Rangers to safety. Brad was a former K Company guy, but Lail did the same thing, for men he did not know.

They flew into tiny places where one small error could rip the chopper apart. They flew at night when we could hardly see, but they came. Gunships, while armed to the teeth, would put themselves at risk in ways a slick might never do. They had guns and could bring brutal destruction to anyone attacking a LRRP team. It was the weapons that they had that often put them at risk. They would slow their speed to keep rounds on target longer, adding to the risk of being hit by small arms fire. They would approach a target so as to best support the team, ignoring the fact that it might be the worst approach for their safety. They did the most dangerous part of our missions, inserting and extracting.

The war in Vietnam was unique in many ways, but at its core, it was like most other wars. It brought out the very best in many men. Men did things that seem impossible to believe. Men risked their lives for other men they didn't know. They did things that had never been done before. They saw others as heroes and themselves as just guys doing their jobs. But for me, and for many like me, the pilots and crews that flew for us are heroes and we owe them a debt of gratitude and respect. I have made contact with many of these men over the years and it is an honor to count them as friends. They are special men.

In my mind, I can hear the slapping of the rotors and the distorted, rattling voices coming in to get us. It sounds something like, "Romeo 5–Blackjack 34 inbound ETA two minutes. Got snakes alongside." There may not have been sweeter music to this Ranger than that. Thank you, gentlemen. There are lots of us who feel this way.

CHAPTER 27

Brass Balls

❖

Helicopter pilots were well known and respected by Rangers. They were very good at what they did, and they were willing to take incredible risks to get LRRP teams out of trouble. As a group, they were just about as cocky as we were. There were some that were legends. One such pilot provided this story.

After extracting a team in contact, this pilot had flown a damaged ship back in to get another team. His battered chopper was masterfully persuaded to fly long enough to get back to An Khe. Unfortunately, the battered machine lost power as it started to set down at the Golf Course and was left visibly bent out of shape.

Who the pilot was or why I was on the Golf Course has left my memory long ago. I was there with several LRRPS who gathered to survey the damage. After accepting many thanks for the extractions, the pilot led a tour of the now dead Huey. Bullet holes were noted, fluid leaks identified, and the last seconds of the flight recalled. The discussion turned to the pilot and to the metallurgical composition of his testicles. We agreed they must be brass.

About this time, a senior officer arrived and proceeded to ream the pilot for risking his crew and damaging the chopper. Apparently all this happened after he had been told not to go after the team. All the Rangers thought it had been well worth the risk, but were smart enough to remain silent. The pilot stood silent as well, taking his medicine like a man. The officer stopped his tongue-lashing and asked the pilot somewhat sarcastically, "What do you think I should do?" The young Warrant Officer thought for a second, smiled, and then replied, "Well Sir, as I see it, you have two options. Send me home because you need good choppers or buy me a new slick because you need good pilots. Either is fine with me"

Brass balls indeed! The officer undoubtedly decided to buy another helicopter for the pilot, because getting to go home, as punishment for destroying Army property would have become a very common event.

CHAPTER 28

On Killing

◆

Most American men are taught from the cradle on that killing is almost never an acceptable way to solve a problem. They are taught the value of human life and they accept that as truth. War destroys that basic understanding of truth, at least on some level and for a time. The taking of a human life is a fearful thing. A man must be trained, or more correctly untrained, to do it. Killing takes careful preparation, unless some pathology is present. Nothing was more difficult for many of us to make peace with than killing another human, another man.

Ingrained in the heart and soul of most Americans was the concept of life as a divine gift, a priceless thing, an irreplaceable treasure. Some exceptions were made for the defense of a loved one, defense of the country, or the defense of your own life, but for the most part we learned not to kill. This lesson became part of us. Most looked for a way to avoid the act of killing. Many came to the war with the conviction that God did not take the act of killing lightly. The commandments said, "Thou shall not kill," and for the most part we took that seriously. The bulk of our upbringing made the act of killing a very difficult thing to even imagine.

As we found ourselves in the Army, we were forced to deal with the very real possibility of killing. Our training substituted "silhouettes" for the circular targets we had shot at back home. These were very roughly human-shaped targets. We did not shoot at a man's chest. We shot at center mass. Our language was changed, subtly, but significantly. We were taught to call the men we would fight by some neutral name. We marched everywhere to cadences that called these men the enemy or Charley Cong. The same cadence incorporated the word kill over and over, deadening our aversion to the word and eventually to the act. "I want to be an Airborne Ranger, I want to go to Vietnam, I want to be an Airborne Ranger, I want to kill old Charley Cong," was repeated over and over, day after day, mile after mile, until we hardly noticed what we were saying.

Bayonet training, the grenade pit, and the rifle range all had targets shaped like people, but they never had faces. They were always a target, nothing more. The process started to change the way we saw things. Anything on the other end of our weapons was a target, not a human. It was not long until some degree of disassociation became evident. I felt it on a bayonet course one day in Basic Training when I suddenly found myself relishing the commands of "vertical butt stroke, parry and thrust." I twisted the bayonet in the target before I pulled it out. I was beginning to change, I was beginning to gain the traits needed to fight and kill.

I am convinced that the process of training was then, and is today, absolutely necessary if men are to go to war. Nothing I write here is to be taken as an attack on the Army's training. I am not saying that there is some sinister plot here to create mindless killers, but the very nature of what men will be ordered to do requires a very fundamental change in how they view killing. Firing a weapon at a human-shaped target was needed to train the eye to see and shoot accurately. Many hunters today use very realistic targets to train their eyes to see and hit the vital areas of an animal. They know there is a very big difference between a round circle and a spot on the chest of a deer. The Army knew the same thing. We had to be able to shoot, and we had to do it quickly, without hesitation, and accurately.

Later in Vietnam, when killing became a near certainty, we went further. Our names for the enemy became less personal. Gooks, dinks, and Gooners replaced the more human names. We had targets in an ambush, we counted confirmed, rather than say we killed someone. It was a very thin layer of protection, but we did it anyway, probably without thinking anything about it. We fired artillery at lights, ignoring the fact that each light was in the hand of a man. Artillery was called on tree lines, bunkers or snipers, but rarely on people. Clearly some of this came about because of the need to be brief and concise on the radio, but the nature of most of these communications was always impersonal.

Once we were in combat, the focus shifted from killing the enemy to protecting our teammates and ourselves. What happened here compounded the problem in some ways, but simplified it in others. First, killing to protect your fellow soldiers was not only approved by most in society, it was our duty in the Army. You were expected to do that, you were trained to do that, and it was far easier to kill in that situation than in any other. Now, in a contact, there was no hesitancy to fight because the other side was human and there was huge motivation to fight and kill to save one's buddies. Now, the average All American Boy became a deadly opponent.

Without the constant reality of the war, of killing or being killed, the ability to accept the killing left quickly. For me it became something that I had to make peace with. On one level, I had to go back to the very real truth that I had to protect the men I was with. I had to accept the fact that I had no other options at that point. I had to accept that killing was part of what we did. All of those things were true, but I eventually came to the realization that they might not be totally valid and that I needed more.

It was not until I admitted to myself that I might be wrong, and asked for God's forgiveness, that I experienced real peace.

I still wonder about killing and the effects it had on us. I still struggle with the enormity of what it means to take a life. I am still haunted by some of the faces of the dead. I will never be the same, but I am sure that if I can be forgiven for this, God's grace is sufficient for everything.

CHAPTER 29

The Most Dangerous Missions

K Company used tiny four-man teams in areas where it was not uncommon to find VC or NVA units of ten to 120 men. The terrain was so difficult that movement was restricted. Booby traps were a constant threat if you walked the easy path. All of our missions involved flights into and out of areas where no one knew what we might find. That was why we were there! Contact with a larger unit was so dangerous that the words "contact" shouted into a radio hand set was the most dreaded event a LRRP could imagine. The words "LRRPs in contact" set the whole chain of command into action. Defending yourself presented many dangers as well. A short artillery round, a grenade that bounced back on you, or an errant mini-gun run from a Cobra gunship added real danger to the mission.

For me, and I believe for many team leaders, there was an even more dangerous mission type. The most dangerous missions were those where boredom, discomfort, and frustration tried to take over. As I wrote earlier, you did develop a sixth sense about what might be in an AO. After a day or two in your little patch of the country, if you didn't see any sign of the enemy, it was easy to let down. If you saw nothing, heard nothing, and had no sense of imminent danger, missions became horribly boring. LRRP teams moved very slowly and often for very short distances, then stopped to listen. If the team was hot or cold, and wet, frustrated and tired, as they almost always were, these stops became almost irresistible nap times. Adding to the problem of these quiet missions was the fact that if you found nothing, you needed to move more. This added to the fatigue and frustration. Nighttime was never a good time to sleep, and at best you were on guard duty one out of every four hours. Staying fully alert in this situation was next to impossible.

Teams could fall into this trap and fail to maintain the level of alert needed for any LRRP mission, even a quiet one. Everyone struggled, but as Team Leader you had total responsibility. We often used a modified alert cycle during the day that allowed two of the team to sleep while the other two remained awake. Boredom seemed to be worse when you were in very thick vegetation. You could not see more than ten to fifteen feet at times. Imagine being in a room that is ten feet by ten feet and staying there for four or five days. Discomfort was just part of the deal. You slept on the ground, no pad, no shelter, and no opportunity to clean up.

Everything seemed to grab, scrape, and chop at you as you passed by. Scratches and cuts from the "wait a minute vines" and elephant grass were soon infected. Leach bites itched and bled. Any body parts that touched, also chafed and had jungle rot in a matter of hours. There were several nasty critters that would feed on you if any skin were exposed. The fabled bug juice, insect repellant, was used liberally. It worked well, it was probably pure DEET, but it burned any cut or scrape. It was oily and smelled dreadful. Once on your hands, it seemed to come off only in your food.

Dehydration was a given, you were always thirsty. We ate only what we carried, so most guys were almost always hungry. In a situation like that described above, add something like a mission extension or a request to move a long distance, to move rapidly, and the team was in the most dangerous situation they could face.

After a mission on the Highway near the famous hairpin turn on QL 19 east of An Khe, I nearly paid the price for falling into this trap. We had walked into our assigned AO. It was a very steep walk of 2,000 or 3,000 meters. The terrain was difficult and covered with brush and elephant grass. After one day, we were tired, hot, and already short on water. We saw nothing for several days. We had asked to be extracted because there was nothing in the area. We were denied the extraction several times before being allowed to leave the AO. Once given permission to extract, the result was not a chopper ride out on a Black Jack slick as we expected. We were told to walk out to the road. We did walk out, but because I was tired, angry, and convinced that there was no threat in the area, we went too far, too fast. We made it to the road safely, despite my foolish actions.

Adding to the danger in these situations was the distinct possibility that not only the TL, but also everyone on the team was affected the same way. That is what happened on this mission. Fortunately for us, I was correct that there was no one in the area, and we made it to the road without incident.

As we walked along the road, a helicopter saw us and landed, offering us a ride. I was so angry that I forgot to clear my weapon as I got on the ship. I climbed aboard, pointing my loaded Car-15, with the safety off, directly at the pilot who had rescued us. Again, God must have been watching over me, because the weapon did not discharge. I rode to An Khe with a very angry aircrew. On these missions, the NVA or the VC was not the real enemy. As Pogo said, "We have met the enemy, and he is us."

CHAPTER 30

Top Keller and Taking Care of Snuffy

F ew words can command the fear and respect of a young soldier more completely than the words "First Sergeant." The men who hold the rank are usually more than worthy of that respect. There were many very good men among Senior NCOs and officers in K Company and the man we called "Top" Keller, we all knew, was exceptional. He was a professional soldier, the personification of what it meant to be a 1st Sergeant. The Army slang used the term "Top" in place of First Sergeant.

1ST SERGEANT DON KELLER, A CONSUMMATE PROFESSIONAL.

My first encounter with First Sergeant Keller was probably on my second day in Vietnam. A fellow Ranger School graduate and I were assigned to the 4th Infantry Division and had been shipped to the "repodepo" (replacement depot) at Pleiku. We had been assigned to a regular line unit and were hustled through the process despite our protests that we should be going to the Ranger unit. My compatriot and I were scheduled to depart for our units the following morning. We contacted the Ranger Company and Top rescued us from the line units. We were in the company area at Pleiku for two days for a short orientation program and to draw weapons and equipment. We were assigned to our platoons

121

and I, in my brand new camouflage fatigues, went to An Khe. Larry Bergman went to Ban Me Thout.

I saw Top very little until the company moved to An Khe and even later during the Company Mission described in Chapter 23. It was during the training for this mission that I think I saw him at his very best. I believe that he was, like many of us, highly suspicious that the POW rescue mission was a trap. Many of us thought there was a good possibility that this was a setup to kill a bunch of Rangers. Top never let the very real possibility of a trap interfere with the mission preparation. I don't recall him ever addressing the issue, because it would have been irrelevant. Top didn't do irrelevant stuff then, and he doesn't now. His focus was to prepare us. The best way to take care of the company was to train us well for the mission. He and the other leaders did that.

At one point during the preparation for the mission, I expressed some doubt about my ability to do the job I had been assigned. Top's response still rings in my ears. "You are a Ranger, son! If you couldn't do this, you would not be here now." Not the warm fuzzy reply of the self-esteem movement, but clear and effective. No time wasted and no doubt about his decision. I recall thinking, "Oh $%^&, I better get back to work!"

During the assault portion of that mission, Bob White was wounded. There was no way to get him out, and we were scheduled for extraction the next day, so Bob stayed. Top prepared the company for the night. One of the important elements to these larger defensive positions was the establishment of observation posts. These were two or three-man positions sent out in front of the larger unit to act as an early warning system. "Put your best people out there." That included Bob. I knew it and I suspect that Top did as well. That was the best way to take care of everyone. He made no apology to me or to Bob; he simply did what was needed to take care of all of his men.

1st Sergeant Keller was available when teams made contact or were in any trouble. If someone got hurt, he was there. He could inspire fear and dread in any of us, but it was not until many years later that I saw him in a different light. I had always wanted to ask him about being a professional soldier and leading a "rag tag bunch of kids." My words, not his. I knew as soon as he started his reply that I was speaking to 1st Sergeant Keller. "You were as professional as any soldiers anywhere!" He still refused to let me doubt myself or anyone else who served in this company. He said that he had a daughter who was seventeen while we were there. She would have been a bit younger that most of us, but not much. He thought of us as his kids and tried to treat us a he would want his sons treated. Forty years later, we can all see that more clearly than we did in 1970.

He was instrumental in ensuring that we had what we needed to do our jobs. We always had LRRP rations and C-rations in abundance while other companies had trouble getting "stuff." We used ammunition at an astounding rate, but we always had new ammo for the next mission. I recall being reluctant to carry claymore detonators for more than one or two missions. When the supply sergeant was not impressed with my extravagance, Top saw to it that we had new detonators. In fairness, it probably was not required to have new detonators, and the supply sergeant was probably justified in his concern. Typical of Top, he credits the supply sergeant with getting all the stuff that we needed.

His concern for and support of the troops continued after his service. He was a significant part of the Special Forces memorial at Fort Bragg. He has spent untold hours researching unit and individual awards, not only for K Company, but for all of the 4ID LRRPs as well. He is a proud man who always manages to make you feel like a "good soldier" even today. He was and still is capable of being tough, even seeming hard, but I always sense that he is still thinking of the best for the troops.

He was "Top" then, and is to many of us today. He has asked us to call him "Don." Many of us can't do it, or do so with difficulty. Like Fonzie of *Happy Days* fame, trying to say, "I'm sorry," it just will not come out. Many of us have taken his example into our lives and our jobs. You can see it in the way we care for each other, for modern day Rangers and soldiers, and for our families. Top sometimes used the term "snuffy" to refer to some lowly soldier somewhere. It is generally used as a derogatory term, but when Top used it, I understood it as a term of respect. He instilled and modeled for us that even "Snuffy" deserved your best. Many times over the years, I have been reminded to do a bit more than was required for someone. Often it was Top Keller's example that prompted my actions.

CHAPTER 31

Rangers and Race

I n 1969 and '70, there was some very real and sometimes violent conflict between black and white troops in Vietnam. While it may not have been as significant in combat units that were actually in the field, it was part of the war in other places. The press surely found some awful examples of racism in the army. Whether it was intentional or not, it was made to seem commonplace. Admittedly, my experience was very narrow in time, and limited by the nature of K Company. I served one tour in a company that could hardly be considered the norm in any way, but I saw very little racism.

The assassination of Martin Luther King Jr. had its effect on the men in Vietnam, regardless of race. The North Vietnamese used the radio and "Hanoi Hannah" to exploit the tension. The propaganda radio from the North had the best rhythm and blues music available to Americans, and they would frequently ask the question of black soldiers, "Why are you fighting the white man's war?" They pointed out that the black soldiers were being denied rights at home and that the white man was trying to oppress both the black Americans and the Vietnamese. Some in the antiwar movement in the US said the same thing.

The situation in K Company was, or appeared to me to be, different. There were black and other minority soldiers in the company. There were black and Hispanic team leaders and several black senior NCOs. I was fairly close to Lowell Tidline and Ed Mobrey. SFC Griffith and others, I knew only in passing. I don't recall any problems in the company over race. There were racist remarks made from time to time, but always in the heat of the moment, from someone who was young, angry and unthinking. I recall a good bit of back and forth banter between black and white solders, that would have been considered racist (both ways), but it seemed to me to be part of the gallows humor of young men at war.

I know of no time when any team leader refused to take someone out due to race. Mixed race teams were common. No team ever refused to go to the aid of another team for any reason. I can state without any fear of contradiction that Top Keller and Lt. Martin would never have tolerated that behavior. I did not know some of the other officers and NCOs as well, but I do not believe they would have either. After the war, there was a book written that accused K Company teams of refusing to respond to a team in contact, asserting that another LRRP company had to rescue the team. I know of nothing that made any of the men in K Company more upset than that. For the record, that incident never happened, and the accusation was later rescinded by the author.

There was a social separation in K Company. It was not hard and fast, not unfriendly or racist, but clear and evident. Today at the reunions, the black faces are conspicuous by their absence, as are many of the other minority members of K Company. There may be reasons that I am not aware of that keep them away. I am always reminded of these men at our reunions, and wonder if my recollections are accurate or ignorant. Am I engaging in wishful thinking or was there a bond that transcended race in K Company? I suspect that race was like many things in the Highlands. I suspect it was totally irrelevant to the missions we had and to staying alive, so we were not very aware of it. What I can say, with absolute certainty, is this: There is a list of forty-two names, men who

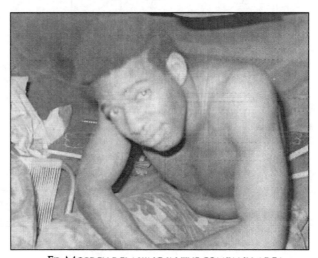

ED MOBREY RELAXING IN THE COMPANY AREA.

died while serving with the 4th ID LRRPs, Brigade LRRPs or K Company Ranger teams. Each LRRP/Ranger Company has a similar list. The names prove that there was no discrimination in one area. Death neither knew nor cared about race.

After this was written, I made contact with both Lowell Tidline and Ed Mobrey. Ed attended the 2013 reunion and I treasure the time we spent together. I think it would be very safe to say that our bond still transcends any difference in the color of our skin.

Ed and I had only a moment or two to visit, but it took very little time to see that our time in 'Nam, our pride in the job we did, our respect for the men we served with and our faith were all we needed to be fast friends after forty-three years. Lowell Tidline was another of the men I came to respect as a soldier and fellow LRRP. For me, the fact that he was a black soldier was never an issue, and I have no reason to think he felt any different.

CHAPTER 32

Chow

————◆————

An Army travels on its stomach, or so the saying goes. After water, ammunition, and radios, food was the major issue. It was critical to all troops in the field, but doubly so for LRRPs. We had both advantages and disadvantages when chow time rolled around. The disadvantage was simply that we had to carry everything from the beginning of every mission. Re-supply was almost never done because it compromised the team's location and thus the mission. That fact limited the amount and type of food we ate to what we could carry. Line units did not carry all of their food, and were re-supplied each day. They usually got at least one hot meal each day. Hot meals like those were never on the LRRP field menu.

The advantage for us was that we had more options to choose from in the first place. We had both C-rations and LRRP rations. The C-rations, known as "C-Rats" or simply Cs, were canned food. Each meal contained a can of meat, some type of canned fruit, a tin of crackers or hard biscuit, a condiment pack, and a dessert. The LRRP rations were freeze-dried meals. Light and easy to carry, they also came in several menus. You simply opened the plastic package, put in some water, and you had a meal. Chicken and rice was not too bad. There was a beef ration that I thought was actually very tasty, but the C-ration, ham and lima beans, was almost universally detested. They were called a profane name that is best left to the imagination of the reader. The freeze-dried scalloped potato meal was nearly as bad. They were salty and nearly impossible to re-hydrate in the field. Many LRRPs believed that they were waterproof. Re-hydrating any of the "LRRPS," as we called them, was difficult. There was a chili con carne LRRP that some of us liked. The beans did stay hard for a long time and at least one team member of mine thought the best use of these rations was to put it in front of a claymore mine. He reasoned that the beans were at least as hard as the steel balls in the mine and that the chili seasoning would make the wounds more painful or blind them if it got into their eyes. There was some merit to the thought.

The forerunner of the modern MRE (Meal Ready to Eat) of today's army, LRRP rations were in many ways an improvement over the C-Rats, but they had one problem. The whole point of carrying a freeze-dried ration was that it was lighter than the C-ration. The problem was that you had to carry extra water to re-hydrate them, thereby defeating the purpose. Consequently, most of us carried them only when we knew we could get water on the ground or in the rainy season. A few ate them dry, but then you had to carry and drink more water. If you put water in the pouch and then carried the pouch inside your shirt for a while, the rations would be soft and easy to eat, but not hot. If you heated water and poured it into the bag, after five minutes you had a hot but slightly crunchy meal. Even with these issues, LRRP rations were carried often because they were filling and a change from the C-rations.

The C-ration was the mainstay of our fieldfare. The meat was highly processed, full of fat, and not easily identified without a label. The consistency was about like that of canned cat food, except for the beef, which was more like an over-done pot roast. There was always a layer of congealed juice around the edge of the can, very much like you see in Vienna sausage cans. When heated, this melted and the meat was reasonably palatable. When cold, as we often had to eat it, it served its nutritional purpose, but offered little else in a culinary sense. There was beef, turkey, and pork, with turkey holding the top spot in my favorites list.

The fruit was always popular. Fruit cocktail was the most prized, but peaches were a close second and the pears were also very good. In the economy of K Company, you could get two peaches for a fruit cocktail. Fruit had the advantage of being nutritious, tasty and having liquid all in one can. It was not uncommon for teams to pull the fruit out of several C-rations and not use the rest. This was a luxury afforded to K Company that grunt units never saw. They took what they got.

The pound cake was the absolute prize in a "C." It was a small dense cake in a can. It was really good, and when soaked in fruit juice it was the high point of a field "dining" experience. There was a kind of cookie and a chocolate bar that also made good desserts. Each C had a condiment pack consisting of cigarettes, coffee or hot chocolate, cream, utensils, salt and pepper, toilet paper, and other assorted items. The cigarettes would usually burn down in a matter of seconds and the plastic spoon broke after a few bites. Most of us carried a metal spoon or fork. The coffee was the nastiest, bitter instant kind that foamed the minute you put water in it. I drank it, but only for the caffeine. The hot chocolate was good, but much harder to find.

MISSION PACKING ROMEO 7, (L TO R) RICHARD BEAM, ROGER CRUNK, DREW FATTEN AND EVEILO (AL) GOMEZ KIA 8/19/70.

To make some of these rations more palatable, a whole system of doctoring arose. Tabasco sauce was always part of the LRRP's field kitchen. Enough Tabasco could cover up the taste of and kill whatever else might have gotten into your meal. If you took a coffee creamer or two and mixed them in with a hot chocolate mix, you could make a pretty good hot drink. Jam or jelly from the cracker tin could be combined with some pound cake to create a tasty mid-day snack. While many Rangers worked hard to create new meals, most of us eventually accepted what we had and ate it.

Some teams carried indigenous rations from the South Vietnamese Army. These were always rice and either dried fish or sausage. They were easy to fix, open, and the packages could be closed if needed. They were very light to carry, and once re-hydrated, very filling. The sausage was much like the dry sticks you could get today at any convenience store. The fish were whole dried fish that you ate just like the sausage. With the addition of some sugar, raisins from home, and a few coffee creamer packets, you could make a kind of sweet rice that really was pretty good.

The doctoring of the food was minor by comparison to what we did to water. Water was the heaviest part of our load. Teams always tried to carry as much water as they could from the base camps because it was clean, pure, and drinkable water. It was impossible for most of us to carry enough water to drink on a four or five-day mission during the dry season. Re-supply from whatever source you could find was the only option you had when you ran out of water. Teams were sometimes extracted because they could not re-supply with water.

129

While some creeks and rivers had fairly clear and clean water, these sources were not always available.

Water from any source other than the base camp required halizone or iodine tablets to make it safe to drink. Unfortunately, these made the water taste absolutely awful. Both gave the water a metallic taste. If your water came from another source, like a pool or a bomb crater, the result was often undrinkable. Drinking from these sources was not a good idea, due to all sorts of possible chemical contamination, but sometimes you had no other option. Wyler's instant lemonade and Lipton's instant iced tea were the weapons of choice in this battle to cover up the taste and provide a reasonable drink. I preferred the tea because it was not sweet, and I must confess that neither really did much good. It tasted different, not really better.

In base camp, we had it better than most infantry units. The mess hall provided a good selection of food and we used it well. Almost everyone was hungry when they came in from a mission, and we always had something to eat. We could get something from the mess hall even if we had missed the regularly scheduled meals. The PX had snacks, soft drinks, beer, wine and liquor if you were twenty-one and an E-6 (Staff Sergeant) or above. Prices were cheap and we stocked up. It was rare to see anyone on stand down who did not have a pop and a snack in hand. I weighed about 114 pounds when I left Vietnam. In spite of our efforts at increased calorie intake, our calorie expenditure was even greater, and very few guys managed to keep up with their needs. Care packages from home were eagerly received and shared. My Grandma Watt, famous for her angel food cakes, sent me one in the mail. By the time it got to me, it was as hard as a rock. No problem for a hungry bunch of Rangers. We broke it up and ate it like hard candy. The popcorn packing was consumed as well.

Perhaps the most endearing and enduring artifact for LRRP chow time in the field was the ever-present P-38 can opener. It was a small folding version of the old style side-cutter can openers. It was about one inch long and the cutter hook folded out to engage the top of the can and cut around the lid. They were everywhere! Most guys had several because they did get dull and you lost them. At almost any reunion, someone will have one that is "genuine from 'Nam" and display it proudly. Why this humble little piece of metal is so revered is a mystery to me. Perhaps it is a reminder of a simple, effective tool whose function was no more sinister than to provide you with a nice pound cake or can of fruit cocktail, something that could not be said for most of the rest of the stuff we carried.

CHAPTER 33

Extended Missions

There was something somehow very comforting about having an ending time for a LRRP mission. Conversely, having a mission extended un-settled everyone. A long-range recon patrol was always a hard, uncomfortable, and dangerous task, but the upside for most of us was that the missions were relatively short compared to the ninety or more days endured by line units. Anything that lengthened the normal five-day mission was dangerous and never well received.

Extending a team's time in the bush was never done lightly. Officers and NCOs knew all too well the costs and dangers involved. They were not always in control. Higher up in the command, extending a LRRP team might not carry the same gravity. Weather, availability of helicopters, and other tactical needs could force the extension of our missions. Teams might be extended because they were needed to do radio relays for other teams. Teams were extended because another team was in contact and their evacuation exhausted the slick's ability to reach other teams.

Whatever the reason for an extension, it presented many problems. Some were very obvious. Food and water were always a major concern. The weight of the combat loads did not allow the luxury of extra food or water on most missions. In fact, the common five-day mission was determined in large part by the maximum amount of weight that a LRRP could carry. It was very common for teams to be out of water, or very nearly so, on the fifth day of a mission. Any longer time on the ground became a severe hardship on teams. Re-supply was dangerous and often impossible.

Food and ammunition was not as big an issue. Several days without food were miserable and maddening, but survivable. Ammo usually would not be a concern. A team low on ammo would have been in contact and extraction would become a priority. In that situation, an extraction would usually be attempted at all cost. The batteries for the radios were another story. The PRC-25 required two batteries for most five-day missions. Most team leaders changed batteries on the third day. That meant that one radio was nearing the end of the battery life on the fifth day. The ATL did not have his radio on all the time and that made at least one battery available in the event of an extension. The batteries varied wildly in how long they lasted and it was not uncommon for them to be used up in two days. Operating with only one dependable radio was doubly dangerous.

Any mission change that happened while the team was on or near an extraction LZ was a team leader's nightmare. These late events meant that the team had not been alerted in time to prepare for the change in orders. A very late change in the extraction forced an unhealthy choice on the TL. Staying on or near the extraction LZ could compromise the security of the team and the mission. The longer a LRRP team stayed, the greater the chance that they would be discovered. The alternative was no less appealing. It meant moving to another LZ if one was available.

These secondary landing zones were secondary for a reason. They had already been deemed to be less safe than the primary locations. Staying on the LZ was universally considered a poor option, but at times it was the only option available. The areas assigned to K Company teams frequently had no more than one or two suitable LZs. If the NVA or VC were in these areas, they watched them for any activity and an extension gave them time to deploy men and weapons to the area. If another LZ existed, it might be a significant distance away. Moving not only presented water concerns, but also exposed the men to added danger of discovery. In any case, the options could be very bad for a team forced to stay in an extra day.

The mental effect on the team was difficult. It took away the comfort of the known end time of a mission. Once a team was extended, it was a given that extraction was no longer predictable. That presented a unique set of dangers. Anger, frustration, thirst, and hunger could distract teams. Wet weather made the discomfort even worse and added to the unpredictability of getting out. The missions required complete concentration, especially near the end, and all these distractions worked against that focus.

Sometimes the tactical situation required a team to stay in the field. These extensions typically could be anticipated and better managed than the last minute events. There was time to work around the many problems of a late extension. They were never pleasant, nor were they well received, but they offered some better options. It was easier to stay in if another team or some other American unit needed you there. A well-hidden Ranger team could be a huge benefit to a line unit in contact by directing artillery and providing information to other units. Whatever the reason, staying an extra day or two in the bush was still better that being out for ninety days. Few of us ever forgot that for very long.

CHAPTER 34

Flying formation

❖

Huey pilots loved to show off by flying close formations during the trips to and from LRRP missions. On one memorable trip, my point man tried his hand at this normally powered aeronautic skill. During any insertion, our teams stood on the skids of the Huey and held onto either the bulkhead at the front of the doors or the door gunner's post at the rear. This precarious perch was dangerous, but allowed each man to see the landing zone and keep his weapon at the ready. The usual approach on an insertion was fairly steep and fast. The pilots spent as little time on the ground as possible. Some of these pilots got very good at these controlled crashes and could put a team on the ground by simply rolling the skids from back to front. Teams loved this because they didn't have to jump and the aircraft was exposed to ground fire only while moving. The Huey was capable of taking a significant amount of punishment, but it was also susceptible to total destruction by a single well-placed rifle round. Anything that made that shot more difficult was considered a good thing for all of us. The altitude of the Highlands, the heat, and accumulated wear and tear on the machines made it necessary to operate the aircraft at or beyond the limits of design capacity. The result of all of these things coming together in one event made for some very wild rides into an LZ.

On just one such insertion, I was at my customary place on the front right and David Siglow (known to most as "Siglow") was behind me. The LZ was sloped into the approach and we were carrying extra supplies for a long radio relay mission, so the load was heavier than normal. The pilots were working hard to get us in, but the aircraft was struggling and was expressing its unhappiness. Powered to the maximum, the torque on the main rotor caused the Huey

134

to switch its tail like an angry cat. The wind burbled over the top of the ridge, altering the approach speed every few seconds. The old Huey was at the absolute limit of its ability to fly. It bucked and dipped its nose wildly. Just a normal LRRP insertion.

At an altitude of about ten feet, the nose snapped down hard and Siglow lost his hold on the post. I heard a scream and looked back. There he was, legs spread, arms flailing, eyes wide and weapon in hand, flying perfect formation six feet to the left and three feet below the chopper that he was supposed to be riding in.

He hit the ground hard, his pack rolled up over his head and he ate a lot of dirt, but unbelievably, was not hurt. He scrambled up the hill to the rest of the team, who had exited the ship in a more conventional manner. Bob White was on the other side of the ship and unaware of the fall. A soon as I was sure Siglow was okay, I laughed hysterically. Siglow soon saw the humor in the situation as well. Bob assumed that we had both lost our minds and made an effort to get us off the LZ. A very good idea, by the way. When I told him what had happened, he too was laughing.

Fortunately for us, the LZ was quiet and no enemy activity was apparent. We gathered ourselves and moved on to our mission. Had there been anyone on the LZ, I am sure we would have been able to defend ourselves, but I am convinced that we would have been laughing as we fought. I still get a smile on my face as I recall my point man on short final approach to an LZ without a helicopter in hand.

In January 2007, I learned of David Siglow's death. He battled his demons for many years after 'Nam. I located him in the mid 1990s. I talked to his mother, but never to him. He talked to a few other members of the company, but he had no interest in talking to me. His mother told me he had been doing well and that he feared that returning to see some of us might ruin the peace that he had achieved. I respected that and never tried to contact him again. Siglow was arguably the best point man in the company. He was, like all of us, not without his faults, and the demons were after us even in the days of Romeo 5. His name is not on the The Wall, (The Vietnam Veterans Memorial) but perhaps it should be. For me, he is a reminder of the horrible price that is paid by those who go to war. I pray you have found real peace at last, my Brother.

CHAPTER 35

Speed

❖

I think it is safe to say that I had a reputation as being "straight" in Vietnam. The term at that time, meant that I did not use drugs or alcohol, so this is one of the strangest stories of my tour. It happened during one of the moves that K Company made from An Khe to Pleiku. The whole company loaded up lock, stock, and barrel, and because we had a somewhat permanent base of operations, most of the guys in the company had collected small refrigerators, stereo equipment, and other creature comforts. All of this had to be moved along with all of the rest of our gear. We loaded up in the open trucks and started on our way.

The trip along QL 19, the major east/west highway in the Highlands, was long and uncomfortable, so the refrigerators all had a supply of cold drinks, and mine was no exception. I grabbed my Coke and set it on the canvas top of the truck as we pulled out of Camp Radcliffe. Another team leader did the same, setting his drink beside mine. As we moved out, passing LZ Schuler and LZ Action, I drank my Coke and, in all probability, pondered the likelihood of getting ambushed on the Mang Yang pass. Somewhere along the route, I became aware of a strange desire to talk a lot more than normal, a great deal more than normal! I saw smiles, smirks and heard giggles, but finished my Coke unfazed by the commotion.

By the time we were on the Mang Yang, I was the cause of much amusement and still not fully cognizant of what had happened. I was the only one who was not fully aware of what happened. Exactly! I had picked up the wrong Coke; one spiked with Speed, and had unwittingly consumed it all. I don't remember anything else about the trip, or the arrival at Camp Enari at Pleiku. Apparently someone took me aside and kept me out of trouble.

Many years later, the NCO who had spiked the Coke apologized to me. That was the first time that I knew for sure who did it. He was relieved to know that I was a forgiving type and we had a good laugh. Rick Noble apparently was the one who took me under his wing while I was on my one and only foray into illegal drugs.

RICK NOBLE RIGHT AND "KID" HOLTON ON THE LEFT.
MALARIA PILL REMINDER WITH A TWIST!

CHAPTER 36

Yards

——————————•:•——————————

They raised their glasses and saluted those they served with in Vietnam. Men spoke the friends' names with the reverence of brothers at arms. They were not fellow Americans, but Montagnard scouts who served with them. Men named Apeck, Ky, Dewey, Jack, Kim, Chuy, Doc and others were remembered. Forty years or more after they served, the men of the 4th Inf. Division LRRPS and Rangers honored men who most Americans never knew even existed.

Americans universally respected the "Yards" in the Highlands of Vietnam. That was especially true of the men who served as Rangers and LRRPs in the Highlands. Ethnically different than the Vietnamese, they were treated poorly by both the North and South Vietnamese governments. They were despised by the Vietnamese, who believed them to be subhuman, to have tails and to be very stupid. They were the historic people of the highlands and wanted nothing more or less than to have an autonomous homeland of their own.

The Dega, as they called themselves, were to all outward appearance a primitive people. They practiced a form of slash and burn agriculture that rotated crops from plot to plot with the passing seasons. They seemed totally dependent on the weather to water their crops. I don't know if the rice they grew in the small, dry fields was the same as that grown in the flooded paddies, but it produced much less grain. They had a kind of yam growing in the same fields. They hunted with crossbows and gathered food as they found it. They raised chickens, dogs, and pigs for food. Woodcutting was a common task for them. They cooked with wood and I think probably sold some to the Vietnamese in the area.

They occupied the strategically critical Central Highland of Vietnam. It was no accident that the earliest American advisors in Vietnam were in the homeland of the Dega. It is also no coincidence that some of the earliest major battles of the war occurred in the Highlands. Americans and Vietnamese alike understood this simple fact: whoever controls the Highlands, controls Vietnam. If the Highlands were to be lost, the South Vietnamese government would be doomed. The Americans also knew that without the Dega, control of this critical area would be difficult, if not impossible.

"KY" A YOUNG MONTAGNARD WHO SERVED WITH K COMPANY.

In the early stages of the war, Americans were able to convince the South Vietnamese that they had to stop alienating the Dega, or the Highlands would fall. Indeed, after working in the area and working with the Yard scouts, I have no doubt that holding the Highlands without them would have been a bloody task, and an absolute terror for LRRP teams. The Americans started militarizing the Highlands from the coast to the Cambodian and Laotian borders, and from Ban Me Thout to Kontom. In the process, they developed a close alliance with the Dega. Most were very pro-American and were technically allies of South Vietnam. In reality they were fighting for their homeland. A pragmatic decision was made: they would first fight the North with the help of the Americans and then fight the South later if they needed to.

There were some Yards who were VC, but not many. Because of the relocation to strategic hamlets, contact with them was fairly common. They were around most bases, selling bananas, pineapple and souvenirs. During the time that the 4th Division was in the Highlands, they supplied scouts and intelligence to the Americans. Other American units, the 1st Cavalry and the 173rd Airborne also used them extensively.

Many of the missions that we were assigned came from Montagnard reports. They knew the country and were very aware of anything unusual or out of place. Reporting to the Americans was a good way to fight the North Vietnamese. Their somewhat primitive ways led to interesting situations for us. They counted, "One, two, three, many," so if you were looking for "many NVA," that could be four or 4000, you never knew. Their reports were usually reliable and often the only reliable information we had.

They were a gentle and civil group of people as a rule, but they did fight when it was needed. They fiercely defended their women and were vicious fighters in the field. They learned to use modern weapons quickly and efficiently, and combined that with a stealth that was unnerving to many of us. They used primitive farming tools, but by the time I was there, they were adopting more modern methods. With the help of the American military's Civic Action Groups, they had more productive gardens and some improved water and sanitation facilities. The consolidation of villages under the Strategic Hamlet program dramatically changed how the Dega lived. We would occasionally find small groups in isolated areas living in the traditional manner, but most of them were in the hamlets.

They may have been primitive and uneducated, but they learned free enterprise very quickly and very well. They wove baskets and colorful cloth. Americans sought after these. They made headbands and wristbands from this cloth and sold those as well. They picked wild bananas and pineapple to sell to Americans. Little kids or bare-breasted young women inevitably offered these to us, but an older "Mama-san" collected the money. Real Montagnard cross-bows were highly prized and difficult to get, but they did make some smaller ones for the souvenir trade. They were adept at some kinds of metal craft and turned brass from American artillery casings into gongs.

The traditional long house was becoming less common by 1970. These communal houses were built on logs and had floors raised about six feet off the ground and thirty to fifty feet long. They had a thatched roof and walls. The floors were covered with woven mats made from grass or reeds. A single log with stairs carved into it led to the door.

They still wore traditional dress. The women wore the brightly colored skirts, and sometimes went bare-breasted. The men wore only a breach cloth, although bits and pieces of American military and civilian clothing were worn. Hats and T-shirts with strangely out of place American slogans were common. It was common to see a small child proudly wearing a Notre Dame ball cap or a T-shirt with some obscene message on it.

We were told that they were animist, worshipping all types of animals and nature. I was aware that there was a snake god, but saw little to confirm that, reflecting my own ignorance more than anything else. I do recall seeing burial huts in the cemeteries around An Khe and on QL 19. In these cemeteries were markers made with a cross inside a circle. The cross was symmetrical and centered in the circle. I remember thinking it looked like some Christian symbols I had seen. The thought was fleeting. There was a Catholic church near An Khe, the presence of Catholics in Vietnam was well known, and I assumed that any church I saw was Catholic. Many years later, I learned that there had been Seventh Day Adventist missionaries in the Highlands as early as 1948. In 1967, two American missionaries at Ban Me Thout were kidnapped and apparently never seen again. There was a fairly large Protestant Christian population among the Dega that I was unaware of. Today, they are one of the most persecuted Christian groups on earth.

I thought, as did many Americans, that the Yards were a totally uneducated people. The Army's own handbooks treated them as such. While this was generally true, there was a substantial group of educated Dega. We knew that there were different tribes, but were unaware that there was any kind of unifying government. We were told, or assumed that they were an unorganized gaggle, and treated them as a single group. In fact there are thirteen tribes, each with its own unique identity, and these tribes made up a fairly strong federation. This national government was unknown to me. Educated as they were, they lacked the sophistication needed to fully deal with the diplomatic complexities of the final settlement that allowed the United States to withdraw from the war.

The Dega leadership expected the United Sates to continue full support of their fight for independence after the Army left. The diplomatic language used led them to believe that there would be real, substantive support. Of course, they were wrong. The statements that meant "keep fighting, we will support you" to the Dega meant, "good-bye, good luck," to the Americans. The result of this was an astonishing struggle.

From the end of the war for Americans in 1975 until 1992, the Dega fought a war of independence with the Vietnamese Army. No one knows how many died. Estimates range from 25,000 to four times that number. Even today, the unrest in the area prevents travel into many parts of the Highlands. Religious persecution is common and the Dega have been reduced to a shadow of what they once were. Their numbers have fallen, their cultural identity is being destroyed, and they struggle to maintain their existence as a people.

Today, many former LRRPs and Rangers from the Highlands find the treatment of "their Yards" a painful and shameful thing. They struggle with the fact that we left our brothers to fight alone. There was deep respect for them then, but even deeper respect for them now. No one knows for sure how many served with the 4th ID. Estimates range from as few as thirty to as many as several hundred. Almost every one of us can name several of these proud and fierce warriors. We know that, almost certainly, all of these men died in the war after we left. They are seen, by most, in the same light that American casualties are seen. Many consider the abandonment of the men and their people to be one of the more painful memories of the war.

CHAPTER 37

Head Hunters

———————◆———————

L ate in my tour, I pulled some missions with new team leaders. I was on one such mission with a TL who was rapidly becoming a very good team leader, when I experienced a very memorable situation. The mission was in the steep and dangerous mountains east of the Mang Yang Pass. The mission was probably security for the road. We must have been in the area for a while, because I remember the care that the TL took in selecting the night location. I also remember a very unpleasant rainstorm during the night.

After enduring a miserable night in the rain, we started to get ready for the day's movement. In sequence, each man retrieved his claymore mine. I moved forward slowly and carefully, scanning to see if the claymore had been tampered with. The VC and NVA had been known to turn these mines around on teams, aiming them at the team. The sixth sense kicked in and I took more care than I might have normally. My care was rewarded. Unbelievably, I saw an NVA soldier, no more than ten meters from me and he had not seen me. He was wearing camouflage and was obviously looking for us.

There were always rumors of bounties on LRRP/Ranger teams and we enjoyed the idea that the NVA would put a bounty on us. There were also stories of special units that were counter LRRP teams. I never put much credence in these stories. Now as I looked across the claymore at this soldier, the legend seemed fairly plausible. I knew he would see me, and the rule for survival was to react first and most violently, and you had a chance. Hesitate, and you gave the other guy a chance. In one motion I raised my weapon, clicked the selector switch to rock and roll (full automatic) and fired. The Car-15 responded with one shot and stopped! I was already sprinting toward the team.

As I got back into the night location, we fired the claymore and waited. The TL called in a contact and we waited a little longer. This was not the time to move. I don't remember a lot about the mission after that. If we searched the area, I don't recall finding anything. I do recall taking some grief later for missing the guy. A possible explanation was that we often aimed low and let the gun work up over the target when firing on automatic. I had other things on my mind, not the least of which was getting my weapon re-charged and ready to fire.

After we were sure that we were fairly safe, I did a more thorough inspection of my Car-15 and found nothing wrong. As we were extracted, I fired again, and again the weapon shot one round and jammed. When I was able to inspect the rifle more completely and disassemble it in base camp, I found the problem. A small piece of debris had worked its way into the recoil tube. The M-16 was designed to allow the bolt to unhook from the breech and travel backward down this tube, pulling the spent casing out, and then a spring in the tube pushed the bolt forward, chambering a new round. The debris had plugged the hole in the rifle butt, and apparently stopped the bolt from moving far enough to clear the spent round,

I kept this mission stored for several reasons. One was because of the very close call. Another was because the care in selecting the night location probably saved my life. But mostly, there was just something about this NVA soldier that was very different. His cammo was very good. The NVA were good at that, but it was usually to hide themselves from aircraft more than other soldiers. This man was also very obviously looking for us. Again, that was not totally unheard of, but this was somehow different. It just was not in any way normal.

Sometime in 1985, I purchased a book called Inside the NVA and VC, a carefully documented book, highly thought of by many historians. In this book, a North Vietnamese officer tells of one of his assignments. He was to recruit and train volunteers to hunt and kill Ranger teams in the central Highlands! There is no doubt in my mind that these soldiers were hunting us that day.

Addendum:

When I wrote this piece about the strange and nearly deadly encounter with a camouflaged NVA, my recollection of the contact was that I had fired once at this soldier and missed. I recalled being ribbed about that and even had a plausible explanation as to why I missed. In July of 2006, I was given a copy of the after action report on this mission. The report states that I saw two men, not one, and that my first shot hit and probably killed one of the men. The detail in the report would seem to indicate that I saw that happen. There is a description of checking the area and finding blood and drag marks. I did not recall nor include that in the first writing. There are significant differences in the two accounts. As in <u>Perceptions, Chapter 43</u>, the explanation seems to be that my psychological state filtered out some of the emotion and pain.

CHAPTER 38

Uneasy Decisions

One of the purposes for training Rangers in Ranger School, and in fact a stated part of the Ranger mission, was to pass this training on to others in the unit. In the regular line units this meant training squad and platoon level NCOs and officers in patrolling techniques. In K Company, it meant training everyone in LRRP techniques. Special attention was paid to the Assistant Team Leaders who would eventually take teams of their own. Those of us who had attended Ranger School started as ATLs and after five missions took over teams. Most of the rest of the team leaders in the company started as team members and moved up to ATL and then to TL positions. These men probably had fifteen missions or more before they took teams. This On the Job Training was very effective, but led to one uneasy decision on my part.

Bob White had been my ATL for a long time. He took over the position when Wayne Mitsch took a team. Like most team leaders, I tried to train everyone on my teams in map reading, radio procedures, artillery and chopper use, and the general basics of a LRRP team With Bob, I started to increase the responsibility that was placed on him. The obvious skills of map reading, artillery skills, pre-plotting, security and safety were all pretty standard, and he mastered them easily. He had the other leadership skills and the confidence to take a team, and I had to move in that direction. Bob was ready for me to do a check mission, a final exam of sorts for the TL spot.

When we discussed this mission, I told Bob to run the mission as if he was the senior TL, and he was to assume I was a brand new ATL. Bob, in fact, had a few more missions than I did. I am sure that I watched all the mission preparation closely, and the lack of any recall certainly means he did that well. I don't remember anything special about the mission except that we were going to be in the field longer than normal, that we had a stream for water re-supply, and Bob could be very forceful as a TL.

We had refilled our water supply at the creek in the bottom of what we called Happy Valley, near LZ Hard times, and were taking a break. I had taken out my pocketknife for some reason. This knife, my compass, map, and shack code, were always tied to my uniform with a black shoelace. The theory was that in a contact or at night or if you fell, you would not lose them. In theory and usually in practice, this was a good idea. It was so good that most of the guys on my team used the practice with weapons at night. On this mission, however, it caused a problem.

I was using the knife when someone on the team moved, catching the string and pulling the knife through my hand. It sliced my finger to the bone. It was painful, but quick first aid stopped the bleeding and I was ready to continue the mission. Bob was concerned about the wound getting infected and said so. I would have none of it and was going to "Ranger on." By mid-afternoon, the finger was beginning to swell and show clear signs of infection. Bob decided to get me out and try to continue the mission with a reduced team. This was no small thing on his part. Our teams were small already and reducing them increased the risk considerably. The extraction of a team member was sure to attract the attention of any VC or NVA in the area, compromising the team's location and increasing the threat further. I argued that it would be safer to extract the whole team the next day.

Bob would have none of that. He persisted and I arrogantly told him that this was my team and I was staying! He responded by reminding me that I had made him the TL for the express purpose of demonstrating his capability to lead a team and to make good decisions. He was the team and I was the ATL. He said, "Go," and I was going.

Once the extraction was arranged, Bob had me distribute all of my ammo, my compass, map, shack code, and radio to the new ATL. He had already reassigned his pre-plots for his artillery and planned the exit from the LZ. He had located potential areas for new night locations and rally points. He briefed the team carefully and the new ATL specifically about his plan for the rest of the mission. Much of what he did was designed to make it look like the entire team had been extracted. He executed the extraction and I left the team, headed for Camp Radcliffe.

A quick trip to the medics confirmed the wisdom of extracting me. The wound was already infected and I would have been very ill by the morning. They cleaned the wound, gave me a shot of something, bandaged it up, and sent me on my way with instructions to return in the morning. Walking back to the company area, I realized that Bob's actions were not only good ones, but pretty much what I would have done if the situation had been reversed.

The next several days and nights were spent listening to the radio transmissions from the team in the company TOC. It was a very uneasy feeling, knowing that "My" team was out there in the bush without me. I need not have been concerned. Bob did his job well, the mission was completed, and they all returned safely. Bob passed that check mission and soon had his own team. I was assigned a new ATL, and we both continued to pull missions. We stayed close, talked often about missions and compared notes. Bob and I have remained close over the years and I would trust the guy with my life today as I did in 1969 and '70.

CHAPTER 39

What Have I Become?

I sat in a room with eight to ten other men and listened to them tell "war stories." Some were clearly exaggerations, but some were the gut-wrenching confessions of men who had done or believed they had done horrible things. Uncharacteristically, I said little that night. Some of what they said forced me to re-live one of the worst parts of the war. I was forced to re-live the events that revealed how much I had allowed the war to change me.

These are small events in the overall picture, I suppose, but they reveal one of the reasons that cause me to hurt like I do. This is a common theme among the guys I talk with. The question of "What have I become?" or "How could I have done that?" still haunts us. I know of no American who wishes to be known as being cruel to children, but I can recall several times when I was. I don't like to think that I could be totally disrespectful of women, but I was. I don't think anyone ever wants to be so hard that they cannot feel human suffering, but I was. I was aware of these things and I was uncomfortable with them, but 'Nam did not allow the time for soul searching. Time, however, would eventually require that I make some sense of these events. At some point in my life I would have to make peace with these issues.

My team and several others were in the back of a "Deuce and half" truck for some reason. As we traveled out of Camp Radcliffe, several kids ran alongside, hoping for candy or food. We had neither. The result was that one of the kids flipped us off and cursed at us. Someone on the truck responded in kind and then said something to the effect that it didn't matter because "we were going to kill his dad anyway." I doubt the kid understood a word of this, but I did and I laughed out loud and shouted in agreement.

I saw a group of medics working with some Vietnamese near the main gate of Radcliffe and found myself angry that they were not out with some American unit taking care of them. It was the only time in my life that I can recall having hatred toward someone solely because of his or her skin color. I felt hatred for these people. I was stunned that I felt that, but I told another Ranger about it, and he agreed. I had not changed my feelings several hours later.

After returning from a mission, a shower was always in order. After de-briefing and cleaning weapons, we went to the shower room and cleaned up. The hooch maids and laundry women used the same spaces to wash clothes. It was a simple matter to wait until they were done, but often I did not. I walked into the shower, stripped, and took a shower in front of several older women. They were clearly not happy, rightfully offended. I could not understand the words, but I knew exactly what they were saying. I was greatly amused at their discomfort and made that clear to them.

Events like these have haunted me. I often helped kids with food. I avoided killing if I could. I tried to respect people, but there were times when I did not do the right things. I look back now, with some very real pain, on those times when I failed. Killing was to be expected, and I still struggled with it. These events were not expected and it seemed to be worse in some way. I had no choice in the former, but I did in the latter, and I made the wrong choice several times.

I was not always that way. I did many good things and all of us risked much to save the lives of noncombatants. Many stories could be presented to support that. Even so, the realization that I could be reduced to that level even once was and is a painful thing. I believe that this is a common reason why many vets do not want to talk about the war. Someone said that talking about your war was painful because no one wants to know that his or her friend or Sunday school teacher or brother or son was a "cold blooded killer." They soon quit listening to the vet's stories. The vets soon quit talking as well. The statement is true and we don't want to know that about ourselves either. I don't want to know that I could joke about killing a kid's father, or show total disrespect to a woman, but I did.

I believe that the most important factor that helped keep me from doing even worse things was my faith. I was a very young Christian, but I had been raised in the faith. I was not perfect by any means, but I was aware of a tempering in my actions. There were times when I could have done some heinous thing and did not. I failed as noted, but I never lost some sense of right in these situations. There is no doubt in my mind that I came home mentally healthier than I would have without my faith. I know I have been forgiven for

149

my sins of war, and I know I need not dwell on those. And yet, it appalls me, that the voice that I hear reminding me of these things does not stop talking, and I can't stop listening easily. I know a terrible truth about myself and I live uneasily with that truth.

CHAPTER 40

Monsoons

—◆—

The dry season was hard on LRRP teams, but the rainy season had its own special brand of misery for us. It never got very cold in the Highlands, perhaps sixty-five degrees was the lowest temperature, but if you were wet and the wind was blowing, you got cold, sometime dangerously so. Some team leaders would use ponchos to make a small hooch or tent to try to stay dry. Some teams used ponchos as they moved. I never did because Rick Williams was so adamant about the danger. The ponchos could obscure vision, they were noisy, and they lacked camouflage, all major concerns to me. As a result, my teams always got wet.

Moving during the day, even if it was not raining, would soak you to the bone. When you stopped and set up a night location, you were already wet. Hands and feet were wet, clothes were wet, and weapons and equipment were wet. The jungle boots we wore had vents in them to allow water to drain from them, but it seemed that only added to the discomfort as warm water drained out and cold water came in. Leaches loved the wet weather and found any bare skin you might expose. Woe unto the LRRP who tore a hole in his uniform.

In the dry season, the night provided a break from the heat of the day. In the rain, night only made things worse. Hooches were safer at night, but I did not use them. We would put the poncho liner inside the poncho and use it as a blanket. The ponchos were waterproof and the liners would work as an insulator, wet or dry. Hypothermia could be a problem, so we used the ponchos at night. My point man had a brush with this problem, and we warmed him up by burning all the C-4 plastic explosive we had under his poncho. He hunched over with his poncho over his head and legs, dug a small hole in the ground between his legs and lit the small balls of C-4. The method worked and he was ready to go the next day.

Vision was not an issue at night, neither was the lack of cammo on the poncho, and the danger of getting too cold was larger than the noise they made. I am not sure that it would have been possible to survive without the poncho and liner. The drill at night was to get into a comfortable position and be very still. If you stayed real still, you could warm the poncho liner and be reasonably comfortable. Staying still was effective, but eventually you had to move. When it was your turn to be on watch, you had to move. The movement usually dumped cold water off your poncho, down your neck, onto your back or into your crotch. There was not a single way to sit up that did not, sooner or later, send a river of cold-water downhill in a very uncomfortable way.

Once you were inserted in the monsoon season, extractions became problematic. The winds and low ceilings often prevented the choppers from flying. Scheduled extractions were often not possible. Drinking water was not a problem in the extensions; it was easy to collect plenty of water. The cold made food a much bigger issue. Weapons were susceptible to the water. They were hard to maintain in the wet weather. Mud was much harder on the M16 than dust. Water in the recoil tube could cause a miss-fire. This was true of all of the weapons, except perhaps the M-79 grenade launcher. The electrical storms of the Highlands could cause the detonators on the claymores to fire. More often the water would short out the detonators and they would not fire. The water raised havoc with the radios. The PRC–25 was an AM radio and very weather sensitive. Keeping batteries, handsets, and radios dry was critically important and nearly impossible. The normal solution for poor commo was to use aircraft as a relay, but the weather frequently prevented them from flying. Use of the "long whip," a fishing pole-like antenna, was more common in the rain. It was six feet long, ungainly, and in most places you could not move with it on the radio, but it helped at night and if you stopped during the day. Generally the normal dangers and discomforts of the dry season were magnified in the rain.

There were a few positives during the monsoons. Water was not a problem, so the loads could be lightened a bit. We carried less water and the availability of water made the freeze dried LRRP rations an attractive option. The weather made it hard to smell things at any distance, which allowed the teams to heat meals, coffee and chocolate. The process for a hot meal was simple. A small ball of C-4 in a small depression in the ground, light it, heat up a cup of water in a canteen cup, pour it in a LRRP and wait a few minutes and eat. A ball of C-4 about 1-1/2 inches in diameter would heat a canteen cup full of water in about one minute. The hot water made a hot meal or drink, and was often not a luxury but a necessity for cold Rangers. This use of C-4 explained the Zippo lighters carried by even non-smokers. Their only use in the field was to light C-4.

Leaches loved the wet, but most other insects did not. Consequently, the misery from those critters was lessened, as was the use of the bug repellent. Vegetation like elephant grass was beaten down by the rain, which made movement easier. This grass would cut like a razor when dry, but much less so when wet. Extractions and insertions were not as dusty as in the dry season. This made it easier to see, and I think a bit safer.

Upon returning to base camp, the teams would have to debrief and clean weapons as always, but the order for the rest of their activities changed. The shower was not the first thing to do after the weapons were cleaned; food was number one on the list.

ONE OF THE VERY FEW BENEFITS OF THE MONSOONS.

We grabbed a dry towel; a dry set of fatigues, and went to the mess hall. We consumed hot food, coffee, tea, or chocolate with enthusiasm. Our mess hall was very good about having something to eat when teams came in at any time, but in the monsoons, they went out of their way to see that we had hot food and drinks.

Vietnam was actually a very beautiful place at times, in spite of the war. The monsoons could match their misery with their beauty. The cloud formations were stunning. When the sun could be seen, the light on the massive cloudbanks was spectacular, much like those over the Colorado Rockies in August. One of the most memorable sights I saw in Vietnam was early one morning on the edge of a valley far north of An Khe. The sun came up in a fairly clear sky, revealing several jungle peaks rising up through the fog on the valley floor. The fog was so thick it looked like you could walk on it. The sun's light made the green peaks shine an iridescent green. The war seemed to slip away. It was a hauntingly beautiful sight that disappeared as quickly as it came; leaving no doubt in my mind that I was back in the rain, back in the war. That happened several times while I was in country, but never more spectacular than that day in the midst of a monsoon storm.

CHAPTER 41

Where Am I?

————— ❖ —————

After the mission on Bob's birthday, north of LZ Hard Times, Romeo 5 was dropped at the firebase. I was transferred into a LOACH and returned to the mission area to help direct an air strike. This started one of the strangest and most painful nights of the war for me.

I was flown back to LZ Hard Times after this action. For many years I wondered why I was dropped off there and not taken back to Camp Radcliffe. I thought that I was at Hard Times by myself, but others assert that the team was at Hard Times waiting for me and we all spent the night at the noisy firebase on the floor of the Vinh Thinh Valley. The artillery people at Hard Times may have been impressed at having a real live LRRP team in their midst, or more likely they took pity on the poor wretched souls they saw before them, but in any case they put us up for the night. We were fed and given a place to sleep.

I have no idea where the rest of the team was, but my cot was in one of the many above ground bunkers on the firebase. These were built primarily for munitions storage, but served my purposes just as well. These bunkers were no more than five feet tall, made with logs and metal planks called PSP (perforated steel plank). The roof was covered with four to five layers of sand bags over a layer of logs and PSP. The walls were dirt-filled ammo boxes with sand bags stacked around the outside. The door, if you could call it that, was a slit about two feet wide in the wall. The top of the door was about a foot lower than the ceiling. Outside the door was a blast wall. It was another section of wall wider and taller than the door. It was to allow easy access to the bunker and still keep shrapnel from entering through the door.

With my belly full, hydrated, and being fairly safe, I settled into my cot, pulled my poncho liner over my head, and went to sleep. Some time later, unknown to me, the battery outside got a fire mission. The first round out of the tubes brought me to some state of consciousness, although not quite a high enough level, as it turned out. My brain knew I was not in the field, because there it would have said, "Get flat, and stay still." I was supposed to be in An Khe, and the sound got translated to incoming fire. That meant my brain sent the "get to the blast bunkers outside fast!" message. I immediately jumped to my feet and slammed my head into the ceiling. I had not accounted for the low ceiling. The barracks at base camp had a much higher ceiling. I guess I thought I was hit, but it had still not registered that I was not in the company area. My brain was still saying that I still had to get out of there. I managed to stand up without hitting my head and sprinted to the door. Again I failed to compensate for the lowered door top and took the second blow squarely on the forehead. The blow laid me flat on my back. Bloody and confused, convinced I was wounded, my total survival mode kicked in.

One last time my sleepy and battered brain issued the escape message. Again I struggled to stand, and sort of sprint to the door. I managed to miss the ceiling and doorpost, only to run full speed into the blast wall outside the door! Three brain-rattling, gut-wrenching blows in just a few seconds seemed to be the limit of my survival instinct, because I turned and crawled into my cot and prepared to meet the Lord. I was convinced I was hit and dying! At that moment the second rounds went out of the tubes, and since I was already dying, there was no need to leave, so I just stayed flat. With no additional blows to the head, I started to think a bit more clearly. I soon realized what was happening, and more importantly, where I was. The guns fired the rest of the night and I slept very little.

The next morning the "Red Legs," artillery crews, saw an even more bedraggled Ranger than they had sheltered the night before. I had a knot on top of my head, a gash on my forehead, and a spectacular scrape on my face. I muttered some feeble explanation as I got on a chopper and went back to An Khe. I wish I had told them that I had gone through the wire that night and wiped out a platoon of VC or something. I suspect that I did not tell them that because my team was standing there laughing at me. I have often wondered what they really thought and if there are grandkids somewhere who have heard this story from one of the guys on that gun crew. I'll bet they have a very different view of Rangers than some others.

CHAPTER 42

FNG

The data available today seems to confirm what we all knew in 1969. New guys were dangerous. They were a danger to themselves and to anyone around them. It seemed that a disproportionate number of casualties happened in the first three months of the tour. It was always an added stressor to have a new guy on a team. We were all an FNG (F___ing New Guy) at one time.

My first mission with Rick Williams in September of 1969 was apparently uneventful by most standards. I was well prepared by Rick and I thought he knew his stuff. He had done what I came to know as his usual thorough job of prepping the team. As the new guy I was to walk slack, third in the line of four LRRPs. He finished the lesson with an Army version of "listen and learn," combined with "shut up and do what you are told." I remember only three things about the mission.

As we lifted off from the Golf Course, it was the most surreal experience I have ever had in my life. I was going into combat! The fear was unreal. I did not have the experience needed to be confident in myself. I was not psychologically conditioned to focus on the mission. I had no idea what to expect. The flight to the LZ seemed very long, and I looked to Rick for some reassurance. He appeared to be asleep. Eyes closed, leaning on his ruck, he might have been on his way to a picnic, except you don't paint your face and carry an M-16 to go on such an outing. I looked back out the door to the trees below and realized this was terribly real.

I glanced back after a few minutes and his eyes were on me now. He gave me thumbs up and charged his weapon. I did the same. On cue the pilots started the descent. The view of the LZ from about fifty feet is still clear in my mind. It was long and narrow, sloped upwards to the right side of the ship, and covered with elephant grass. We moved away from the chopper, and it lifted up and out of the LZ, leaving us alone! We found a spot with good cover and stopped, "laying dog" for what seemed an eternity. Laying dog meant that we simply stopped, got very still and quiet, and listened.

Nighttime brought a whole new set of terrors. I stood my watch, but I am sure Rick was awake with me. It was probably on this mission that I heard something and reached for Rick. He whispered, "It's okay." I am certain that I did that many times over on the next few missions. That was one reason why new guys caused problems; they simply did not know what posed a threat and what did not. Rick seemed to understand and never made an issue of my false alarms. Later when I heard something at the end of a long and noisy night, I reached out to Rick and felt his hand reaching for me. Instantly I understood that this was a real threat and that I was becoming attuned to the sounds of the night in the Highlands.

Unlike many of my LRRP buddies, I do not remember my first mission as a TL. It probably was uneventful enough to have been lost in the clutter of the rest of the time there. Like Rick Williams, however, I was to have new guys on my team. Those are strong enough to stand out. My first mission with a new team member was probably a radio relay mission with David Siglow. David was not a new to the company or to LRRP missions, but he was new to the team. I found myself being hyper-vigilant with him. I was awake when he was on watch. I checked his weapon and safety closely. Fortunately, he was a good Ranger and maybe the best point man in the company. Until I knew that, I watched him, like Rick had watched me.

Another time Romeo 5 took a man into the bush as the fifth man on a five-man team. He had been with another team and they had rejected him, asking that he be placed on another team. This young soldier was a good man, I am sure, perhaps even a good soldier in another setting, but he was not cut out for K Company. Twice during the mission he simply froze in critical situations. We were moving in tall grass and brush when there was a sudden and loud movement to our front. All four of the rest of the team instantly went to the ground. The new guy was still standing. The movement was just one of the wild chicken-like birds, but had it been an NVA or VC soldier, this man would have probably died.

By mid-April of 1970, both of my long-time ATLs had their own teams, and I was back building a new one. I had an ATL who had pulled many missions and I was very comfortable with him, but the rest of our team was brand new to our world in K Company. Both of these men eventually became good at the game, but suffice it to say my ATL and I got very little sleep on the first few missions. The missions where Rick Williams was the old vet and I the FNG, had come full circle.

CHAPTER 43

Perceptions

I n May of 1970, K Company had teams near the Cambodian border in preparation for what would become the famous Cambodian Invasion. Once the teams were out of the area, larger American infantry units from the 4th Infantry division were sent in to complete those operations. These larger units were then not available to protect the base camps in and around An Khe. As a result, Camp Radcliffe and other smaller bases were vulnerable to attack. One way to prevent this from happening was to use the LRRP/Ranger teams as screening forces. Essentially, these teams were placed in areas that were likely routes of approach for NVA units seeking to attack these facilities.

My team and several others were assigned the picket line in the Animite Mountains northeast of An Khe. I was one of the old guys in the company, so my team was in the center of this line of teams. I was also the most familiar with the terrain because I had pulled many missions in this general area. It was, to say the very least, a difficult place to work, and therefore a place that the NVA used frequently.

Navigation was very difficult in the dense double canopy jungle and on the brutally steep sides of the ridgelines. Teams not experienced in this type of terrain could fall into great difficulties. The vegetation and infamous wait-a-minute vines slowed movement. They distracted you as you moved, and while you were distracted, the steep sides of the ridges pulled you down and away from the top and toward the low ground. Climbing back up could become almost impossible.

One team, led by a well trained but somewhat inexperienced team leader, fell into this trap while trying to move along the razor back ridgeline. As he tried to move parallel to the top, his team drifted down the side of the hill. They found themselves far down the slope when they started to hear and see signs of NVA soldiers in the area. Compounding the problem were the spotty communications, and the near non-existence of any landing zones on the north side of these ridges. The team had packed heavily, expecting a five-day mission. A team in contact would have only one chance to get out. They would have to climb up the slope and find an LZ on the other side.

As darkness fell, the team realized that they could only communicate with my team. It became obvious from the radio traffic that they were going to have to move at night to avoid contact. Moving at night was done only in dire situations. Navigation in this area was impossible at night without some sort of light, and that was out of the question with NVA in the area. Since I was sure I knew where they were, I covered my head, map and flashlight with a poncho and talked the team to the top of the ridge and to a new night location. During the rest of the night, most of the teams in the picket line had sightings of lights and heard sounds indicating NVA units were actively using the area. Once that was established, our job was done and the teams were to be extracted. I don't recall much about the first team's extraction. There was a team pulled before mine that received some ground fire, but we got out without incident.

The next team pulled was the team we had talked out the night before. They were on a grassy LZ on the bottom of a small valley. I was watching the extraction from our chopper and saw the ship flare and begin to settle into the tall elephant grass. At that moment, the team was attacked from the hillside above them. Two of the Rangers on the ground were wounded in the initial burst of firing. I could hear the team leader asking for help and the slick pilots were calling for the gunships to make gun runs on the hillside. Two LRRPs jumped from the slick and sprinted to the two wounded men on the ground and pulled them into the ship. Both teams were lifted out with two wounded Rangers on board. Several times after the incident, I wondered why there was a team on the extraction ship. This was very rare, because the ships often could not lift two teams. Vietnam provided very little time for reflection on such things and I soon was onto other missions.

About thirty years later at a Ranger reunion in Fort Lewis, Washington, I was reminded of this mission again. Janet and I were at the pool when a vaguely familiar face appeared at the table. He introduced himself and thanked me for "saving his life." I was confused and assumed that he had mistaken me for someone else. He assured me that he was not mistaken and related a story to me that was nearly identical to the one written above. Nearly identical, but not quite.

161

His story and mine matched up well until the extraction of the team in contact. While I watched the extraction from a chopper 800 feet above the LZ, he saw something very different. As the team moved to the LZ, they knew contact was imminent. They were right and they were hit at the edge of the LZ. He says that the chopper that went in to get them was the one my team was on. He was one of the LRRPs wounded on the LZ and I was the one who got him onto the extraction ship. My assistant team leader was the other guy I saw leaving the Huey. I again tried to tell him that I was not the right person. Bob White has confirmed the story as told by the wounded LRRP. I have no reason to doubt either of them.

More than forty years later, I still have no ability to summon up any picture of this event other than the first. I think I could pass any test of truth about it, all the while knowing that what I recall is not what happened. Later in the process of this work, I discovered that this memory might well be a melding of two events. One was certainly SSG Duke's team and the other may have been another team that was pulled during a VR that Bob and I were on. The confusion in my story is almost certainly some psychological disconnect from reality as a result of the stress. I know now that this is not uncommon. I wonder what else I have remembered or forgotten because of this. It is an eerie thought.

CHAPTER 44

LZ Hooper

———————◈———————

L RRPs never dig in. At least that was usually the case. Most of us also hated being anywhere near a line unit or firebase. It was not that we didn't like or respect the other grunts; they were brothers. We just found the noise and commotion of these large units and facilities very disconcerting. We relied almost totally on stealth for security; they relied on their volume of firepower. We tried to make as little noise as possible; they were willing to make any amount of noise to get dug in. It was total culture shock for a Ranger team to deal with these units.

In March of 1969, I had been given a mission of radio relaying for a number of teams in an operation well north of An Khe. We were told that we would be on a firebase called LZ Hooper. It meant nothing to us, and we prepared as we normally would for any mission except that we had light rucks and lots of radios, antennas, and batteries. We flew for a very long time before we were alerted that we would be landing at Hooper. I don't know what we had been told about the place, other than it was a brand new firebase and there was a larger operation going on in the area. As we turned onto the final approach, it was very apparent that LZ Hooper was still being built. Four Rangers were dumped unceremoniously onto a half-finished firebase on a bare hilltop. The hilltop, really two small hills and the saddle between them, was totally open and exposed.

There were certainly infantry troops in the surrounding area providing security, but the firebase itself seemed very vulnerable to us. There were American troops scurrying all over the place. There was a small caterpillar tractor running around the perimeter, digging holes for the bunkers to defend the place. Chopper after chopper dropped off troops, and supplies. Several Chinooks brought in sling loads of timbers, perforated steel planks, and empty sand bags to complete the overhead cover on the bunkers. A big sky crane helicopter brought in several loads of concertina wire, steel posts and other material to build the perimeter. Some engineers were putting up wire around the place while others pounded posts to anchor the wire. Someone was building a garbage pit. There was a mortar pit in the center of the LZ and the crews were busy setting the tubes and aiming poles. All this activity did nothing to comfort the Ranger team stuck in the open. My first instinct was to flee into the jungle outside the perimeter and disappear into the security of the bush. That was not our mission, so the next best thing was to get a bunker built and get the radios up and running before the teams were inserted. There was a small bunker being built near to the large command bunker, and after introducing myself to the CO of the place, I was given the smaller bunker. The engineers who had just finished it were not pleased, but they had many others to build, and left us to our mission.

Once underground, we felt at least a bit safer. We immediately set up the long-range antenna, the 292, or "two-inner-two" as it was known. Even this had an unnerving effect on us. For men used to concealing everything, placing an antenna twelve feet high right next to your location seemed a lot like advertising your presence. This was totally irrational, since we were about ten meters from the command bunker with at least three or four more of the 292s and one even larger antenna. Once the antenna was up, common checks were made and we waited for the first of our teams to be inserted. The duty was not bad, plenty of food, water was plentiful, and the bunkers offered some comfort not usually available to us. Still, the amount of noise and activity kept us on edge.

David Siglow, my point man was determined to make the best of the situation and had carved out several shelves in the wall of our bunker and was busy making a comfortable home on LZ Hooper. We watched with some concern as troops moved about totally in the open and without any apparent attempts to conceal their movements. After a while, several men near our bunker sat down and cooked up a meal, again without any consideration of the possibility of getting shot at. It was a strange experience for LRRPs.

After a few hours, we started to relax a bit and even decided to join the troops outside the bunker. We watched with interest as they busied themselves with the building of the base. Interesting things were happening, things I had never seen before. One bunker just a few meters from ours was home to a 50-caliber machine gun, mounted with a Starlight scope. The scope was the new night vision equipment that allowed the user to see in almost total darkness. This setup was to be used as a night sniper. Further away, the mortar crews were beginning to register final protective fires. They were dropping rounds around the perimeter in preparation for any attacks on our temporary home. I had made further contact with the command bunker and we were all set to start working teams in the area. We had some time before that happened, so we braved the exposure and sat on the bunker, eating and taking in the spectacle.

L TO R: SGT. WAYNE MITSCH AND SGT. WALTER DUKE
ON RADIO RELAY AT LZ HOOPER. NOTE THE TALL WHIP ANTENNA AT CENTER.

As we watched all the hustle and bustle, a Chinook came in with a 500-gallon bladder of water slung under the ship. As it settled into a hover over the drop area, a poncho was blown into the air, through the rotors and over one of the engine intakes. The Hook pilot instantly dropped the bladder, which burst and sent water everywhere. The aircraft landed hard, but apparently was not damaged because they flew it out after a quick inspection. Not long after that excitement, the mortar crews dropped a round well short of the perimeter and directly into the garbage pit. The result was a shower of trash and shrapnel that sent not only the LRRPs, but also many others back into a bunker. I think we spent most of the rest of the day inside, wondering what we had gotten ourselves into. Night was coming and we had a team on the way, so we had no more time to worry about those things.

We were on Hooper for three or four days. I don't remember leaving. We had several teams to relay for, at least one team was in contact and another was in a very difficult spot, and contact was imminent. We were a long way from the choppers, and with all of the other troops being moved around, getting ships was difficult. Communication was not good from teams in the field to us, and they were even worse from Hooper to our Zero.

At some point during the stay on Hooper, I diverted a team that was being inserted and then used those ships to pull the two teams mentioned earlier. After they were out, I was able to get the other team inserted as planned. This action, seen by me as "decisive, creative and tactically prudent," was seen by a more senior officer as "an arrogant overstepping of authority." I had a run-in with this officer earlier, and had he seen me, he would have realized that I was a second time offender and really gone after me. Fortunately for me, he did not realize who I was and he had the CO on Hooper chew me out. After I had my butt chewed, the CO looked at me, smiled and said, "You are just one in a long line of guys who have pissed him off. Glad you got your guys out."

Two other events remain in my memory from this mission. The first involved another team on a tiny firebase called LZ Blister. It was no more than a few meters wide and ten meters long. I saw it only because I saw it when we pulled a team off of it some time after we left Hooper. Roger Crunk had a team there while we were on Hooper, and they were also a relay team. During their stay on Blister, I was manning the radio when I heard a huge explosion from Blister. Mariano, an excellent LRRP, well known for his difficulty with the radio, got very excited and was trying to tell us what happened. In his excitement, he became very difficult to understand, and in this case, he was very excited. He thought, understandably, that they were being shelled. One of the teams in the area needed the frequency and whispered into the handset: "Get him the hell off the radio," and we did. Bob White was on Blister with the relay team and remembers the incident well. Engineers were trying to blow a hole in the ground for a sump and apparently used far too much explosive. It collapsed several bunkers!

The second thing I recall was waking up one morning to perhaps the most beautiful sight I ever saw in Vietnam. It had rained during the night and I was on watch as the sun came up over the mountains. The early light of day revealed the valleys around Hooper filled with fog and the green peaks of the Animite Mountains pushing up through the fog. It was beautiful! It lasted only a few minutes, the fog burned off, and we were once again just on a bare hilltop in the middle of a war. Hooper had provided a snapshot of the war for me. I saw strange things, felt fear, and got mad, laughed, marveled at the ingenuity and power of an American unit. I wondered at the thought processes of some commanders, and appreciated the honesty of others. In fairness, I did not know a lot of things and that certainly made my perspective very limited. I felt gratitude from some for what I had done. I felt the wrath of others for the same actions. It was all wrapped up in the fleeting beauty of a highlands sunrise and a return to the things I would soon forget as I returned to the normal work of a Ranger in the Highlands. I did not know, and probably never will know, what the bigger operation was or what it accomplished.

CHAPTER 45

Numb

T his is the most difficult story about combat that I will write. It was very late in my tour, perhaps my last mission at the end of May. I was with a heavy ambush team and I was there to evaluate team leaders. This was an eight- or nine-man team, and the mission was Hawkeye, an ambush mission.

The AO, steep mountains north of LZ Hardtimes, was well known for its brutal terrain and large numbers of VC and NVA. We found a rice storage hooch very near our insertion point. There was ample evidence of enemy activity in the area, including a very wide and heavily used trail. Before we had been on the ground long, a VC soldier had seen us and fired on the team. Had this been a more normal LRRP team mission, with four men, the team would have been extracted. In this case, our job was to make contact and this initial contact did nothing but enhance the prospect.

The team found a good night location and in the morning set our ambush. This was not a hasty ambush. This was well

ONE OF THE WATER FALLS IN THE MISSION AREA.

planned, well supplied, and well executed. The primary weapons were the clay-more mines and the M-60 machine gun. The mines were a curved plastic shell filled with hundreds of one-quarter-inch steel balls and an explosive charge to fire outward in a lethal fan of death and destruction. Several of these mines, placed carefully, formed what we called the kill zone. Our kill zone probably covered twenty to thirty meters of trail. With the ambush set, we waited.

We did not wait long. Two groups of VC approached, carrying weapons and large baskets. They seemed unaware that shots had been fired in the area the day before. They walked into the ambush, totally unaware of the presence of American Rangers. The ambush was blown and those in the first group went down. Some in a second group managed to escape the mines. As soon as the ambush was executed, each team member had a specific job to do. Some were to provide security for the rest of the team, some searched the site, gathering whatever they could find that might have intelligence value.

I was to sweep the kill zone and be sure that no threat existed. The clay-mores had been brutally effective. I checked one body and moved to another. The second soldier, lying face down in the trail, moved slightly and groaned. He was mangled horribly from his lower chest down and was clearly dying. Wounded VC would at times hold grenades under their bodies when wounded, trying to kill Americans. I placed the barrel of my Car-15 behind this man's ear and fired, moving on to the next. We finished our job and the birds took us home.

I don't know if we found anything of importance. Little memory remains of the actual mission except what I have just written. The most vivid memory of the mission is not what happened, but what did not happen. It is not what I felt that day, but what I did not feel that haunted me for years. What I recall is that I felt nothing on this mission. In the initial contact I was very close to being hit. I felt nothing. During the ambush I felt nothing. I felt no fear, no concern for the VC, no guilt, nothing. It is that lack of emotion that I recall. I know they were armed, I know they were enemy soldiers. I know I acted responsibly in protecting my teammates. Still, it took over thirty years to finally come to grips with this lack of emotion.

I know I was shutting down at that point. I know it was common for men to do that. It becomes too painful to feel, to know you are capable of such behavior, so you don't feel, you just don't allow yourself to think about it. In the second Gulf War, there was a tape played over and over showing a young Marine shooting a man in a situation very similar to what I have described. I don't know this kid's name, I never met him, I share only a few seconds of vid-eotape in common with him. In spite of that, I know him well. We share this. At one time we were forced by the situation we found ourselves in to do the unthinkable. We were both numb to the pain. I know now that the numbness cannot last, must not last forever. We will both be forever changed by what we had to do and by the numbness that allowed us to do it.

CHAPTER 46

Gifts from 'Nam

———✦———

It took a long time for me to recognize them, and even longer to embrace them, but Vietnam gave me several gifts. There are many clichés that get thrown around when veterans get together and talk. There are many versions of the "It made me a man" theme. There are several versions of "I grew up in a hurry." All are probably true for most of us in some way and to some degree, but I believe there are at least three great gifts that God gave me through the experience of the war.

After the first day of Ranger School, I had survived and was convinced that I had endured the worst that they could offer. I was wrong, very wrong! Each day after that, I was convinced it could not get worse and took that as a comfort and an encouragement. Each day I was wrong. Vietnam was not consistently like that, but the principle was the same. Each time a mission went badly, I was convinced that I had endured the worst and could make it. I was often wrong, but I was able to keep going. Each time some unexpected change in plans threatened us, and it seemed that it could get no worse, I drew strength from the fact that I had survived and could go on. After many of these experiences, I became confident in myself, in my team, and in our ability to make it through the war. Confidence was not something that I came by naturally. It was in the crucible of the war in the Highlands that I was given this gift.

I was, and still am, a fairly trusting person by nature. In K Company, I learned more fully what it meant to trust another person. I learned a better definition for trusting someone. I trusted the men who worked with me in a way that I trusted no one else.

The gift from 'Nam was not just learning to trust others, but rather that others could trust me. There is no single moment that I can point to and say, "This is when I knew I was trusted." It was a process that happened without me knowing it. As I learned to trust the men of K Company and those on my teams, they learned to trust me. As I realized that, it made a deep impression on me.

One incident that illustrated this to me was when David Sunglow asked to be on my team. It was very clear that he trusted not only me, but my team as well. Later, when I doubted my abilities to function in the point element of the company POW rescue mission, Top Keller curtly set me straight. It was a shock to me that he trusted me as he did, but I do remember that I was very motivated to do the job well. The effect of this has been an awareness that what I do matters. I like to be trusted and have tried to be trustworthy. I learned the basic lesson from my parents, but I learned the real value of it in 'Nam.

I think the most important gift was that my life could end at any moment. I knew this before Vietnam, but I did not fully grasp the reality of that fact. I knew that everyone died; I had lost friends and family before I went to Vietnam. I knew what the *Bible* taught about death, but I had not accepted those realities as something that applied to me. Like many young people, I knew with my head, but denied with my heart.

Unlike my experience with trust, I know the specific moment that I realized that my life could end. It was on my very first mission. As we flew out of the Golf Course, I looked down and saw the perimeter disappear behind the Huey. After a few more minutes, I could see that we were flying over unsecured ground. Still later, Rick Williams told me to charge my M-16 and we started down to the LZ. I realized that this was very real and I knew that I could end up dead.

Over the next ten months, I would have several missions that came close to making this a reality. I did not fear death particularly, but I knew that it could happen and that I had some control over that. I planned carefully. I trained constantly. I tried to learn as much from as many people as possible. The truth of the matter was undeniable and it motivated me. Not only was it real for me, it was real for those who were on my team. I resolved to do all I could to keep that from happening. By the grace of God, I was successful.

When I returned to the US, this understanding never left me, but it did change in the way it affected me. I lost some of the vigilance, the immediacy, the urgency of the situation and became more aware of the gift that I had been given.

Now I believe that I enjoy my time here more. I appreciate my life, my family, my faith, everything, more than I would have without that lesson of the war. I know that it could have all been taken from me. I know it was taken from so many. The end of life here on earth is for me so real and so certain that it holds little fear. Surely, my faith in Christ is at the center of this, but there is more to it. I know how fragile life is and how quickly it can end. I try not to waste any of the time I have been given.

Vietnam was for the most part an awful experience. Many of the problems I face today may well be a result of the war experience. I know I am a different person because of the war. I have some "' 'Nam demons" that I battle and there are surely negative effects. Would I have learned any of these lessons another way? Could I have learned them from different people? Probably, but I did not! I learned them from my experience in 'Nam.

Lest anyone think that I glory in the war or the horror of it, I count the cost of these lessons. I see the cost in others around me, in my family, in my own soul. I know I have not learned the lessons completely, nor have I lived by them perfectly. They are, nonetheless, gifts from God, sent through a soldier's experience in a war. I can be confident in myself and in others. I can trust and I can be trusted. I know my life is fragile and finite, and I should not waste it. I count these as gifts from God.

CHAPTER 47

Why Do Men Become Rangers?

❖

W e sat a table, forty years after the fact, and wondered, "What made us do what we did?" What was it in us that made us become LRRPs and Rangers? What did we have in us or what were we lacking? Was there something special about us, or were we just ordinary guys who rose to the occasion? There were several opinions expressed that morning, but no real agreement.

One suggestion was that we came from situations that drove us to seek "family" in the Rangers. There can be little doubt that that sense of family was, and still is, a major reason why we are Rangers. Some thought the reason

ME WITH A NEW TEAM LATE IN MY TOUR. MISSION CAMMO.

was our seeking of excellence and the desire to be recognized as someone who was special. I can attest to this personally, and know several others who acknowledge this as well. Some came out of a sense of duty and wanted to serve with honor. Most of us look back with pride and know that we did have a sense of duty to the mission and to each other, that we did honor our predecessors and our country. There were some who sought the notoriety and reputation of the Rangers. Some thought that having two days of stand down out of every six or seven days was better than being in the bush for ninety days at a time. Some thought it safer than duty in a line unit. Many team leaders will tell you that they sought the control offered by

172

LRRP units. Some, knowing that the Ranger Units were being re-constructed, saw the opportunity to be a part of something important–history, if you will.

At the foundation of the question is the assumption that what made us become Rangers happened before we joined. I would submit that what made us become Rangers was not what caused us to volunteer, but it is what kept us there doing the job. It is what we did that made us Rangers. There were many who volunteered for the LRRP units who did not stay to pull many missions. Many came and went without ever making the connections that we have with each other today. They did not feel the gut-wrenching fear as we listened on the radio to a team in contact. They never sprinted to the choppers as a four or five-man reaction team. They never learned to trust three other guys with their lives like we did.

They did not know the assurance that your senior NCO and officers would be there for you. They did not know and accept the fear of contact in these tiny teams, or the exhilaration of surviving a contact. They did not know the real deprivation of a LRRP mission extended. They didn't commit to the team and put the well being of the others in front of their own. They didn't commit to the men or the mission. They shared none of the deprivation, none of the pride, none of the pain, and none of the sacrifice that made those who stayed Rangers.

There is nothing in what I am saying that is derogatory to those who never volunteered, nor to those who, having started, decided to leave. My premise is that the act, doing the job, makes men Rangers. My point is seen in the Tab/Scroll controversy. I have a Tab, and I believe I am justifiably proud of it. I have a Scroll, and I am justifiably proud of it as well. The first symbolizes a significant amount of perseverance and effort, to make myself a better soldier. It made me a better LRRP than I would have been otherwise, and I hope it made others better as well. However, the scroll symbolizes for others that I actually did the job; I was a LRRP/Ranger in fact, in action, in deed. Had I earned the Tab and not served as a LRRP, I would not have the relationship with the men of K Company, the men of the 4th Division LRRPs or the other LRRPS from Vietnam... Had I not earned the Tab, but served with these men, I would still have the connection. I would have been a Ranger in the sense that we all understand. Likewise, when someone left the company after pulling missions for a time, they remained a part of the brotherhood.

Whatever the reason for joining the company, there was something that kept us there doing the job. That is what made us Rangers. When asked, "If you had to choose between your Tab and your Scroll, which would you keep?" I said without hesitation, the Scroll! It denotes one of the most treasured titles that I carry. It tells me that, whatever it is that makes men Rangers, I am one of the Brotherhood!

CHAPTER 48

Coming Home

AWARDS PRESENTATION OF MY BRONZE STAR AND AIR MEDAL.
SFC MOTT (L) AND CAPTAIN OLMSTEAD (R).

Returning to the "World" as Nam vets called the United States was the goal of everyone there. By the time I left K Company in June of 1969, there were hundreds of stories about vets returning home to mobs that spat on them, cursed at them, called them baby killers or worse. I had some concern about this, but I never experienced that to any significant degree. Perhaps I was just lucky or naive. I had good support from my family and especially my dad. I had friends who truly welcomed me home. An old girlfriend, a very vocal antiwar person, never attacked me. We remained friends with very different views. I was asked to leave a barbershop once because I was part of "the first generation of Americans to lose a war." There were a few snide remarks in college classes, and lots of flags sewn onto someone's butt. I saw more fatigue jackets on campus at Mesa College than I did in An Khe, but I experienced nothing that was really painful. On the way to Vietnam, our plane landed in Hawaii to refuel. We were not allowed to leave the immediate area. These places were used as rally points by protesters and the potential for conflict was apparently pretty high. I was reminded again, soon after arriving home, that I should not expect or seek a warm welcome most places.

I recall almost nothing of the flight home. The plane erupted in wild cheering when the wheels cleared the runway and we were no longer in Vietnam. I must have slept much of the way and really only vaguely remember refueling in Alaska. Cheering was no less enthusiastic when the wheels touched down at Fort Lewis, Washington. We had survived. Now all that was left was to out process and go home.

After the long flight on a World Airways freedom bird, we were warned about protesters. In my haste to get home, I paid little attention to the Captain as he spoke, and instead enjoyed the steak dinner that was the last Army meal I would ever eat. There were a few protesters as we left the base in a taxi bound for the airport and home. Once at SEA-TAC airport, I had some time to kill. One of the things I had promised myself I would do as soon as possible was to get a civilian cup of coffee. I bought a large cup and soon had to use the restroom. I entered the restroom, and in the corner near the trashcan was a pile of uniforms. Perhaps twenty Army uniforms were piled in the corner. There were several Air Force uniforms as well. Dress Greens, Khakis, boots, shoes, caps, and medals all strewn on the floor. I was stunned. The image has remained with me to this day. I did not consider leaving my uniform there and I had no civilian clothes anyway, but I understood the meaning of this. The message was now brutally clear.

"Be very careful about telling people that you were a soldier in Vietnam," said the Captain at the out processing center. Those words, hardly noticed a few hours earlier, now were a new, hard, and clear reality to me. There are some today who have not forgotten that message, nor have they broken the silence. They have paid an unnecessary price. I have been blessed in my ability to talk and heal, but that image in that restroom kept me from healing as fast as I could have. It kept me guarded and it kept me from being honest with myself and with those who truly cared about me. I did not want to be hated, so I talked only to those who I knew would accept me. I told only the funny stories. I tried to convince myself that the war was not that bad and those who seemed to struggle were weak. I was different, I was stronger, and I had not changed out of my uniform.

But I was ultimately forced to admit that I was wrong. I wasn't different, or stronger. I had not changed the uniform, but I had not been honest about my struggle, either. I was eventually forced to deal with my issues. I was more arrogant, a bit more proud, a lot more stubborn, but I was finally able to come to grips with my war. I now understand what I saw that day, and why that pile of uniforms was there. It seemed to be a good way to erase the past, to separate themselves from the war. I hope they have found their way. I pray that those men have found the peace that I have found.

CHAPTER 49

PTSD

———————◆———————

It would seem to be a very easy thing to write about. After all, most of us have it. It has been around, using different names, for many years. From the Civil War to World War I and II, from Korea and Vietnam, to today, the names changed, but it seems to be pretty much the same thing. It was probably even present in much earlier times. Jonathan Shay contends that it is at the very heart of *The Iliad*! So why isn't it fully understood, accepted, treated and healed? It is, I suspect, much more than the sum of all of its parts. It presents in everyone differently and everyone deals with it differently.

When I returned from Vietnam, I was determined to move on with my life. I was certain that my war was over and there was nothing to deal with. That sentence in itself reveals a conflict that I either could not or would not recognize. I was determined, probably because I had some understanding that it was not over, and yet I tried hard to convince myself that there was really no problem. My actions seemed to be indicating privately that I had things to work on and yet outwardly I seemed to most to be "doing well." In rare moments I did confide in my dad and with my first wife Ethel. Roger and I talked some, but everyone else got to see me covering up the doubts that I had.

To most people, I talked only about the good times in 'Nam, the friends, the funny stories, and only occasionally the tough times. Even those were carefully sorted and edited to reflect the physical and mental challenges, and to minimize the psychological and spiritual challenges. I knew some of the things that I did when I got home were strange.

In the first few months after I got home, I worked for a guy who was surveying in the eastern Utah Mountains. I was basically a pack animal for him, but I was used to that and it was a job. In the remote area, I found myself very much at ease with the work, but deeply uncomfortable with being there and not being armed. I was constantly looking for the possible threats, mentally plotting the possible dangers and escape routes. I frequently spoke in a whisper. I once started to tell my boss that we needed to move before we ate lunch. I caught myself and that prevented me from saying anything, realizing that the spot would have not been a good one in 'Nam, but was perfectly fine in Utah. Some of that continues to this day.

I did some pretty strange things elsewhere as well. Several times in those early months, I drove home late at night. There is an intersection near my parents' house that has very limited visibility, especially if you are going north. More than once, I turned my lights off and drove through the stop sign at that intersection, going well over eighty miles per hour! I saw, pretty quickly, the insanity of this and stopped, but I would often think about doing it again. There was something very attractive about that. I went out with friends when I got home and it seemed that there was often someone who decided that it would be a good idea to fight a Vietnam vet. I eventually stopped going to these places, because "some idiot" always wanted to fight, but I now know that I intentionally, subtly, provoked many of these events. Only once did this end in a real fight. It took me years to realize that I was doing this.

I have come to believe that the underlying cause of some of these things was simply that I wanted to be treated with the same respect that I had received from the men in K Company. That kind of respect was not generally forthcoming for Vietnam Veterans. I was busy with school and soon found myself moving on pretty much as I had planned, never suspecting the anger that was building inside of me.

Probably the first time I really recognized this was after I started teaching. I dealt too harshly with a student and I got a reprimand. I deserved it. As I was sitting there, I got very angry and thought "I was leading combat missions while this man was playing basketball in college!" On one hand, I was aware of the ludicrous nature of this thought, but on the other hand it seemed perfectly reasonable. Fortunately, I had the control to keep my mouth shut.

Some time later I did the same thing at home, losing my temper totally. I threw a hammer at the TV set because my wife had complained that we watched too much TV. That was the beginning of my journey toward some healing.

I made contact with a local counselor who worked with vets and started attending one of the groups. At the time these were called "Rap groups" and my experience was helpful, but also disturbing. John, the counselor, was able to start me on the path of healing and I was able to begin to move on in a more positive fashion. He pointed out that people probably did not "understand the hurt" because I never really shared the very bad times. I started to do that with a few close friends and it helped. He suggested that I start reading about Vietnam, and for the next twenty years, I read everything I could get my hands on. The one negative about this experience was to be dealt with years later.

In the group, there were several guys who were either imposters or very ill mentally. The stories they told got wilder with each passing week. John had made me commit to twelve sessions before he would let me in the group, knowing that I might not come back after one or two. He was right. I stayed, and two of the men in the group and I became friends and we made progress. The others in the group, imposters or not, convinced me that PTSD, (Post Traumatic Stress Disorder) was an excuse and a sign of weakness in all but a very few cases. My Ranger training still kept me from admitting that I might have a real issue and that I might need help. I was willing to make exceptions for a few of the men I knew who had suffered horrible situations in 'Nam, but I was not ready to place myself in that group. Life was busy. We had kids and work, and I buried things in work and family and reading. It worked for many years.

When I retired, I was not prepared for the return of the anger. Sixty-hour workweeks were a thing of the past, and while I did not realize there was a problem, Janet certainly did! After a particularly rough stretch, she kindly, lovingly and strongly suggested that I go to the VA and see if I needed help. I know I had the attitude that I was "fine," but something must have told me that I might not be fine, because I went. I went to "get my hearing checked," still denying or not recognizing the reality of the situation. I was told I needed to do a PTSD evaluation. The statement made me mad, but I did take the evaluation. I went home and promptly forgot about that whole thing. I knew my hearing was not real good, and I was now "in the system" as the VA says. Not much else was said until some months later.

Janet handed me a letter from the VA, and I said, "Well, maybe we are going to be rich," still making light of the possibility that I might have PTSD. I opened the letter and read that my hearing was bad, but not bad enough to get hearing aids and that I was awarded a 30 percent disability for PTSD. I still did not really think I had an issue, but I was already scheduled for an appointment.

The doctor was ready for me. He understood that I was a doubter, and he knew pretty well how to deal with that. By the time I left, I knew I needed help and accepted it gladly. It was not the end of things by any means, and I still struggle with things at times, but it has been an upward path. What I had to learn was that self-medication with books, work and activity was okay when I was younger, but I could not do that forever. Relearning ways to react was not easy. I had long ago asked for forgiveness for anything I had done wrong in Vietnam and believed that I had been forgiven. I felt a deep sense of God's grace in that, and I knew I had been spared some of the worst traumas of the war, and I was grateful. I know now that it is not a single weakness that we suffer from; it is that we all have different vulnerabilities and experiences. So when we are involved in these things like a war, we all respond differently. We even respond differently at different points in our lives. Early on I could "charley mike," continue the mission; later I had to admit that I could no longer do that and I was shown another way.

I have heard all kinds of explanations for PTSD. They run from weakness of character to insanity before the war; from justified guilt for war crimes to lack of guilt for war crimes; from not having faith to having faith in something that is not true. Fear of death, wanting to die, wanting sympathy, faking, lying about the war, and telling the truth about the war. I suspect that somewhere, there is someone who might fit any one of these, but it is not my place to say. We all have to find our way. What I believe is true of all of us is this, not one of us came home the same after 'Nam. We were all changed in some way. We all had some vulnerability when we went, we all had something difficult that we had to deal with, and most of us managed to deal with things pretty well. What we did in the LRRPs probably just intensified some of our vulnerabilities; I know it did that to me. We all carry something from those days and we all have something to give to those who are returning to us today. We don't have all the answers, but we do need to listen to the young veterans. They need to know that we do understand their pain and we will be there when they need us.

There is another pain that I am just beginning to understand. Our pain carries over onto those who love us. I have caused pain for those who love me most. I can only pray for forgiveness and say I am sorry.

CHAPTER 50

Recon: A Piece of Cake

———————————◆———————————

Chapter 50 and 51 are fictionalized stories based on several missions and events during my tour with K Company

The characters are all composites of men that I knew. The missions are based very broadly on several of my missions. I have added details from other teams' missions and stories. The stories are fiction, but I have attempted to portray the mission in a realistic fashion. The physical, mental, and emotional stress portrayed are real. I have attempted to let the reader see a bit of what it was like to be a LRRP and to see something of the kind of men who I served with. If you know some of these men, I hope you can recognize them and understand them a bit better as you read this

This was the kind of mission that Sgt. Ben Gordon and his teams were good at. It was pure recon, deep penetration, and exactly what Gordon had asked for. He took the normal briefing, made his normal notes, gave the Op order to his ATL, and headed for the Golf Course to meet with SFC Miller for his VR. The visual recon from the chopper was the first step in mission preparation for the twenty-one-year-old Ranger. He had done it enough times to earn an Air Medal, but he thought little of that. Almost everyone in the company had as many hours in the air. Many had more missions and more contacts, and that was fine with him as well. He climbed into the Huey and leaned back against the co-pilot's seat.

The platoon Sergeant, SFC Bill Miller, had shown the pilot the area to be over-flown. This AO was bigger than normal, 3,000 meters wide and 4,000 meters long. It was well north of LZ Hard Times and covered with heavy jungle. It was flatter than most of the areas he had worked, and that probably accounted for the larger AO. Both Gordon and Miller had seen what appeared to be two small landing zones on the map. They were located near the center of the AO and in some of the flatter ground. Miller assumed that one of those was going to be the primary insertion point, but Gordon knew this part of the Highlands well and he did not want to use those LZs unless he had to. He had already located a larger LZ just outside of his assigned AO and was probably going to use it, even if it meant that his team had to walk further to get where they needed to be. He would reserve the two smaller clearings for extraction.

SGT RUSS TEMPLE, DRESSED FOR A RECON MISSION.

The door gunner yelled and pointed to something on the ground. Gordon leaned forward and let his legs dangle out of the door. He followed the gunner's eyes to the right side of the aircraft and saw a large, high waterfall. There were several falls in the Highlands, but this one was a real treat. It had three falls, two smaller ones framing the third larger one in the center. The beauty of the place took in everyone on board. The pilots apparently were impressed, and they made a wide circle over the area, while the copilot took pictures. Gordon and Miller looked at each other and just nodded. Both knew that the view from the air was probably not even close to the reality on the ground. Still, both wondered what it was like down there. It might be an interesting place to visit. The thought disappeared with the pilot's warning that the AO was coming into view.

The pilot flew about 1,500 feet above the treetops and followed the western boundary of the AO. Gordon searched for anything indicating enemy activity, while Miller looked for the two small clearings. The first of the possible insertion points was tiny, and surrounded by tall trees. It appeared to be little more than a "hover hole," but it might be usable. The general lay of the land was much flatter than the areas they usually worked, but it was far from flat. Gordon noted the high ground running diagonally from northeast to southwest. There was a rocky area on the west side of that ridge and the trees were smaller near that outcropping. He noted three possible locations that might hide some kind of large unit base. Miller tapped his shoulder and pointed to the second LZ. Both men looked and shook their heads. The clearing was too small to accommodate a Huey. Any extraction or insertion there would be on ropes or rope ladders. Romeo 5 had done that once and Gordon had no desire to do it again.

As they neared the northern limit of the AO, it was apparent that there was not going to be an easy way of getting to where they needed to be. Getting out quickly was going to be difficult. Looking back down the ridgeline, Gordon could see several areas that were likely places to find trails crossing over the high ground. He did not like the look of the largest of the flat areas and was concerned about the distance that his team might have to move. He made a note on his pocket notebook to carry a maximum load of water.

The Huey flew on to the north for about five minutes and then turned back south, this time flying over the eastern side of the AO. Gordon paid special attention to a larger LZ just a few hundred meters east of the AO. It offered more room for the choppers, and if they had to get out quickly, it was far safer than the other two he had seen. He pointed to the break in the trees and Miller responded with thumbs up and marked the insertion point on his map. He again saw the rocks at the top of the ridge. There was a smaller, steeper ridge splitting off to the east here and another on the west side, splitting the whole area into four smaller sections. This might be something the Rangers could use to their advantage.

The rest of the flight over the recon target offered very little of value. It was covered with heavy triple canopy jungle, had no landing zones and no significant terrain features. The team leader started to slide back into the Huey when a fairly large open area caught his eye. It was 200 meters south of his AO, but it was a good LZ and he noted it on his map.

The ride back was filled with a little small talk and some business. SFC Miller was now aware that Romeo 5 wanted to use an LZ outside the assigned AO. He would have to clear that with the Brigade Tactical Operations Center, but there would be no problem from the TOC. The mission was so far north that it was very unlikely that any other friendly units were close by. Artillery coverage was going to be spotty at best. Gunships would be available, but they would be at least forty minutes away. Communications would be impossible without a relay, arranged by the K Company communications guys. The team would get those call signs and frequencies when Gordon returned. Miller noted the location of the southern LZ and knew without asking that Sgt. Gordon was probably going to try to use it to extract his team. He left nothing to chance and asked.

Gordon acted like there was nothing to it. "Dang right, Sarge, stroll right down that ridgeline, map out all the bad guys' hideouts, hitch a ride home and take a shower, eat, nothing to it. Piece o' cake!"

Miller knew his TL was having some fun, but the basis of his recon plan was contained in that bit of bravado.

The Huey dropped the two Rangers off as close to the company area as they could and left to refuel. Miller looked up two more team leaders and prepared to begin his second VR flight of the day. Gordon returned to his barracks and found the team packing. Sgt. Timmerman was the ATL for this mission. He was an experienced LRRP team leader with twenty-five missions to his credit. A shortage of manpower had limited the number of teams and placed some strain on those who could lead teams. Timmerman was serving as an ATL on this mission, while two men on his regular team were on R and R. Gordon was glad to have him because the other two members of Romeo 5 were inexperienced and new to the company. Neither had been around long enough to acquire a nickname. Most of the men in the company had one, but it took some time to figure out what it was to be. SSG Gordon was often called "Gordo" for obvious reasons, while Timmerman had earned his nickname differently.

Randy Timmerman was from Minnesota, and after a few beers one night was telling the story of Paul Bunyan. He was a good storyteller, but forgot the name of Paul's ox. Someone yelled at him, "Babe, his name is Babe!" Someone heard that, and asked, "Whose name is Babe?" "Timmerman!" "No shit? Is it really Babe?" "Yep." And he was instantly known as Babe for the next eleven months. It took only a few cans of beer and a badly told story.

The other two men, Stevens and Chandler, had only six missions, but had been with Romeo 5 on four of those. They were inexperienced, but had been trustworthy and they were learning fast. Sgt Ed Stevens would be the ATL after Timmerman went back to his team, and PFC Brad Chandler would be the team's point man. He was an outdoorsman and learned quickly. Stevens was, perhaps, a little too careful at times, and Chandler a little too confident, but Gordon was glad to have them. He had experienced one light contact with them and they performed well.

The team had already drawn rations and ammunition for the mission. He had anticipated the need for more than the normal basic load, and as a team leader was able to get the extra material without any questions. Gordon got the team together and briefed them on the mission. He took extra time to cover the ammo and ration loads to carry. His old team would not have required this much direction, but he was careful with the new men. He was pleased when Chandler asked about extra water. Stevens, thinking like the ATL he would soon be, was concerned about the radios and wondered if he should carry an extra battery or two. They were learning quickly. The veterans on the team continued the briefing, stressing the need for great stealth and total sound, light and cammo discipline. Air support might be slow getting to the team and artillery was going to be of minimal value, so remaining undiscovered was critical to the team's survival.

Communications were going to be a challenge, and they were totally dependent on the relay. Everyone was nervous about this because a relay was always an adventure. Any relay added at least one, sometimes two places for communications to break down. They did not know who their relay was going to be, and that did nothing to calm them. Gordon left Timmerman with the packing, and went to draw four extra flexible gallon canteens, and two extra batteries. He returned to find the team involved in the inevitable battle over the choicest items in the C-rations. Very few Rangers carried everything in a C-ration because they had the luxury of cherry picking the best from several rations and rejecting others. They drew more rations than they needed, but there was a limit, and the choicest items like peaches and pound cake were always in short supply. Chandler had already tried to steal a second can of peaches and had to agree to carry one of the extra batteries to keep Timmerman from taking both cans away from him. Sgt Stevens enjoyed the good-natured scuffle and then returned his second pilfered pound cake to the pile. Sgt Gordon was a bottom feeder when it came to eating in the field. He only ate twice each day and then only small meals. He struggled under the loads that the Ranger teams carried and always chose to carry more water than food. The extra canteen of water in his ruck would cost him some food because he could not leave anything else.

After packing the rucks for the mission, the team now turned their attention to their weapons. There was none of the light-hearted atmosphere here. Each twenty-round magazine was filled with eighteen rounds, each round carefully seated at the back of the magazine. Each magazine was then placed in the ammo pouches on the web gear. When that was done, the grenades received their own special care. Pins were checked and spoons taped and each grenade was placed on the web gear. Each man kept a magazine out to use at the weapons check. Timmerman and Gordon would both carry a PRC-25 radio and two batteries. He would add an extra hand set to his load for this mission. Both radios were tested before they went into the rucks, and again after they were secure. The packing for the mission was completed and the team prepared to test weapons.

There was a firing range of sorts on the green line, and the team hitched a ride to test fire the M-16 and Car-15 rifles. Each man loaded and charged his rifle and tested the safety. They switched to semi auto and fired three or four rounds, and then to full automatic. When they were satisfied that all was well with the rifles, they returned to the company area and did a light cleaning and returned the rifles to the armory. Gordon was now ready to do the rest of the preparation for the mission. He returned to the company area, directing the team to return the equipment to the supply rooms. He gave them thirty minutes to get something to drink. All four men gathered at Gordon's hooch for the rest of the preparation.

Timmerman was a team leader, and like most of the more experienced LRRPS, he was a teacher. He and Gordon both had trained several team leaders, just as they had been trained. The briefing and Operations Order that they gave was as much a lesson on how to prepare, as it was preparation for the mission. Stevens was a sponge, jotting notes, asking questions, and rechecking his answers. He had adopted the check list that the TL used and was very interested in how to use it. The nearly maniacal focus on the list would have bothered either the TL or ATL, if they had not been the same way when SSG Rick Williams had taught them. It was the way that replacements were trained. When the subject of artillery pre-plots was to be addressed, the two senior men had Stevens tell them what he thought they should do. His work was well done, he had considered all the requirements, and he had accounted for all the concerns with the AO. He probably had more pre-plots than needed, but Gordon was not about to say anything because he had a reputation for the same thing. When they gave the two young LRRPs a chance to plan the mission movements, both were eager to show a grasp of the skills.

After the teaching session, a few details were still to be clarified. The decision to insert on the large LZ to the northeast of the AO determined the basic route the team would have to take to do the recon. They would move west to the higher ground and then generally follow the higher ridge to the south. Then several rally points were pointed out for the initial day of the mission. A fair amount of time was spent pointing out any area of special interest or concern. Chandler saw the three flat sections and expressed his concern about bunkers. Everyone shared his concern.

"Where do you think the trails might be?" Chandler had a quick answer. Stevens scanned the map carefully, in his analytical manner. They came up with the same places. They would eventually make a good team, one very careful and thoughtful, one very quick and intuitive. The rest of the time was spent on the issue commo.

The relay for the team was an unknown station with the call sign, "X-ray 12." The team knew only that it was an infantry unit and they were on a remote firebase. Additional help would be available in the form of a FAC plane. The

Forward Air Controllers were often part of these deep missions. If required, choppers from other 4th Division units could be made available. The frequencies for the team's communications with X- ray 12 would not be available until the team was nearly ready to insert. Artillery and other support would go through the relay, so at least for the initial part of the mission, they would talk to only one unit. The aircraft frequencies would be used only for a few minutes after the insertion. All four men would have these before the team inserted. The TL took one more chance to stress the importance of complete stealth on this mission. Their best chance of making it out of this mission was to get in and out without the NVA ever knowing they had been there. The briefing ended with, "Be at the mess hall at 0600, we will saddle up at 0700 and get on the birds at 0730. Questions? No? Good, see you then."

Insertion

The Huey was late. SFC Miller was on the horn, asking where it was. On one hand, the team was in no hurry. In fact, if it never came they would not complain. On the other hand, they knew they would go some time and the waiting was an irritation. Twenty minutes passed and the sun started to beat down on the team when they saw and heard the Blackjack Hueys hovering toward them. The lead ship settled to the ground and the Rangers climbed on board. The chase ship lifted off and the insertion bird followed. They climbed to altitude and turned north. They were joined in a few minutes by two Cobra gunships. The Gamblers would be the team's only real support in the event of a hot insertion. If the team encountered enemy troops on the LZ, only the Cobras would be able to respond quickly. Gordon knew that they would be his only hope if the worst happened.

The team was going to use an insertion technique that they called the "LRRP death spiral." It was not as bad as it sounded, but there was some validity to the name. The insertion bird made a steep, descending turn to the left and sometimes completed several full turns before they touched down. It could be a wild ride, especially for the men on the left side. Those on the right or high side could not see much until the last seconds before touchdown. The method limited observation of the LZ, but also made detection of the insertion more difficult. It was one of many tradeoffs that the Rangers in the Highlands made every time they played this game.

Miller signaled to the team that the LZ was near. Romeo 5 was committed to insert now. The nose dropped, tucked into the left, and they fell out of the sky. The ship made one-and-a-half turns before beginning to slow and set up for the final approach. The nose was still down but the ship was beginning to slow its decent. Gordon saw the LZ for the first time, and was pleased. The nose started to come up as the pilot cleared the trees. The team now had only seconds before they were on the ground. The men were now totally focused, searching for anything that might warn them of a threat.

The insertion went smoothly. The team was down and they moved quickly toward the edge of the LZ, seeking a spot to hide and wait. Timmerman found an ideal spot and moved the team into a small depression with heavy elephant grass around it. Gordon was doing radio checks with Miller and confirming that they were on the correct LZ. Miller confirmed good commo and a good LZ. He told the TL that no fire had been taken on the insert.

"So far so good," thought Gordon. He now went to his radio relay. He whispered into the hand set, "X-ray 12, Romeo 5, commo check over."

It took only a few seconds for the response, but it seemed like hours, "Romeo 5, X-ray 12, we have you 5 by 5. How me?"

Gordon was not surprised, he had expected some issues, and 5 by 5 was adequate. "X-ray 12 you're good, I will be quiet for thirty minutes." X-ray responded with "understood."

The team now had time to wait to see if they had been detected. The birds would stay in range for a while and then depart. All four men were now quiet. Their potentially deadly game of hide and seek was on!

Silence. Ten minutes. Twenty minutes. Thirty minutes. A whispered commo check was followed by a relayed situation report to the company. A whispered exchange between the two veterans would change plans for the initial movement.

"Chandler thought he saw trail east of the LZ," whispered Babe.

Gordon grimaced and asked, "How far?"

"200 maybe 300 meters, he wasn't sure."

Chandler had seen something, but he was not sure what and no one was interested in moving away from the LZ until they knew they had not been spotted. They decided to wait another fifteen minutes before they did anything.

The time came and went with no indication that they had been compromised. The trail might not be a problem, but it did raise the risk that they had been observed during the insertion. They should have a look because a trail was a threat to them and to anyone who might use the LZ in the future. They would go away from their assigned area to confirm Chandler's observation.

Babe called in a sit rep and let K Company Zero know their intentions. Gordo pointed out the rally point for the day and had each team member confirm that he knew where it was. A quick check of equipment and weapons and the team moved into the trees and then turned back east toward the trail.

Babe Timmerman was on point, Gordon was next, Chandler walked slack, and Stevens was the drag. Gordon had Chandler third in line because he wanted him close. He wanted him to be able to help identify when the team was close to the trail. After about 150 meters, the team stopped and rested. Chandler was sure they were close, so he moved up with the point and the team moved forward at a creep. Chandler reached up to tap Timmerman on the shoulder. Timmerman froze, not sure what Chandler had seen. The younger Ranger slipped forward and pointed to a small break in the trees in front of them. Chandler whispered in his point man's ear, " I saw that broken tree on the way in." "The trail is close."

Another five meters and they stopped again. Timmerman's signal brought the team to a knee. He could see the trail. Chandler's reputation was beginning to take shape.

Each man slipped out of the rucks and quietly found a spot to lie down. The team leader and Chandler would check the trail. Together they moved forward in a crawl that took them fifteen minutes. They stopped about one meter from the trail, and listened for any sounds. They heard nothing. Both stood and in unison leaned out toward the trail, looking in opposite directions. Neither could see more than a few meters, but they would not risk getting closer to the trail this early in the mission. Any sign that they had been there could spell disaster for them. They pulled back into the brush and settled into the cover of some bamboo. The men whispered a quick comparison of what they had seen and decided to move back to the team. They could not see the others and Gordon keyed the handset three times, signaling Timmerman that he was returning. Gordon backed away while Chandler meticulously removed anything that might reveal that they had been there. The young Ranger was becoming good at this business already.

With the team together, the TL made notes on the trail. It was about a meter wide, it was apparently used regularly, but there was no indication that it had been used in the last few days. The surface was well packed, but there was enough dry dust on the surface that any recent use would have been apparent. There were no visible tracks at all. Gordon pulled out his map, marked the location of the trail, and copied the grid coordinates onto his notebook. He pulled the overlay paper out of the plastic map case and marked the location before replacing the fragile tracing paper. He let the others see the notes to be sure they all knew what was going on. Everyone nodded and the information was sent to the radio relay. It was a tedious process; each word had to be encoded using the Shackle code cards, copied and sent to the relay, and they in turn had to copy it. To prevent an error, the most critical information like the location had to be repeated back to Romeo 5. The message was sent and the team's movement was also reported. Romeo 5 reversed direction and moved up the hill toward the LZ.

Nearly four hours after they had inserted, they were about fifty meters from where they started. Timmerman found a suitable place to rest and eat. Chandler, then Stevens and Timmerman ate quickly and repacked everything. Gordon ate a can of peaches and quietly put the can into his ruck. He took a long drink from his canteen and hoped they would not run out of water before they were finished. They were still about 250 meters from their actual AO, and it bothered all four of the men. They needed to be closer to all of the pre-plots, rally points and other points of interest that they had carefully selected. None of them had ever seen this place, but those points on the map were somehow familiar, somehow comforting. The teaching never stopped, and the veterans on the team handed the map to Stevens and whispered to him, "Where do you think we should go now?"

It was a trick question in many ways. There was no right answer and everyone knew that. It was really more important how he came to the answer. Stevens looked over the map and thought for a minute. He then pointed to the top of the ridgeline directly west of the team. His answer contained all critical issues, night location, mission considerations and the well being of the team.

Stevens whispered, "November Lima tonight here, or close, it will be a long day, but we need to be ready to follow our plan, water will be a problem if we have to extend."

Gordon smiled. It was not exactly what he would have done, but it was a sound plan. Timmerman was more aggressive and suggested that they push to the top even if it meant moving very late in the day. That had merits. They might be able to rest and observe the valley on the other side of the ridge. That was the original plan, but it now required the team to move nearly 1,200 meters in one day. That was twice the normal movement.

The route was uphill, but it was not a brutal climb, the team was fresh, they were in the shade of the large trees, they might make it. With Timmerman back on point, Chandler moved to the number three spot and Stevens walked drag. Gordon told Timmerman to keep the pace slow until they had some idea what they were walking into and did a commo check on both radios. After turning off the ATL's PRC-25, Gordon alerted the relay of the movement and started to climb toward the ridge. He was very comfortable with his ATL on point, less so with the other two men. He chided himself at that thought. They had never let him down, and in fact they had done most things very well. He recalled Rick Williams and realized that he probably once felt the same about him. The thoughts went away as the move started to grind on his body.

After about an hour, the team settled down for a rest between two large downed trees. It offered cover, concealment and shade. The ground was damp and cool, but soon revealed a healthy population of the small land leaches common to the highlands. Chandler, for all his apparent skill and courage, was totally freaked out by the things. He used most of a bottle of insect repellent during the stop. Timmerman could not believe it and silently shook his head.

Each man took the opportunity to drink and to refill the quart canteens on their web belt. Quickly, quietly, and one at a time they opened their ruck and used the one gallon collapsible bladders to fill the hard-sided canteens and then slid them back into the rucksack. Gordon watched as the two new LRRPS carefully removed the air from the bladders before stowing them. He did not like the sloshing sound they made, but sometimes felt silly about insisting that it might give them away. Timmerman spotted an ammo pouch open on the TL's web gear and motioned for everyone to check the others equipment.

Chandler was looking for some sign that he might be allowed to walk point, confident that he was ready, but not sure how to say so. Babe Timmerman had done his time on point and really did not want to do it if another option was available. Gordon had no desire to walk point because it was brutally difficult work. He leaned forward and pointed at Chandler, and signaled to Babe to switch positions in line. The smile on his face told Chandler all he needed to know, but Gordon got the finger from a grinning Timmerman. Pleased with the exchange and relieved to be off the point, he slid into line at slack.

X-ray 12 called with a message from Zero. Apparently the CO was happy with the discovery of the trail. Romeo 5 reported that they were moving. Chandler stood and looked for a direction. The TL pointed and then made a mental note; he needed to anticipate that kind of thing. It was not fair to the younger man, and he knew it.

Fifty meters, one hundred meters, the pace would have been agonizingly slow in any other setting, but here it was fast enough to bother the two veterans on the team. They stopped and reported their location. The radio signal was adequate, but it was not as strong as before. Gordon asked Timmerman to try his radio and got the same result. He slowed his young point man down with a hand signal and started to move. Another fifty meters and he stopped the team; he was not going to go far without checking the radios. He contacted X-ray 12 and had better signal strength. Good news, because he was now 400 meters or more from the only LZ he could easily reach, and he did not want to get into contact with poor radio contact. It was about time for a water stop, so the team again knelt down and rested. He handed Stevens the map and indicated to him to locate the team. Stevens, as always, took his time, and correctly located the team. The TL pointed to a pre-plot and Stevens signaled the direction and a distance to the position. He was correct. He again pointed to Stevens and had him check to see if the others knew where the rally point was. They all did. Another step in the training program seemed to be nearly complete. He would never stop checking, because that was the Standard Operating Procedure, but it would no longer be teaching. The team started to move again and this time it seemed more natural, more like a veteran team, more like a single organism than four individual men.

The two veterans felt the ground under their feet start to level off and knew they were nearing the top of the ridge. Gordon stopped the team and looked at his watch. It was nearly 1730, about an hour-and-a-half before dark. He checked his map and had the other two men confirm his mark on the map. Both agreed they were within twenty meters of the top. Should they stop here and find a night location, or move up and see what was there? They had time to get to the top, but eating and finding a good night location would stretch them. Staying here put them closer to the LZ, but really provided no opportunity to recon any new areas. It might push them to move faster later. This area seemed quiet and they had seen no sign of enemy activity. Stevens reached for the map and with his pencil pointed to a small hill, just a hump about thirty meters away. Wrote NL on the map case and pointed again.

Timmerman agreed, writing on his note pad, "See both ways, good trees and bamboo. Commo #1." There was no reason to fault the plan, and in fact Gordon wanted to be on top if possible. He signaled for the team to eat. He shackled his location and relayed it to Zero. After that, he added two artillery pre-plots to his back trail. The first was on the point where he had intersected the trail off the LZ; the second was near the LZ. If he had to use that LZ, he wanted a plot on the north side. He showed the new information to the team and then sent them in.

"X-ray 12, Romeo 5, new pre-plots number 8 and 9, I shack." What followed was a string of letters and digits that needed to be translated with the same card that the team was using. It worked well, and made the TL feel better about being this far away from any help. The others had finished eating and were resting but on alert, while Gordo finished his meal with a candy bar from the C-ration, washed it down with water, and packed up. He pointed to the hilltop on the map, and Chandler pointed the direction. The team now started to move, more slowly now than ever.

After only twenty-five meters, they saw the hill and it looked like a good location. The team turned to the north, then back to the west, then south, and still again east. The final move was into the night location. It was right on the top of the small hill, and offered something very unique for most locations. It had both cover and concealment. Again the team had found an area with some fallen logs and some brush. The small hill offered the team some view of the areas below them. There was another small hill, slightly higher, to the north. The path the team had taken into this location meant anyone following the team would pass by the team three times before they could follow the team into the night location.

Stevens had done his job of concealment as they moved the last few meters, making it difficult to follow the trail. The team settled in, and then just before dark placed their claymore mines. Each man followed the direction of the TL as to the placement and firing direction for their own mines. They ran the detonating wires back to the team and secured the detonators, called "clackers," to the wire. These were nothing more than a small handheld generator that produced enough electrical charge to detonate a blasting cap in the claymore, causing the mine to spew its deadly mass of steel balls toward an unfortunate enemy.

With the defensive mines in place, the weapons were checked and rechecked. All four men tied the rifles to their belts with a black bootlace to prevent them from being lost in the dark. Grenades and magazines were checked, and then the radios were checked again. Both radios worked fine and the backup radio was again turned off. The frequencies were again reviewed. All the rally points were again located. Gordon pointed to the men in order of the night watch and then started the last light full alert. Everyone had their packs off, but they would sleep with everything else on. X-ray 12 called for a situation report and Gordon was surprised to hear them ask for two squelch breaks of negative and green. This was SOP for Ranger units, but not something that he expected from his relay. He clicked the rubber-covered button twice and then joined the rest of Romeo 5 in the alert. It passed without incident and Chandler took the first watch.

Both Timmerman and Gordon were awake during most of the first watch. Timmerman had the second, then Stevens and the TL. Most team leaders were awake at least once during any watch period. With two newer members, they were awake more than normal. It was like the rest of the training that went on during the day. It was training, but they also just habitually checked everything. The night went on without any excitement and the steady stream of negative sit reps was uninterrupted.

The only excitement of the night happened around 0300, when a Korean radio operator started using the frequency and insisted that the Rangers get off of "his radio." He was making it hard to hear, forcing X-ray to change the frequency. They instructed Romeo 5 to "add 1.5 for the new freq." Babe turned on his radio and in the dark turned the radio frequency knob, counting the clicks on each knob. He then tried to contact X-ray and got them on the first try. They did the same thing on the other radio and made sure it was on the push. They turned the second radio off and tried to go to sleep. It was no use, first light alert was coming soon and he was thinking about the next day's activities.

Day Two

The team quietly sat up and all four men focused on the morning sounds of the jungle. The thirty minutes came and went with nothing to concern the team. They ate, one at a time, filled canteens, checked their equipment and prepared to begin the day's work. The first order of business was to move toward the rock outcropping. It would be a short move and the jungle would provide plenty of places to hide. They would approach the rock with great care and again go silent. During the briefing, each man had pointed to this place as a likely spot to find a trail. The point stopped the team, indicating to the TL that he could see the edge of the rocky cliff. Gordon alerted the others and they moved the last few steps. Chandler dropped to a knee and the team disappeared into the bamboo.

Their care was soon rewarded with the sounds of men on a trail below the team. There was no indication that they suspected the presence of Romeo 5. Their weapons banged against packs, voices were not hushed, and none of the normal discipline of an alerted NVA troop was evident. Stevens' vantage point allowed him to see several meters of the trail. He counted twenty men, armed with AK-47s and wearing new uniforms. He whispered the information to the TL. Romeo 5 would not be moving soon. This was a very good place to gather information, and it was very clear that the team had arrived without alerting anyone. That was the good news. The bad news was that Stevens was sure he had seen troops from the NVA 95 Bravo regiment. If so, Romeo 5 would do well to stay undetected. As the information was being readied for sending, Stevens alerted the team again, as another group of troops moved past, totally unaware of the presence of the Rangers. Timmerman had moved toward the rocks and was now able to see the trail. The look on his face confirmed Stevens' assessment, they were in the home of some very capable enemy soldiers.

There was no reason to change the location; they were perfectly positioned, so they would wait. The parade of NVA soldiers continued for several hours, and then appeared to stop. All that they had seen was shacked and sent to X-ray. The relay soon had several messages for the team. The company Zero was pleased with their work and Brigade wanted the team to get a closer look at the trail. Gordon was sure that the trail crossed the ridge somewhere below them, but he was also sure they would find a camp or something in the flats to the east. The whole team knew that they had seen only a few of the soldiers in the area. They were about to engage in the most dangerous activity a LRRP team could do. They were going into the home ground of a large NVA unit. Despite the danger, they had the advantage. They knew they were undetected, they knew the enemy was there.

Chandler took point and felt genuine fear. Gordon was next, too busy to feel anything. Timmerman was glad to be third in line, but wanted to be on point. Stevens simply went about his job, but watched the two veteran LRRPS closely. The team silently started down the slope. Gordon forced his attention toward the trail on the team's right and trusted the front to his point man. They advanced a step at a time, stopping, looking, smelling and listening. Time meant little now, it had really ceased to exist as far at the men were concerned. It mattered only that they find any threat before they themselves were found.

They crawled along, covering less than fifty meters in thirty minutes, stopped for water and started again. The process was repeated five times before Chandler lowered his hand to his side and slowly lowered his body to a kneel. The team followed his lead. He motioned for the TL to come forward. He pointed to a few broken twigs and a wet spot on the soft duff of the jungle floor. Someone had taken a pee in the brush. Chandler was sure the trail was close, perhaps within five meters or less. The information was passed back to the other two, who remained in place as their point man inched forward. The TL stayed close, and then stopped as the other two moved forward. Like an inchworm they moved forward, until Chandler stopped, turned, and pointed to the trail. He had found it and still had plenty of jungle between him and the trail.

It was not where they expected it to be, but they had found it without walking into it. They backed up a few meters and found a spot to hide. Stevens passed the team's location and information to X-ray while Gordon whispered to Chandler.

"What made you think we were close?"

"Sigler told me that the dinks never pissed very far from a trail."

Gordon was surprised. "You talked to Sigler?"

"Sure, he's a crazy SOB, but he knows how to walk point!"

Gordon trusted his young point more after the quick exchange. Timmerman was looking over his map and pointed out the smaller finger going to the east. Without speaking, he pointed out a series of loops that would move the team along the trail without walking parallel to it. They would intersect the trail at several more points and still keep some distance and cover between them and anyone on the trail.

Stevens was on the radio, but both men knew they were going to be told to try to map the trail further. Stevens was scribbling on his notepad and showed it to Gordon. He pointed to his ATL and then to the map where the route was already drawn on the map case! It matched the new orders and it was Stevens' turn to appreciate the skills of the men in charge of the team. Gordon had the team pull back from the trail and stop to eat and rest. He put the new information on his overlay, looked over the map, tried to anticipate the risks to the team, and then put the team on half alert. It was 13:00 hours and the heat was beginning to wear on the men. The NVA often rested during the heat of the day. Romeo 5 would rest as well.

Mapping a trail was dangerous work for the Rangers. They could not just walk down a trail and see where it went. There was too much risk of being seen and compromising the mission. Walking parallel to the trail posed the same risk, and was nearly impossible to do anyway. The method of choice was to move away from the trail a safe distance, move on a generally parallel track, and then approach again at a perpendicular. This was simply a probing technique and while dangerous, it minimized the exposure to the team. The team would follow this plan with a series of three of these probes. They all drank once again and readied themselves for the moves. Gordon was nervous about the mapping, not because he doubted the men with him, but because of the risk of being detected. At least this part of the move would not take them away from the LZ, he thought. With hand signals only, he directed the team to move.

The Rangers moved away from the trail, turned to follow the finger for fifty meters, turned back toward the trail, and probed. Chandler saw the trail from about five meters away and stopped. There was no reason to get closer, so they marked the map, backed away and repeated the process. On the second probe, the undergrowth was getting thicker and they did not see the trail until they were right on it. Romeo 5's point man also saw a small trail branch off to the south, telling the team that there was probably some kind of NVA compound to the south of the main trail. They backed off and rested while the new map coordinates and information were sent to the relay. They had made two probes without exposing themselves. With any luck, the third would be just as easy. Romeo 5 was now in increasingly thick brush, bamboo and vines. Moving here was safer, but difficult. They slowed and moved, sometimes literally, at a crawl.

The work was beginning to tell on Chandler. The camouflage on his dark face was washed off with sweat and his fatigues were soaked. Gordon moved up, taking the point, and the team again inched forward, straining to see, hear or even smell something that might tell them what they needed to know. They stopped often, moved a few feet, and stopped again. It was frustrating, stressful, and in a way boring work. They did not know if the trail had turned away from them or if it was just a few more steps away. Gordon stopped and leaned his ruck against a tree, appreciating the work that Chandler had to do, when he heard voices. All the men heard and responded in unison, dropping slowly to a knee. The voices got louder and then faded, a clear indication they had walked by on the trail. Gordon had all he needed to locate the third spot and moved the team back to the relative safety of the finger.

Once he was sure that they were still undetected, he put the trail on his overlay and showed it to his ATL who agreed on the mapping. Stevens and Chandler got a look at it as well. He was teaching again, because he knew the next time they went out they would have a brand new member on the team, and he had to be sure they were ready. He scribbled "NL?" on his noted pad and showed it to Stevens. He was not sure and picked two possible areas, one close to their present spot and the second back toward the top of the ridgeline near the previous night's spot. Both offered some opportunity to monitor the trails close by. The advantage here was they would not have to move, while the higher location offered better opportunity to see anything of interest in other areas of the AO.

Timmerman was watching and resisted the temptation to interrupt. Stevens' choices were not wrong, but one was a far better choice than the other. The veterans were now sure they would need to work farther south along the high ground, and that in fact was the plan for the start. Staying in this location for the night would mean several hours of moving before they could begin to go south. They needed to be as fresh as possible for the next day. Gordon and Timmerman pointed to the rocky area and the team started the climb back to the top. All four men were beginning to feel the wear on their bodies. It had not been as difficult as some missions, but it was draining them nonetheless. With Chandler back at his post, they found a spot near the rocky opening and made ready for the night.

Like the morning before, the team had movement on the trail, and could see lights on the far side of the valley to the west. These were reported. Stevens looked at his watch when he first saw lights and again when he heard a group of men pass. He estimated the distance the men had traveled, using that information. It might not be important, but they never knew what was important to the men in command above them. The lights and movement still indicated that the NVA thought they were alone on the mountain. Good news for the team, who had now counted nearly 100 men on the trail. Gordon could not help feeling just a bit pleased with his team; they were beating the NVA at their own game.

Just as he had the thought, he felt Timmerman's hand on his arm, a silent alert that there was a problem. The ATL whispered to him, "X-Ray is not on the radio!"

For the first time on this mission, the team leaders felt very vulnerable.

"What happened?"

"Don't know, they just went away," Timmerman hissed. He was clearly stressed and Gordon's gut tightened.

"How long ago?" Gordon asked, and Timmerman was not sure.

"I did a sit rep at 01:30, and they missed the next one."

"Okay, try your radio, I will wake the others up."

The ATL quickly turned on his radio and found no contact with X- Ray 12. Their only communication with the rest of the world was gone. A full alert was now in order as the team tried to solve the radio problem. They could hear each other on the two radios, meaning they were working, but maybe the signals were weak. Gordon whispered the situation to his team and returned to Timmerman.

"We have to sit tight for now, just wait and see." Gordon wished he hadn't said that. His ATL knew. They had no choice. The lights on the far ridge now seemed far more threatening, and Gordon no longer felt so smug.

An hour went by, and the team was still alone. Then Gordon heard the faint voice of X-Ray 12 calling Romeo 5. It was as sweet a sound as he had ever heard. He answered and was further relieved to hear a reply. Minimal radio contact was back.

"X-ray where the hell have you been? You scared the shit outa us!"

"Romeo 5, we got shelled and they blew the hell out of the place, they got my 292 and that was when I lost you! Give me a sit rep, I'll let your Zero know you are okay."

"Roger that, X-ray," and Gordon whispered the news to the rest of the team. It was good news to have the relay back, but for how long? If X-Ray was on a firebase that was about to get overrun, they might go away again. The radio came to life again and the relay had a message for the team. They expected to get hit again, they did not have another long-range 292 antenna and they had no way of getting one. They were trying to get some kind of aircraft to relay for the team if they went down again. Zero was aware and had a ship on stand-by. They would be able to relay in about an hour. In an hour it would be light and without the radios, Romeo 5 might have to abort the mission.

"Romeo 5, X-Ray 12, we are taking fire, I will hang on as long as I can, Over!"

There was nothing to do now but wait, and pray that Romeo 5 was still undetected. There was no need to do a first light alert because everyone was totally alert and ready. The rally points were checked, located, and re-checked. The location of the LZ was pointed out; pre-plots were selected for the move to the LZ if needed. All this was necessary, but everyone involved knew that the best scenario was for the Rangers to stay put and just hide. X-Ray called for a sit rep, and the team replied with two squelch breaks. Gordon could hear gunfire and explosions in the background.

"Cool customers," thought Gordon, and he turned his attention to Chandler, who was counting a group of VC going by on the trail below.

"Romeo 5, Blackjack 34, do you copy?"

Gordon almost yelled out loud, they had a chopper to talk to. "Black Jack 34, Romeo 5, I have you loud and clear." The blackjack ship was on station 3,000 meters south of the team to relay if needed, and they had the platoon leader onboard. Some of the confidence returned.

Day Three

The team stayed in the night location until they were sure that X-Ray was secure. The team prepared to begin the day's recon and went through the routine like they had done it many times before. The batteries in the radios were changed one at a time and tested. The team leader's was okay, and he had the ATL test his. He whispered into the handset and nodded, then nodded again, then shook his head in disbelief and turned off the radio. His teammates were not sure what to make of the smile on his face.

Gordon whispered, "What?"

Timmerman replied, "X-ray is Charley Rangers, You know the guys we got in a fight with last month? He said if he could get us back in one piece, he'd kick our ass again".

At Camp Radcliffe they would fight at the drop of a hat, but here, they were brothers and Romeo 5 was now X-ray 12's responsibility. The team was glad to know that warriors manned their relay.

With the communications issues resolved, Romeo 5 was now in the process of planning the day's work. They had the trail running to the east well mapped, they had managed to stay hidden, and they still had at least two days of water and food. Everyone was healthy, no one overly tired, and there was no reason to change the basic plan to work south along the high ground. His only concern was that the mapping had put them one day behind schedule and that might require them to move more quickly than they had planned. If they could not do that, water might become a problem. It was hot, but the jungle canopy kept them in shade, they were working downhill, and both of those things worked in their favor. Babe and Gordo selected a route, briefed the others, and warned them to be very careful with their water. All four Rangers used the green cammo sticks to cover their faces and arms. Everyone checked the others' gear. They were ready to move, Chandler took the lead, keenly aware of the burden he carried, but for the first time sure of himself, not cocky anymore, just confident. The men behind him felt the same way.

The first objective of the day was to find a place to cross the trail. They knew where it was and decided to try to cross at the edge of the ridge, hoping to find rocks to walk on. They intersected the trail about thirty meters west of their first encounter. As they suspected, there were plenty of rocks to hide any tracks. Timmerman would cross first, then Chandler, Stevens, and Gordon. The order was designed to be sure that they had a radio on both sides of the trail if they were separated. The team could not see far in either direction, but they could hear nothing and Timmerman quickly crossed the trail, disappearing into the brush on the other side. The point man followed quickly. Stevens was about to cross when voices were heard to the east. Stevens froze and Gordon pressed himself down and against a tree, trying to become small and invisible. Seven men walked by, each with an AK-47 in hand and a pack on their backs. The packs appeared to be for carrying water. Gordon took a few seconds to listen and motioned Stevens to cross. He waited only long enough for Stevens to reach the far side and followed. He had no desire to be separated from the team.

With all four across the trail, they moved a short distance away from the trail and found a good spot to stop and listen. Gordon's heart was pounding as he sent in the team's location, reported the sighting of troops and marked all the other information on the overlay. The initial concern about the move was now behind them, it was time to move again. Stevens asked for a few extra minutes to work on the team's back trail and Chandler had to pee, so they waited.

To make it to the extraction LZ in two days, the team would have to move 800 meters each day, a long ways by their normal standards. Until they were sure what was ahead of them, they could not move that fast. The possibility of having to extend the mission for another day was now a very real possibility.

The large flat area to the east of the team was the most likely spot to find bunkers or a camp. Gordon was concerned about that area, and the openness of the ridge they were on. There was not much concealment, making them vulnerable. By moving to the west side of the high ground, he could hide his team, but it slowed them down. The team was now at least 400 meters from any LZ. If they were detected now, they would be in very deep trouble. They slid off to the right and continued to move.

Chandler alerted the team and Gordon instantly saw the small trail in front of them. They had walked right onto it and were exposed. They had to either move back or cross, and they had to do it quickly. He alerted the two men behind him to the trail and pointed. Chandler stepped over the narrow trail and moved into the brush, going to the ground as soon as there was room for the others. Everyone crossed without issue and they decided to stay quiet for a few minutes. Everyone needed water and a rest. The trail was much smaller than the others they had seen. Timmerman and Gordon knew they might be inside a large base camp. If the larger trails were leading to a complex, the small trail might be an access trail inside the complex. Both men now knew they had to stay undetected. They also had to move to the south, to be extracted. The two requirements worked against the other.

Gordon decided to move away from the trail and toward the west side of the high ground. The risk was walking into a bunker or other structure, but there was not enough vegetation to conceal the team where they were. Chandler took the team to a thick patch of brush and stopped. In front of him was another small trail. Timmerman pointed to the south and they saw another small trail. Romeo 5 was now clearly inside an NVA compound of some kind. The team slid into the brush and flattened themselves to the ground. It was midday and getting hot. They drank quickly while the team leader whispered a sit rep and location. X-ray understood the situation and was already alerting K Company.

The team would not normally move during the heat of the day, but now they would consider it. Gordon asked Timmerman about moving while the NVA might be resting. Timmerman agreed it was probably risky, but they needed to get closer to the tiny extraction LZ. If they were discovered, they would need to be able to defend that LZ for a while. The rest of the team was told of the decision and they prepared to move. Both radios were on, all weapons were checked and cammo applied. Quietly, each man stood and tried to remain invisible. They felt no fear now, only the total focus needed to survive. Chandler bore the greatest burden. Gordon knew he had to trust the young point man. He had too much to do now, and Babe Timmerman would be responsible for the team's tactics if they did make contact

The team moved south, toward the trail they had seen. The point man found the trail with no difficultly and the Rangers crossed without incident. The jungle got thicker in front of them and they were drawn forward by the desire to disappear again. They found a small mound of rocks in the thicker part of the brush and settled in for a rest and sit rep. No one made a sound as Gordon whispered the location to the relay and informed the team of the next move. They had cover now, so they would move again. This time they would be close to the hover hole, the least desirable of the two landing zones available. Timmerman took point and Chandler gratefully took his place in the line behind Gordon. They moved again, slowly, but with an urgency that sapped them mentally, physically and emotionally. X-ray was calling for sit reps at ten-minute intervals, and the team replied by breaking squelch. They had to stay focused on the move, and X-ray was doing their part. Gordon had marked the trails on the map cover. He did not want to take the time to pull out the overlay. He would not risk even that small distraction now.

As they moved along the western edge of the high ground, they found another trail, but this time they could see where it went. It dropped off the edge of the hill and disappeared into a small hole in the ground. The team had found what appeared to be a bunker. They moved away, crossed the trail, and continued south. Stevens needed a rest from the back trail, so they stopped. Without a word being spoken, they drank and filled their canteens again. Gordon was not hungry, but Timmerman pointed to the others and the TL nodded. It was time to stop.

The wisdom of the decision was soon apparent when the team heard voices and movement around them again. They were in a good place to hide and they were now about 1,000 meters from their primary extraction LZ. They hid and took time to collect themselves.

At first the sounds, voices, and other noises were disconcerting to the team, but as they listened, they started to tell a more positive tale. Everything they could hear was north of them, and there was still no indication that the NVA knew they were there. Stevens smelled cooking fires, and again they appeared to be north of the team. The two older LRRPS now considered the possibility that they had actually moved completely through the complex and were actually outside of it. Stevens and Chandler had not yet realized that, but the veterans were already considering that possibility and what it meant. Gordon and Timmerman now risked a quick whispered exchange. They tried to imagine what the complex might look like if they had passed through. They drew the known points on the map cover and then filled in what they thought might be a reasonable guess at the rest. The south edge might well be north of them.

Now they had to decide if they wanted to stay put, spend the night and try to get out in the morning, or move away and try to get to the LZ and extract today. Neither man wanted to spend another night anywhere near the men of the 95 B regiment, but neither did they want to compromise themselves. They decided to see if an extraction was possible. They soon had an answer, no extraction today. They had an answer to part of the question.

Gordon remembered the over flight and that the jungle seemed to be much thicker to the south. He decided to risk moving a little further south, closer to the LZ, and perhaps further from the enemy troops. Timmerman was not sure, but he knew the risks of either decision. Gordon was the TL and he did what he was supposed to do: he sought advice and then did what needed to be done. He prepped Chandler for a move, and instructed Stevens on the critical clearing of the back trail. Gordon again checked and pointed to all rally points and the pre-plots. He made sure that they all knew where the LZ was and told them to make their way there if they got separated. What they felt was a strange mix of fear and exhilaration, of exhaustion and anticipation. Gordon was on what he called autopilot, totally aware, but operating on some level of instinct. He signaled to the team and they moved south.

It was apparent within fifty meters that the team had made the right decision; the jungle told them that they were probably alone. They moved toward the extraction LZ, stopped about 200 meters short, and ate. They took more time at this point and even Gordon filled his belly. He let the team rest with only two on alert. He made notes and sketched out the probable outline of the complex on his overlay. He felt comfortable enough to let Stevens call in the information and he relaxed. Chandler had been looking at the area and had a good idea where to set up a night location. He pointed to the map, indicating that the team could hide and observe from that spot. His choice was solid and Romeo 5 was ready to move again.

The night went quietly, with only the wind and a quick rain shower to bother the team. It was an uncomfortable night, but that was hardly noticed now. After the morning alert they pulled in the claymores and readied themselves for the last push to the LZ. They were about to enter into the most dangerous part of any mission. Extraction made them vulnerable in many ways. There was always the possibility of the LZ being watched. It was a very real possibility with 95 B involved. The air activity could attract attention to the LZ, and there were plenty of NVA in the area to hear the choppers. Booby traps and wires on the LZ were also a threat. There was much to be concerned with as they started their move. X-ray confirmed that the extraction was on for 10:00 hours and wished the TL luck. The team moved now like a single organism, and Gordon noticed.

Extraction

The move was uneventful, and there was no sign that the LZ had been watched or booby-trapped. Chandler had found the edge of the trees and cover for the team. No wires were to be seen. They had made it and things were apparently ideal for an extraction. They hid in the trees and brush at the edge of the LZ, scanning the rest of the area for any sign of the enemy they had so far avoided. Gordon pulled out a pair of small binoculars from his pack and searched the LZ again. He often carried them for just this kind of situation. They waited, listened, and heard nothing.

Stevens leaned forward and whispered to Gordon, "Would you consider extracting without the gunships getting close?"

There it was, the thing he had been waiting for, the initiative and forethought that Stevens needed to be a good TL.

"Why would we do that?" he asked.

Stevens knew what was going on and smiled. "We can really hurt them if we can get out undetected!"

Gordon nodded and told X-ray to keep the Cobras away from the LZ unless they were called for.

"Romeo 5, Black jack 12, we are six minutes from your location, what is your situation?"

Timmerman and Gordon had both of their radios on now. Gordon filled the pilots in on the tactical situation, wind, and condition of the LZ. He quickly told them where he was and how to approach. He wanted them to come in from the southeast and leave to the southwest. They complied. Gordon popped a smoke grenade and the slick quickly dropped into the clearing. The team sprinted the ten meters to the chopper and they were gone. Gordon counted the men, and then checked weapons. Timmerman had already done both, and Stevens was doing the same. It was only a few seconds into the ride when a shout came from the ATL.

"Son of a Bitch, we made it!"

That started a wild round of shouting and laughing. Stevens slapped Gordon on the back, Gordon was laughing, Chandler was yelling something about the NVA being fooled, and Timmerman just lay back on his ruck and repeated his statement over and over.

SFC Miller yelled over the wind in the cabin, "Glad to see you guys all in one piece!"

Gordon let his sense of humor override military courtesy and said, "Hey, I told you it was a piece of cake, never any concern at all for me, were you worried, Sergeant Miller?"

The older man was a career NCO and had very different views of the world in general and the Army in particular, but he respected the young men in the company and he knew that the four men in the Huey had just done a professional job and that not just anyone could do what they had accomplished. He

joined in the celebration, with his own war whoop. Chandler, still on adrenaline and giddy with excitement, told Miller that it was a great mission "Get in,
do what you have to do and get out without anyone ever knowing you were
there," he said, quoting the words of his team leader. "I am glad we won't be
there when the Air Force gets done with that place."

Gordon and Timmerman both smiled at the quote, and tried not to think
about the awful reality of Chandler's last statement.

Four filthy and exhausted Rangers collapsed onto the floor of the slick as
the adrenaline left their bodies. The forty-minute flight back to Camp Radcliffe
seemed long, and Gordon wanted to sleep. The chopper turned on its final
approach and landed. Gordon would leave the team because he had to debrief
at the Brigade TOC and the Company Commander wanted to see him as soon
as that was done. Timmerman would see that the equipment and weapons were
cleaned and turned in. Stevens would always be one step ahead of him, and he
noticed. They would clean up, and eat at the mess hall and then return to the
hooch for some talk. They would not think much about what they had done, not
tonight, they were too tired, and later they could not afford to think too much.
They were alive and they would go back out again in two days. They would
get in, do what needed to be done, and get out before anyone knew they were
there. They would try not to think about what would happen to the NVA if they
succeeded, or about what could happen to the team if they failed.

CHAPTER 51

Contact

❖

H e saw the map in the brigade TOC and the team leader felt the knot in his stomach. He had been in this part of the Highlands before. The Army's name, "Base area 266," did not do justice to the place at all. It sounded like some innocuous motor pool address on a state side base. It most certainly was not. He knew this mission had the potential to be very nasty. He also knew eight months earlier, he had asked for just this kind of deep penetration mission, preferring them to Hawkeye missions. He took his seat and pulled out the ever-present pocket notebook, grabbed his map and prepared for the pre-mission briefing. Ranger teams, Romeo 5, Romeo 9, and Romeo 11 were about to get OP Orders.

Captain Kennedy, the Brigade operations officer, knew the three team leaders and wasted no time or words. Not much was known about the specific areas that each team had been assigned, no 4th Infantry Division units had been near them for at least two years, maybe longer, maybe never. There was no way to know if the 1st Cav or 173rd had been there. These three teams might be the first Americans ever in the vicinity. From reconnaissance photos, Division suspected some kind of large unit activity. Kennedy knew the risks the men would be taking and gave them all the information he had. There was little of substance to give the teams, and they all knew that was why they were going.

Their job was to find out what was there. They received the normal briefing concerning the terrain, the weather, but few specifics of the AO. They were looking for a larger NVA unit. The young captain gave them one piece of operational information that might help them. They would be part of something else, much bigger, and there would be some air traffic in the area. All three of the LRRPS knew what he was doing. He was telling them how to disguise their insertions. It was something that did not always happen, but Kennedy had developed significant knowledge of each team leader's needs. He knew they would need all the help they could get.

With the AO assigned, the team leaders walked back to the company area and alerted their men. All three then left immediately for the Golf Course. There they boarded a waiting LOACH for the visual reconnaissance of the area. They knew it was going to be a brutal area to work. The topographical maps confirmed what they already knew. The terrain was all narrow valleys and steep ridgelines covered with large trees and thick vegetation. Landing Zones were going to be scarce, small, and difficult to use. Even without the briefing, the men knew that they might also be under observation if an NVA unit was working the area. Romeo 5, 9 and 11 strapped themselves into the seats of a LOACH flown by a veteran Warrant Officer, Ed "Wildthing" Mooney, a colorful and well-respected pilot. All the team leaders knew him well. In seconds they were flying northeast over the more settled areas and toward the mountains. The VR did nothing to relieve the concern. SSgt Bensen, Romeo 5, was a veteran TL and he knew what the LRRPs called "Indian country" when he saw it. He and the others resisted the temptation to make a low-level pass over the area. They were very concerned about the LZs, but could not risk advertising the fact that the teams were coming. All three would risk a poorly chosen LZ over being attacked on insertion. He carefully noted three possible insertion sites and marked them on the map. Two small clearings, one very small, and a string of bomb craters along the top of a ridge were his only options. Mooney turned the LOACH around and flew back to An Khe.

Bensen walked back to his hooch and found his assistant team leader packing the team for the mission. The team had been together for a long time, at least by LRRP standards. The ATL, Sgt Anderson, had been on the team the longest, serving as point man and then ATL. The point man, known only as Sigler was on his 21st mission, and his 12th with the team. He knew his job well. The fourth member of the team was younger and less experienced, but he was a very good LRRP and would soon be an ATL. There was not much to the OP Order that Bensen gave to the team. Everyone knew what to do, and Sgt. Anderson had most of the packing done before his TL returned. Bensen decided to add extra ammo and water and cut down on food. Each man was to carry one extra frag and eight additional magazines of ammunition for the M-16s. Water was going to be a problem. The dry season guaranteed no rain and finding water on high ground was unlikely. Climbing to the bottom of the valleys was dangerous and difficult, but climbing out was often impossible, and because of that, re-supply from a blue line was seldom a good option. Each man would carry more water than normal, adding an additional four-quart bladder canteen in his pack. The additional water and ammo would add ten pounds to their loads.

The rucks would weigh in excess of ninety pounds. Food was selected with care. Each man took several of the prized cans of fruit and their favorite meat. Fruit offered calories and fluids, the meat offered a filling meal with the maximum amount of calories and a minimum of weight. Not knowing exactly why, Bensen had two more claymores added to the load. He would carry one; he pulled out one of his meals, lightening his ruck, and gave it to his point man. He handed the other claymore to Chavez, who would be walking drag. The young soldier said nothing, but he knew why he had been given the extra weight. He had walked point enough to know that it took everything a man had. He also knew that Sigler needed more food and water than the others on this team of Rangers.

The team now sat down and planned the mission movements, setting up rally points in case the team was separated. Artillery pre-plots were established and delivered to the Company TOC. They would send them on to the artillery units. As was often the case, the team would be near the maximum range of the big guns. After going over the rest of the details of the mission, the team completed packing, raided the mess hall, and tried to relax. All of the teams had requested a morning insertion. They wanted to have plenty of daylight if they were discovered. A hot extraction in the dark was to be avoided at all costs. They would all sleep tonight, but only because they all knew they would not sleep tomorrow night.

Lt. Mallory was the Platoon leader and he would insert Romeo 5. Platoon Sergeant Danials was inserting 9 and 11. The team was ready. Last-minute weapons, radio and equipment check were made. Face paint was applied and the team boarded the chopper for the flight into the Animite Mountains of the Central Highlands. The insertion bird was one of four slicks flying in a trailing formation. Two more Cobra gunships would follow. The team sat on the floor, legs hanging out the door. All four of the men tried to relax. They looked calm, but they were not. The TL was looking over the map, going over the plans in his mind. He would try to anticipate what an NVA or VC unit might do in this area. He mentally rehearsed his reactions to each scenario, one for a NVA regular unit, and another for the VC. He knew they would be different in most cases. He scanned the artillery pre-plots and felt uneasy about them. They were at the maximum range of the 175 mm guns, perhaps too far away to be of any real help. He felt fear at this moment that he would not feel again during the mission. It nearly made him sick.

Bensen knew his ATL was doing the same things on the other side of the ship. He had the primary control of the team's defensive fire in a contact, and he too was concerned about the artillery. Without thinking about it, Anderson scanned the team one more time, looking for anything that might cause them problems. He had checked each weapon, each safety, and each grenade several times, but he did it again. Anderson looked at the point man. His eyes were closed, but he was not sleeping. He was as good as anyone in K Company when he was in the field. It was in base camp that he battled his demons. He was now transforming himself into a LRRP point man. The fourth team member also seemed calm, but while his face did not betray his concerns, his hands did. He ran them over every bit of equipment he could reach, checking and re-checking, assuring himself that everything was as it should be. So deeply ingrained was the location of each piece of equipment that he never looked, he just felt for them. He knew where everything was, not only in his ruck, but also in everyone else's. If he needed a first aid kit and his was gone, he knew where to get three more.

The insertion officer was only a few years older than the TL. He had done this many times, but he never got used to it. He knew the danger that the team was about to accept; he knew that getting them in was the second most dangerous part of the mission. The only thing more dangerous would be getting them out, especially if they were in contact. He had gone over the insertion with the team and the pilots several times, even though all of them knew what to do. Today, the team would use a common technique to disguise the insertion. The four slicks would fly in a trailing formation, one behind the other. Romeo 5 would be in the second ship. The choppers would fly at a normal altitude over the LZ. The insertion ship would drop into the LZ, the Rangers would step off, and the Huey would lift off, taking its place at the end of the line. The noise of the three helicopters flying straight and level overhead would help cover the distinctive slapping sound of the other Huey landing. The team and the pilots had agreed on this technique because of Capt. Kennedy's statement that there would be some other air operations going on near the team's AO.

Lt. Mallory was now scanning the area in front of the chopper. The insertion was getting close. He looked at the TL to signal for him to get ready, only to find him holding the map and pointing to the primary landing zone. The ship now started to lose altitude and speed, setting up the approach.

Suddenly the ATL yelled at his team leader, "Use the secondary, use the secondary!"

Yelling over the whine of the turbine engine, Mallory asked, "Why?"

Benson had seen this from his good friend before and he had come to trust the premonitions. Benson had only a few seconds to decide.

"Go to the secondary!"

Mallory gave the change to the pilots, and they executed the changed approach. Benson was very glad he knew who was flying. He felt the Huey pull up for a second and then begin a sharp nose up drop into the smaller clearing on the side of the ridge. What they had just asked this aircrew to do was not easy, and a missed approach would have been a disaster for the team's security. The team stepped out onto the skids, each man scanning his sector of the LZ. The two in front were looking for threats on the LZ and the two in back were scanning below and behind the aircraft. The pilots cleared the trees by a few feet and pulled the nose up, and flared to the ground. Both door gunners were watching to be sure the tail rotor cleared any obstructions and manning the M-60 machine guns, ready to fire. The landing zone was flatter than expected, the rear of the skids touched first, and the machine rolled forward, dropping the nose, allowing a second or two for the LRRP team to step off. This maneuver kept the team from jumping off the chopper while minimizing exposure of the ship and crew. Romeo 5 stepped off and went to the ground.

Bensen was already making a commo check. He confirmed with the insertion officer that he was on the secondary LZ and that the choppers had not taken any fire. All four men of Romeo 5 were now searching everything around them for any sign that they had been detected. Eyes, ears, and even noses searched for the slightest indication that an enemy might be near. They were also looking for a good place to hide and observe. The team had planned to move off the north side of the primary insertion site, but this LZ did not offer that option. The concealment was not good and going north here would take them downhill. Bensen would not leave the high ground, not yet. The point man had seen the same thing, and was pointing to a spot up the hill to the southeast. It offered plenty of concealment and some cover in case they needed it. Sigler pointed, Bensen nodded, and as one the men moved twenty meters to the bamboo along the tree line. As they entered the bamboo, they again went to ground and went silent, straining for any hint that they had been compromised. Bensen whispered into the hand set, "Zero-Romeo 5 commo check." Zero, responded quickly, confirming a good radio signal. It was the last time anyone would speak for over an hour. The team was now totally silent, "layin dog" as they called it.

Without a word, the two men in charge of the team checked the maps to be sure they knew where they were. They pointed and nodded, nothing else was required. No one moved, even their own breathing and heartbeats seemed loud to them now. Every ten minutes there was a call from Zero, asking for a situation report. Knowing that the team would not talk, the call was, "Romeo 5, if you are negative and green, break squelch twice." Bensen pushed the transmit button on his handset two times. He hoped to do it at least four more times before he moved his team again. He needed at least two more green sit reps to assure himself that the insertion had not betrayed the team's presence. He looked back to the map, locating the closest rally points and pre-plots. He pointed them out to the team. It was a comforting thing to see that each already seemed to know where they were.

Thirty minutes passed and the team had not heard, seen, or smelled anything. The heat was beginning to be a problem. Each man in turn took a drink from the canteen on his web belt. They could easily have used half of the water, but each took a few swallows and put the cap back on. Refilling them now was out of the question. The sun was starting to bear down on the team. They were running out of shade, they could not stay here much longer. Bensen had spent the last twenty minutes planning the first move. They would stay on the high side of the LZ and move southeast to the crest of the ridge.

Once on top, the Rangers would hide again. The insertion officers and NCOs had anticipated this and called for confirmation. Bensen broke squelch twice and smiled. "Good man," he thought, appreciating the fact that Zero was on the ball. It was nice to know that they were listening if they were needed. Romeo 5's point man also knew it was time to go. He had located two routes even before the TL signaled. Bensen pointed out the direction and distance for the team to move. Everyone else was ready to move as the point man stood up. The team moved slowly, literally one step at a time. They stopped every two or three steps, scanning and listening at each stop.

The point man was looking forward, the TL to the right and the ATL to the left. Chavez covered the back trail. Walking drag was tough work. He had to watch for someone following the team and carefully cover up the team's trail. The team inched up the slope, searching for the crest and for the trail that might be there. After thirty minutes, Sigler lowered his arm, palm facing back to the TL. The signal stopped the team. He could see the top of the ridge, but no trail. They moved on up to the top, hoping to be able to observe the other side of the hill. They covered the last five meters quickly and disappeared into the short brush along the edge of the trees.

Again the team would hide and listen. They had not found a trail, but decided not to move down the side of the hill to look for one. Their packs were still heavy and they all knew that artillery was going to be nearly impossible to bring in on this side of the ridge. There was no reason to risk that now.

Anderson looked at his watch. They had been on the ground for nearly two hours. There had been no sign that anyone knew that Romeo 5 was there. The team sat down in a tight perimeter and the ATL signaled for the team to drink. He scanned the safeties on each weapon, the spoons on every grenade, and assigned a sector for each man to watch, knowing it was not really necessary. There was a chance that the elaborate procedure to hide the insertion had worked, and the team could relax at least a little. The point was already looking for a way to move. Chavez checked his M-16 and he had found a bit of cover, a log, if he needed it. He moved a few small sticks and settled in. Maps were-consulted, rally points pointed out and pre-plots confirmed for this location. The team went silent again. Silence and stealth were the best weapons that the tiny group of men had now. They knew that and they used it well.

There was little need to report a new location; the team had moved no more than fifty meters. The coordinates would have to be coded before they were sent to the TOC. Bensen was not willing to risk even whispering into his hand set. He looked at the pre-plots again and decided there was no reason to change them. Again the doubt about his artillery cover caused more than a little concern.

The only support close enough to reach the team was a long-range 175 mm battery on LZ Bannister. They were near maximum range and that had a negative effect on the accuracy. The 175s were not as accurate as the smaller 105 mm or eight-inch guns. The backside of a hill, sloping away from the guns, could be impossible to hit. The thought of a contact in those areas sent a chill up the spine of the team leader, even as the heat of the day caused the sweat to run down his painted face. Gunship support was available, but it would take time to get them on station. He silently questioned the wisdom of asking for these types of missions.

The ritual of checking safeties, grenades, and equipment was observed again at this stop. Another hour on the ground and everything seemed to indicate that Romeo 5 had been successfully inserted. No sign of any bad guys, either. No team ever relaxed on these missions, but three hours on the ground with no hint of trouble would allow the team to use their weapon of choice. That was stealth. Anyone looking for them now was at a serious disadvantage. It was nearly noon. The team had no specific threat to be concerned with, they were well concealed and positioned to observe.

The team leader signaled for the men to eat. Each man, one at a time, opened his pack and pulled out a meal, opened the C-ration cans, and ate quickly. This was not a real meal. This was only refueling. After eating, the cans were quickly and quietly placed in a bag and secured inside the ruck. A quick drink, wipe off the P-38 can opener and spoon, and they were done. The whole process took less than fifteen minutes and they were all on full alert again. Anderson knew that his TL would not eat, he never did early in a mission, but it bothered him just the same. He knew neither of them would sleep much either. He also had seen Bensen forget to drink, which was not something he could overlook. He scowled at his TL, pointed to the canteen on his belt, and signaled him to drink. Bensen did, knowing his friend was looking out for him.

Anderson had acquired the nickname "Bandit" because he had tried to grow a mustache and had failed. Sergeant Lopez, team leader of Romeo 14, told him that he looked like the "Banditos in those stupid old-time movies," and Anderson had his nickname for the war. Like many of the men in the company, years later, he would still be known by the nickname. In fact, some would never know his real name.

The sit reps were on an hourly basis now. Zero called and the team responded with two squelch breaks. The team would use this technique for most of the mission. They could whisper, and not be heard, but it affected their own hearing, so they avoided it. Adrenaline was wearing off after the insertion and the heat was beginning to take its inevitable toll on the men. They all had to fight the urge to sleep. The team seemed to have inserted successfully, but it was far too early to relax. Bensen and Anderson looked over the map again. A quick whispered exchange confirmed that they agreed on their location and they were done. The team went quiet again. After twenty minutes, Bensen motioned to Anderson.

He leaned forward and Bensen asked, "Why did you divert us to the secondary?"

Anderson's reply, "Don't know, just thought it was safer," did nothing to make him feel better. His ATL and the premonitions were correct often enough to cause yet more concern. They would have to check the primary LZ, he knew that, but it was now the extraction LZ. The possibility of a booby-trapped extraction LZ made him chill again.

The team was safe for the moment. There was no need to move, especially in the heat. Bensen signaled for one man to sleep, each taking a thirty-minute nap. He obsessively looked over his map and scanned what he could see in front of him. He tried to put himself into the mind of an NVA commander. What could they do here? Where would they get water? Where would they build bunkers? Would they be training here? He knew that to answer the questions he would have to put his team in some tough spots. The high ground to the southeast and low ground and the blue lines to the north would almost certainly have to be checked. The topographical map in his hand told him that there was nearly 600 vertical feet between those spots. He prayed that he could do his job without having to move that distance quickly.

They would have to check the flat area in front of them. Artillery would be hard to get into the valley to the north. There was no place to get a chopper in there, either. He also knew that he had to check the saddle to the east. His mind was racing through all of the information he had and making a plan to accomplish the mission. He turned to his long time ATL and pointed to the three locations on the map. Anderson, without speaking, nodded in agreement. They had talked about these areas before the insertion. Both the saddle and the flats were likely places to build bunkers and the eastern ridgeline might conceal a trail. Neither of the men liked the idea of going into the flats, the saddle, or the low ground. They both knew they would go.

Romeo 5's point man was known universally by his last name, Sigler. He was from Tennessee. He was a big man and he struggled with the heat. He needed more water than the other LRRPs. His job was physically and emotionally demanding, and that only added to the need for food and water. His workload would determine the team's actions for the next several days. His transformation into a LRRP point man was complete now, and he was ready to meet the challenge.

Balancing the loads that his team was carrying, the distance to move and the time available, Bensen decided that the flat area was the obvious first objective. He selected the pre-plots for the artillery. The rally point was next, and he pointed them out to his team. He did a commo check on his radio and alerted Zero that he was about to move. He had the ATL check his radio and then turn it off. While Bensen made notes in his notebook, the rest of the team prepared to move.

Three hundred meters, barely three football fields separated the team from the flats. It was a distance that, as athletes at home, they might have run in less than a minute. It would take the LRRPs almost three hours. Sigler rolled onto his left side, pulled his right leg under him, and pushed himself up. Each man did the same, emitting the sound that gave them their generic name, "Grunts."

Spec 4 Eloy Chavez, a strong eighteen-year-old athlete from New Mexico, stayed a few seconds after the other three started to move. He checked the back trail and searched the area for the signs that an NVA tracker would use to follow the team; a piece of paper, a can, a broken twig, or bent grass were such signs. He bent down and pulled a bit of foliage up. Satisfied that he had covered the trail as well as possible, he too started to move. He would spend most of the mission walking backwards, and looking behind the team. It was a physically taxing task, perhaps even more difficult than walking point in some ways. It was critical to the security of the tiny Ranger team.

The point man was a part of the bush now, totally at home in the thing he hated. He moved slowly, carefully, and with purpose. He was so attuned to the surroundings that he seemed to have been in the place before. He would move one, two, or maybe three steps and stop. He eyes penetrated the jungle, seeking threats, and the path he would take next. He seemed to have a map in his head He knew how far he had traveled. Bensen, followed in line, with Bandit behind him. Each man kept as much distance as possible between himself and the next, but they were never out of sight. After twenty-five meters, the right hand of the point came down and the team stopped to listen. So far, the team seemed to be alone on the ridge.

Point men in K Company were highly valued, and Sigler was no exception. He had asked to be on the team, and Bensen had accepted him. He knew both sides of the man. He knew the point man in the field and the man who battled the demons in the rear. As the TL came to trust his point man in the field, he gave him freedoms that he would not give many others. This move revealed one of those freedoms. The point man controlled the team's movement to a great extent. He stopped when he needed, he choose his route and controlled the pace. Today, there was plenty of time. The point man's sense of distance overrode his sense of time and the movement was slow, very slow now. There was no reason to hurry, and every reason to be very careful. He would take the full three hours to accomplish the move.

As the team began to travel down hill, Bensen saw something to his right and stopped the team. The team went to a knee and froze. For two or three minutes, the team remained motionless, but primed to react with incredible violence. Bensen had seen motion, and stopped the team. He soon realized that it was no threat, only one of the tiny deer that LRRPs occasionally saw. The deer was watching them, trying to figure out what strange creatures had invaded his home. It turned slowly and disappeared into the bush. Anderson saw the deer and both men relaxed. The TL signaled to move, reassured by a deer that his team was moving quietly.

The move continued uneventfully until the team reached the flats. There was nothing there, nothing to indicate any activity by any human, certainly not the NVA. Bensen changed course once on the flats. He followed the contour of the ground, not wanting to have to climb too far if contact was made. It was now late in the afternoon and finding a suitable night location was the team's next major task. The vegetation was getting thicker as the team moved south. It promised a good night location.

Sigler knew that was the case and now slowed even more. The team was hardly moving at all now. He would find a place for the team to stop, listen, and eat. Bandit had seen a thick stand of bamboo to the team's left, but it was down-hill from the team. It would be rejected, at least for now. Above them, several breaks in the trees had created some very thick vegetation. Bensen selected this area for a NL and indicated that to his point man. The team stopped to rest and eat. Sigler would be looking for a NL while he ate.

Romeo 5 went quiet for twenty minutes. Bensen confirmed his location with his ATL, and coded the grid numbers. The process of shackle coding information was fairly simple. It was nothing more than matching the actual number or letter to be sent with another character on a card. The cards had several different codes on them and each different code was used on different days. It was simple but slow. It always seemed to irritate the TL, and he was not sure why. "Zero — Romeo 5, new location — I shack," followed by a string of letters and digits that were meaningless without the card, the shackle code. The teams November Lima would be no more than fifty meters from this spot, and there would be no need to code the new location. Canteens were low, so the ATL had each man refill them from the four-quart bladders in their rucks. Sigler had settled on a spot about twenty meters from the team. He knew that Bensen liked to have the back trail below the NL. His spot met all the requirements. There was little need to talk. Bensen signaled to his point man and he in turn pointed to his selected spot. Anderson nodded in approval; Chavez started to check the back trail again. The procedure for entering a NL was pretty standard. Most teams would walk past the NL and make a ninety-degree turn and walk past it again. Another turn would put them in the desired spot. Anyone trying to follow them would have to walk in front of the team. Tracking a LRRP team into a well-selected NL was a very dangerous thing to do.

The veteran point man chose his path with great care, trying to make any change of direction as inconspicuous as possible. Chavez was very attentive to his back trail. He even made several small false trails, further complicating the task of following the Rangers. The team moved very carefully now. When Sigler stopped and pointed, Bensen and Anderson both agreed, giving thumbs up.

The team slid into the thickest part of the bamboo and quietly lowered themselves to the ground, leaning on their rucks. They all went dead silent. It would be dark in an hour and now was no time to be discovered. After thirty minutes, Bensen signaled to the team to set out their claymore mines. He pointed to Chavez first, cupping his hand to set the direction of the mine. He pointed out the direction and his fingers signed the distance. Chavez always covered the back trail. He pulled the mine out of his ruck, carefully extracting the detonator and wire at the same time. Rising quietly, he took the mine, the wire, and his weapon forward to place the claymore. Careful placement and concealment of these mines was the heart of the team's night defense. Positioning them to cover the team and at the same time avoiding the back blast was critical. The wires were never run directly back toward the team. They always had at least one change of direction from the mine to the November Lima. Each team member placed a mine with the same care and precision. Bandit placed his last and his return to the team signaled all of the men to connect the detonator wire to the detonator or clacker. Once connected, the safety clip was closed and the shunt was engaged. The safety prevented accidental firing by the LRRPS and the shunt prevented static electricity from detonating the mines. Both Bensen and Anderson checked the clackers several times.

With the claymores set to do their deadly work if needed, the team's location was confirmed and reported to Zero, based on the last shackled location. Rally points and pre-plots were pointed out to everyone. A radio check revealed a loose hand set on the ATL's radio. That was corrected and the radio was again turned off. Each man checked his own weapon and set it on safe. As a last precaution for the night, each man pulled out a black bootlace and tied their weapon to a belt loop. They could operate the weapons in the dark, but not if they could not find them. In a night contact, losing your weapon was not a healthy option. From now until thirty minutes after dark, the team would be on full alert. After that period of full alert, the team would go on a rotation, each man standing a one-hour watch. Three men would sleep, while the fourth would be awake. At least that was the procedure, but all four men knew that there would be little sleep for them tonight.

The last light alert was uneventful. A sit rep was sent and the team was ready for the night. Sigler was drinking water, trying to stay hydrated. Anderson took the first watch, Chavez the second, Sigler the third, and Bensen the fourth. They would rotate like this until thirty minutes before first light, and then they would go on full alert again. Pulling his poncho liner over his head, Sigler curled up on the ground. He was soon sleeping fitfully, but as well as he would ever sleep in the field. Chavez was a light sleeper most of the time, and tonight he was even less able to relax. The team leader slept in fits and starts, rarely asleep for more than fifteen minutes at any one time. Both men pulled the poncho liners around their shoulders and tried to get comfortable on the ground. The bamboo offered a bit of comfort by shedding a layer of leaves. Holding the handset, focused on the night sounds, Anderson was now the only LRRP on full alert. The team was his responsibility now.

The Central Highlands, and mountains especially, often seemed to be very noisy at night. This AO, in Base Area 266, was no exception. The noise drove new LRRPs and their teammates crazy. It took a while to learn what a threat was and what just the jungle was. False alarms were common with new men, but this team was not new to the jungle at night. Bensen let himself relax and sleep. He was awake in ten minutes, again in fifteen, and again when Chavez took watch. He would repeat this pattern all night long and on every night he was in the bush. Sigler was awake for his watch. Chavez and Bensen heard him take a drink. Both men laughed silently as the point man got to his knees and emptied his bladder. At midnight, Bensen took over. He busied himself with thoughts of tomorrow's moves. He again tried to imagine what an NVA unit would do in this place. Where would the trails be? He reached out and put his hand on his point man's shoulder to stop his snoring. He marveled at how quiet this man was in the daytime and how noisy he could be at night. He felt Bandit reaching out as well, the snoring stopped, and the nighttime routine resumed.

At fifteen-minute intervals, Zero called for sit reps. Every team in the field was contacted all night long. It was partly to get any information that a team might have gained, but mostly it was to be sure that teams stayed awake at night. Everyone had heard a team miss a sit rep, and tonight one of the teams missed the 01:00 call. Zero called three times and got no response. Twice they asked for squelch breaks if the team was in danger. No answer! Bensen felt the sick fear build in his gut.

"Come on! Damn it! Answer!" He felt the anger begin to build. "How can you go to sleep? How can you be so negligent?" But as soon as he thought that, he knew it was easy to do. It could happen to anyone. He slept very little at night, waking frequently to check on his team. He passed it off as good training, good Ranger School preparation, but he knew there was something else. He had gone to sleep on watch early in his tour! The call for a sit rep woke him up and the incident was never discovered, but he feared deeply that it might happen again. The late team responded. Bensen and everyone on the net relaxed.

The night went quietly, not quickly. At thirty minutes before first light, all four LRRPS were awake and alert. A strike at first light was a staple of military strategy. The team had sectors of the perimeter to secure. With only four men it was not really a perimeter, but the term still stuck. As the light filtered into the trees, the team could see a few meters, then ten, and finally the full light of day was on them. Before the team's eyes had adjusted to the breaking light. Chavez reached out to Bandit and pointed to his nose.

The AT and TL both nodded, they could smell the smoke now. The young soldier from New Mexico had detected the smoke before anyone else. Romeo 5 was not alone. Bensen called in the report.

"Zero, Romeo 5, we are negative and green, but we smell wood smoke near our NL."

The natural thermals on the mountains often drew the air up the hills in the morning. The source of the smoke was probably below them, and any thought of avoiding the trip to lower ground was now gone. Romeo 5 was going to the blue line sooner or later.

After the sun was well up and the team was sure they were fairly safe, they ate. The routine of eating was repeated from the previous day. Sigler ate first and he ate the most. No hot food or drink this day, or any day after. The smell of wood smoke made any such comfort a casualty of war. Each man took his malaria pill, washed it down with a drink of water, and then refilled the canteen on his belt. Weapons were checked. Bensen's Car-15 had a bit of a leaf on the bolt. The dust cover had come open during the night. He quickly pulled the charging handle back, checking for dirt in the weapon. All seemed to be in order. The whole process took him thirty seconds. The radios were checked again and nothing was amiss.

The map became the next object of attention as the Rangers tried to plan their next move. The time offered the opportunity to get some more water into his body before they moved, so Sigler took advantage of it. Chavez was looking for ways to hide the NL. Bensen and Anderson, knowing that the team was still heavily loaded, did not want to move downhill. They knew that there was a good chance that they might find bunkers or a trail on the high ground. If they were right, they might avoid the trip to the blue line. Not likely, but at least if they waited, their rucks would be lighter. Staying high helped a little with the artillery problems and both possible extraction locations were closer. They would stay on the higher ground for a while.

Anderson directed the team to pick up the claymores. The procedure was last night's process in reverse. Chavez was the last one in because the back trail was usually the greatest threat. Each mine was stowed in the top flap on the rock and the detonators placed in the top right side pocket. Romeo 5 was ready to move. Little was needed to start the process. They had done this many times. Romeo 5's point was only slightly surprised when Bensen pointed out the route. He knew his TL pretty well and thought they might go downhill while the team was still fresh. He was not disappointed with the decision to stay on the high ground. Zero was informed that the team would be moving. Before the team stood up, Bensen heard Romeo 9 asking for an extraction. Two of the team's four men were ill. Bensen stopped the team and told them what was going on. All four men grimaced at the news. They knew that any activity might tip the NVA off to the presence of Americans in the area. It would take twenty minutes to get the choppers to the team, so Bensen decided to move. Four men with painted faces started slowly toward the saddle.

The ground was fairly flat here, but features that don't show on the map could be significant obstacles to a LRRP team. The point man soon found one of these. A small rock outcropping, about a meter high appeared in front of the men. Sigler wanted to climb around it, but Bensen decided to go over it. One by one the men inched their way over the rocks and when Chavez had cleared the wall, the team rested. Chavez was relieved to stop because the rocks gave him a clear and safe view of the back trail. Bensen reported the team's location, and the men drank water. Zero informed the teams that there was a new firebase going in to the north and that they would have 105 mm guns available within the hour. Bensen thought of Capt. Kennedy and his information. Apparently the new firebase was part of the bigger action. It was a firebase, not a hip shoot, so it would be there for a while. That was good news for Romeo 5 because it eliminated the issues with the backsides of the ridges and it gave them accurate, close support. Romeo 9's extraction was delayed so the team began to move again. The pattern of move, stop, observe was repeated over and over again. After an hour-and-a-half, the team had moved 200 meters. They stopped to rest. Everyone needed water. They settled into a thick area and filled canteens.

Bensen looked over his map and pulled out the overlay. It was a small piece of tracing paper that was used to record teams movements and other important locations. After the mission, it would become part of the report that was given to his commander and to the brigade. As he traced the team's route and NL onto the paper, sweat ran down his face and onto the paper. His hands were filthy and they stained the edges of the paper

He wondered if anyone other than Capt. Kennedy ever saw these, and if they did see them, what did they think of the sweat and dirt? As strange as it seemed, he had thoughts like this, even on a mission like this one. He wondered for a second what that meant, or if it meant anything.

The radio was now busy with the extraction of Romeo 9. Another team member was now ill. Romeo 5 hid, waiting for the commotion in the area to settle. They could not hear the choppers. They thought that to be very positive. If they could not hear them, the NVA might not either. Romeo 9 was out, so they were now even more alone. They stayed still for another twenty minutes, listening for any indication that the extraction had alerted the enemy that they knew was close by. There was none, and the signal to move was given. The ground they had to cover to get to the top of the second ridge was not steep, but it did not take much to make moving very difficult. The point was taking a lot of punishment. Just walking would have been hard work. Staying focused on security, moving quietly and fighting the "wait a minute vines," brush, bamboo, and fallen logs were causing him to expend massive amounts of energy. All four men were drenched in sweat, and they had moved less than fifty meters from the rock ledge. Bensen stopped the team and had them drink. Even he was beginning to feel the dehydration. He thought about putting his ATL or Chavez on point for a while, but decided to wait. Within a few meters, the team had to climb over a large log.

As he struggled to the top, Sigler slipped and fell. His feet shot from under him and he fell hard onto the log, landing on his side. The noise seemed deafening to the team. Bensen got to him quickly and he seemed to be okay. He had knocked the wind out of himself and had managed to stay quiet. His ribs hurt and he had a nasty scrape on his side. His right leg and arm were going to be sore, but he seemed unhurt otherwise. His weapon was not damaged. After it appeared that he was ok, the concern turned to the extra four-quart bladder in his pack. It had split and all the water was gone. Water had been an issue from the beginning of the mission; it was now a major problem.

Anderson reported to Zero while the TL tended to the point man. Chavez was the eyes and ears of the team for now. They rested for thirty minutes. Missions were sometimes scrubbed because of this kind of thing. The battered point man seemed to be regaining his strength. Sigler might still need to be taken out, but that would mean a climb to the LZ above them. He was clearly not ready for that right now. Since the team's route was beginning to take them uphill and Sigler was sure he would be able to resume his position, Romeo 5 would "Charlie Mike" or continue mission. Anderson moved to point, Sigler moved to third in line and the team moved out.

As the team moved, the mid-day heat became nearly intolerable. They stopped for water often. None of them drank enough. Each man was acutely aware of the burst bladder canteen and what it meant. They were now trying to maintain the delicate balance between becoming severely dehydrated and running out of water too soon. Either would end the mission.

They pressed on to the top of the ridge and stopped. The trees were tall and thick. The shade was not just welcome, it was now required. The fallen logs offered both concealment and cover. With his point man injured, Bensen was glad to call a halt to the movement. The base of a large tree provided the team with all the comfort they would get. As Spartan as it might seem, it was a luxury to Romeo 5 now. They did not need to be told to drink now. Each man drank deeply from the plastic one-quart canteen on his belt. Bensen was checking the map, showing each team member where they were.

The SOP for this team was to point out pre-plots, rally points and location at every stop. Like every other team leader in the company, Bensen was always teaching the skills needed to lead a team. He knew that most of them would, at

221

some point, be leaders. He also knew that if something happened to him, the rest of the team would need the information and skills to get themselves out of trouble. Bandit was ready now and would have his own team very soon. The two men had been together for a long time, and neither relished the idea of separating. Both knew it was inevitable. Sigler, had no intention of taking any job other than point, but he also knew he might have no choice, and that was one reason why Bensen made him do the maps and other skills. In contrast, Chavez was a very willing student. He was also ready to take over as an ATL. His opportunity would come soon. Bensen handed the map and shack code to the young soldier and nodded. Chavez reported the team's location and intentions to Zero. Romeo 5 was now resting in a comparatively safe and cool location. A dangerous enemy would now try to attack them.

The lack of sleep the night before, the heat, the exertion of the day's movement, the quiet, the boredom of sitting all converged at once. Sleep now attacked all four men. Their bodies were going to sleep, that was certain. Two men stayed awake while the other two slept. LRRP teams often used this technique to conserve water and strength. Staying quiet during the worst of the heat was sometimes the only way to avoid heat exhaustion. It was a luxury that the line units did not have. LRRPS could usually stop and wait during the worst of the heat.

Anderson and Chavez took the first watch. Sigler ate quickly and went to sleep. In an hour, Benson was awake and Anderson took Sigler's turn on watch. They were both concerned about their point man and decided to let him sleep. The fall could have been more damaging than they knew. They spoke in whispers about how to handle the situation. Where should they go next? Unless they found something of importance on the high ground, they would have to go to the blue lines. With Sigler's condition still in question, going lower now was out of the question. They would move on to the saddle as planned. Everyone on the mission was antsy about this area. It was a prime place for bunkers. They had not found anything in the flats and that made the saddle even more threatening.

There were other issues to consider. Sigler was awake now and was not happy about being allowed to sleep. All three of the others were relieved. It was a good sign. Much could be said about Sigler's motivation in some areas, but he was adamant about carrying his share of the load. The two leaders spent a few more minutes whispering. It was clear to them that there was something going on in the area. The new firebase was a sure sign. The amount of air traffic that they could hear was another. The LRRPS were told that their information was used in the decisions to deploy troops and that lives depended on the information that they gave to the brigade TOC. Lives depended on the information, and the information depended almost entirely on the integrity of the teams. Romeo 5 would make every effort to get the information that "higher" wanted.

After eating and drinking more water, Sigler seemed to be ready to continue. He was sore, stiff, and determined. Bensen signaled to prepare to move. As the team stood, Sigler took his place at the point. His face told Bensen he was in no mood to argue.

The contrast between the man in the bush and the man in base camp was never clearer. The movement was slightly downhill now and it was easier. Each step down meant a step or maybe two back up. Those steps would take their revenge. Each step now took the team away from the two extraction points. Romeo 5 was now doing what LRRP teams had to do: they were moving away from their own safety to help secure that of other soldiers. Bensen stopped the team, ran through his mental checklist, cautioned his point to look for bunkers, and they started the move again. He consoled himself with the fact that they were still on high ground. His point man was able to function and the two men behind him were as good as any in the company. It was no small comfort to him.

After moving about 100 meters in an hour, the team slowed even more. They were beginning to get close to the first of the two small hills forming the saddle. Sigler felt the ground change under his feet and stopped the team. He knew that Bensen would be extremely cautious here. The men all knelt down. They would rest and listen for a few minutes. NVA bunkers were very hard to see, but sometimes the men in them were not as quiet as they should be. It was not uncommon for teams to hear a bunker complex long before they saw it. They heard nothing. Water was taken again, and Sigler had to refill his canteen. He would be out of water by the end of the day.

Approaching an area where the NVA might have bunkers, in many ways was the worst situation a LRRP team could face. LRRP teams could disappear into the jungle and make chasing them very dangerous, but here the roles were reversed. It was the NVA who had disappeared, and the LRRPS who had to find them. The procedure for this moment had been discussed many times at Camp Radcliffe. Each man checked the cammo of the others. Any deficiency was remedied. Every piece of equipment was secured. Bensen motioned the team forward. They all knew the rally points and where to go if they got separated. Detecting the bunkers if they were there was now the sole concern of the team. Chavez turned to the front, checking behind only occasionally. The slightest clue, a bit of discolored vegetation, an unnaturally straight line, a break in the vegetation, all could give away a bunker. The four American infantrymen inched forward, covering twenty to thirty meters in an hour. They stopped every step, and listened, looked and moved another step. Sigler felt the earth flatten again. The Rangers were on the top of the hill and they had found nothing. They stopped, drank, and reported their location to Zero.

Bensen was confused, concerned, and a bit irritated at finding nothing. It was one of the things that he had shared with other team leaders. Many also had this bizarre anger when they were primed and ready for something difficult and it did not happen. Bensen certainly did not want to walk into a bunker complex with his team, but the letdown expressed itself as anger. He didn't know it then, but this reaction would return to haunt him for years after he returned home.

The second hill was less than 100 meters away and the team needed to go there. Bunkers were again a possibility, and they needed to know what was there. The possibility of being able to observe some of the low ground existed. They would need a night location in a few hours. This hilltop could provide answers to many questions.

A quick conference with his ATL confirmed his thoughts. Sigler was moving easily, the stiffness gone for now. The new artillery coverage from LZ Hooper provided support on the east faces of the ridge. The team moved out. Again they executed the dance that was so familiar to them. They moved and again found nothing.

Sigler stopped the team about ten meters from the crest of the small hill. He had seen a NL toward the top of the hill. The team stopped to rest, listen and eat before securing for the night. Bensen realized that he had not eaten since breakfast. Sigler filled his canteen and was out of water. Chavez had a rip in his fatigues, exposing him to the leaches in the bamboo. He taped it up with green tape. Preparations for moving into the NL were made and the team moved into the bit of jungle that would be home for the night.

Nothing was said, just pointing and gestures. Claymores were set. Chavez went first, then Sigler, Anderson, and Bensen. Bensen moved to his area and placed the mine. Before he could cover it, he heard voices. He froze. He could not know if the others had heard the voices. He was already kneeling, so he raised his weapon slowly and tried to locate the voices. They became louder and then he saw movement in front of him. Through the brush, Bensen saw flashes of color and motion. It wasn't much, but it was enough to know that he was close to a trail and that the men who had passed by were NVA and totally unaware of his presence. He moved back to the NL. Anderson was on the radio the instant they had heard the voices. Romeo 5 was within ten meters of a trail. Bensen completed the report, using the shack code and the team went totally silent and on full alert.

Bensen was not exactly sure what he had seen, but he was sure that the NVA had no concerns about a Ranger team in the area. They walked too fast and made too much noise to have known. It was the only real good news. Romeo 5 was committed to this NL. They could not risk moving this late. All of the reasons for moving to this spot were still valid, perhaps even more so. The exhaustion of the day was gone now, as adrenaline took command of the men. No instructions were needed. Everyone knew it was full alert until told otherwise. How long that might be was anyone's guess. Zero went to a sit rep every ten minutes for Romeo 5. Bensen confirmed the team's status with squelch breaks. His mind was racing now. Where should they go if they had to run? He already knew the heading to the Primary LZ, but he checked it again. Pointing to the map and signing the azimuth to each man was all he needed to do. They understood. The same was true of rally points and pre-plots. He picked two sets of targets for the 175s and two more for the 105s, and called them on to Zero, who passed them on to the artillery.

His mind now went to the extraction. He would try for the primary LZ despite the concerns Anderson had. The bomb craters were far too small for a night extraction. He picked out a route for the team to use to get to the LZ. He pointed everything out to Anderson and he showed it to the other two men. Sigler spent a few extra moments looking at the map. He would be the first to leave the NL if they had to move. He would have a copy of the route in his mind if they had to move in the dark.

An hour passed, then two, and then three and nothing new had happened. The team went to the normal nighttime alert cycle. Bensen and Chavez split the fourth watch, allowing their point man time to rest. They all worried about his health and they knew that they needed him to be 100 percent in the morning.

Around 02:00 hours, right after a negative sit rep, Anderson saw lights. He reached out to Bensen and woke him up. The lights were visible through a gap in the trees and appeared to be about 500 meters away. They formed a broken line of light that snaked along a hillside. They appeared to be on a trail, perhaps on the same one at Romeo 5's back. The team reported the lights, and included the azimuth and estimated distance. It was impossible to count the number. LRRP teams would often call artillery strikes onto lights. That would not happen tonight. Romeo 5 was on a true recon mission and the mission would be wasted if they engaged these troops now.

Chavez was awake now and he was told of the situation. He took the handset and started his watch. The TL decided to stay up a while, thinking that the lights might soon pass by the team. Chavez saw more lights and then a third group about twenty minutes later. None had passed the team, nor would they.

Bensen, like many team leaders, slept little at night. Tonight was no exception. He was thinking about what his team had seen and what it might mean.

Anderson was processing the same information. Sigler was on watch now, a good sign. Bensen stayed up. Where did the lights go? Was there another trail they could not see? Were the men carrying the lights still below them in the valley? Was there some sort of camp there? If Capt. Kennedy was right, there might be a staging area there. Could Romeo 5 be as close to it as it appeared? Anderson was awake now and his mind shifted to what the team might have to do in the morning. He knew Bensen was thinking the same things through.

All four men were awake and alert now because it would be light soon. Their hands ran over weapons and the detonators on the claymores. The TL was on the handset, Zero's sit reps came every ten minutes again. The end of the normal alert came and went. Bensen extended it another thirty minutes. Nothing, again nothing. Irritation and relief filled his mind. The team ate and drank water. Anderson redistributed some of his water to Sigler and took some from the TL's bladder canteen to fill his own. Anderson ate next, wolfing down a C-ration and washing it down with a few gulps of water. He ate quickly, partly because he was very hungry, but mostly because it kept him from his duties. Bensen ate next and everything was quickly repacked.

The concern now turned to the point man and his health. How was he doing? Could he function? Anderson was skeptical and had him move, get to his knees and even stand. He was stiff and sore, but insisted he was okay to walk point. Bensen was busy checking his radio. He decided to change the battery. The old one seemed to be fine, but it was two days old and a contact with an old battery was more than he could risk. Batteries in the PRC–25 often gave little warning before they failed. In most situations the team needed only one radio, but in a contact the possibility of losing one was high. Losing one to a bad battery was avoidable, so the risk could be minimized. A team that lost both in a contact was in deep trouble.

Chavez and Sigler were on watch now as Bensen and Bandit studied the map. Anderson was okay with Sigler's readiness. The discussion centered on where the men with the lights had gone. Either they had gone out on another trail or they were still near the blue line in front of the team. If they were still below, what were they doing? Their guts churned at the thought of going down there. Warning bells were clanging in their heads. Both knew this was as dangerous as anything they had ever done. Zero ended the discussion: "Romeo 5 — Zero, Higher wants an eyeball on these coordinates, I shack alpha, echo, delta, niner one, one, seven, bravo, do you copy?" Bensen repeated the coordinates and they were confirmed.

He decoded the message, but it was not really necessary. There were only two places that Higher would want to see. Neither was going to be easy. Anderson saw the plot and shook his head. It was not the worst of the two. Bensen pointed to the spot for Chavez, who just smiled. He knew they were going an hour ago. Sigler saw the plot and without hesitation whispered, "F— — —- Higher!" It was with some effort that the rest of the team did not laugh out loud. He had said nothing that the others had not thought. It wasn't Higher's fault either, but it always seemed to help if they groused about them. The message told them an extraction for Sigler's issues was not going to happen and the outburst reassured them that he was able to function.

Now that they knew where they were going, they settled into the preparation for the move. They had to stay away from the known trail, and as far from likely bunker locations as possible. They needed to stay as close to the LZs as possible. All these were considerations, but recon was the mission, the others were secondary. Higher assigned the task, but left the rest to the LRRPs, something else that line units seldom got to do.

Backtracking kept the team close to the insertion LZ, but might increase the risk of being followed. Staying on the eastern ridge kept them high and close to the primary LZ, but exposed them to being heard or seen from the trail. Going down between the two ridges risked bunkers, but it offered the easiest climb out to the LZs. Bensen decided to backtrack, reasoning that there was no cause to think that the NVA knew the team was near. Therefore being followed was the lesser risk. Anderson and Chavez agreed. Sigler was now the point man and the team was again in his hands.

A point man carried an extra burden, not physical, but mental and emotional. Any mistake could be fatal. Sigler, for all his foibles, was good at his job. He was now literally going to carry the lives of three other men with him as he moved. He hated the bush, he hated the war, he hated the Army, and he hated 'Nam, but he would do anything to see that he and the others made it home. It was not great heroism, or even love for his teammates. It was pure survival. When he came on the team, he had said as much. He was willing to do whatever he had to do to stay on Romeo 5 because he thought it was his best chance to get home. The other three might have been more team-oriented, but they felt the same way about him.

Bensen signaled to bring the claymores in. He looked at the trail behind them. It was a well used trail about one meter wide. He made a note in his notebook and returned to the team. Anderson's check of weapons was complete and he re-taped a grenade on Chavez's belt. The claymore was stored in the top flap of the ruck, this time leaving the detonators and clackers in the flap as well. They could be used quickly in the event of a contact. The claymores would provide a defensive shock and destroy the heavy rucks at the same time. All four men took a last long drink and the team was ready to move.

Chavez was last to leave. He paid particular attention to the place where Bensen had return to the NL. Satisfied, he followed the team. For 100 meters they paralleled the path that they had used in approaching the NL. They turned north, following the contour of the terrain. They moved as slowly as they could, one step, stop, listen, and another step, listen again. They knew they were probably close to more than a few NVA. They were closer together now and could touch each other if they needed to communicate. It was getting hot and the camouflage fatigues were wet with their sweat. Sigler wore a green towel around his neck to wipe his eyes. The sweat removed his face paint. The team put on new paint at each water break.

The point man was again moving easily, his stiffness gone. Bensen felt better about his decision to try to stay in. He was now more concerned with his role as a pair of eyes than with the radio. Zero knew he would be off the radio and left him alone. Anderson as well was now more concerned with patrolling. Chavez was living up to his reputation as a good LRRP. He could not afford to ignore the back trail, but he had to look forward as well. He was strong and tough, but this move sapped his strength. Except for the slow pace, it was an impossible task. Anyone watching them would know this was a well-trained and close-knit team. It was, however, not that much different than most of the teams in the company.

As they moved, the terrain and vegetation changed the route. The underbrush seemed to open in front of the team. Hoping see into the valley, the team turned to the northwest and moved downhill slightly. Crossing some lower ground, not shown on the map, they found the soil soft and wet. The team crossed carefully and again paralleled the elevation along the hillside. Each step now took them closer to the objective and to the insertion LZ. There was some comfort in that thought.

This area had plenty of concealment, but also offered some open lanes to observe the lower areas. Bensen was always very cautious, but this situation required more caution than normal. His team had moved about 200 meters. He needed to report his location and to rest his men. The team stopped and seemed to disappear. They drank. The quiet was deafening. There was nothing to be concerned about specifically, but all four men sensed something. The next part of the route was already planned. Bensen pointed in the direction that his point man had already scouted. Behind the TL, Bandit had selected the path as well.

Sigler moved ten meters and stopped, his hand down, palm back. The slow, controlled nature of the movement told the team that there was no immediate danger. He motioned for his TL to move to him. Looking over the shoulder of the point, he saw a small crater on the hillside with water in it. The general rule for the LRRP teams was to not re-supply their water in the field. If necessary, streams were the best option. Water from a crater was to be avoided. The danger of parasites was very real, but the chemicals from the explosives were a bigger concern. The team was dangerously low on water and contact was a distinct possibility. Bensen did not think twice. He stopped the team and they filled their empty canteens. Halizone and iodine tablets were placed in the canteens and they closed them up, allowing the chemicals to kill any parasite in the water. It would taste awful, and it would be biologically safe. It would serve the purpose.

Again the team moved, not allowing themselves a rest in the heat of the day. It was brutally hot and the tension was palpable. They had to find out what was on the blue line, but they also had to be sure they had time to get back out.

Sigler's body froze. His posture told the team to do the same. They knew it meant they were in danger. They were now fully alert and focused only on their area. They were ready to erupt in a wave of carefully choreographed violence. Bensen, without knowing what had stopped the team, rapidly keyed the handset several times. Zero had taken the other team off this push and they knew it was Bensen. They asked if the team was in "red or yellow" and the squelch breaks answered their question. Yes! Without a word being spoken, a whole chain of events needed to support the team was set in motion.

Sigler motioned for his TL to come forward. He moved slowly, looking over his shoulder. He saw what had frozen the point man. Less than thirty meters in front of the team was the outline of a roof and side of a building. Most of the thatched roof was brown, but it had new green material on the top. Neither man knew exactly what they were seeing, but it meant that other humans were in the area. For LRRPs in this situation, in a free fire zone, anyone else was the enemy. The men were silent, and they could now hear voices! They were not hushed voices; they were normal speaking voices with no attempt to conceal them. The team searched for any other clues. What were they seeing or hearing? Anderson and Chavez had not seen anything, but they had heard the talking. Bensen and Sigler backed up, seeking more concealment. Bensen turned to whisper to the other team members. They needed to know what was happening.

Bensen decided he had to let Zero know his situation. He whispered the message to Zero. Bensen had his map out. He pointed to the LZ on the map and then on the ground. He did the same for the rally points and then for the route they would follow. The team moved as one, keeping as much vegetation as possible between them and the hooch below them. In five meters, they were stopped again. Bensen was close this time and could see what the point saw.

This time there was a break in the trees facing toward the blue line. Parts of several large structures were visible. Voices were audible, but now the team could hear the clink of metal on metal. It sounded like men eating in the closest hooch. There was ample concealment here.

Sigler had found the perfect spot to observe, like he almost always did. It would go unnoticed now, it was expected. Later the others would express their amazement at how their point man found these places. The team settled into the thicket of bamboo and vines. They would be impossible to see now. The noise from below was unnerving and comforting at the same time. They knew they were close, perhaps too close, to these men. The noise also made it clear that whoever they were, they did not know they were being watched. There was some satisfaction in the fact that four Americans had beaten the NVA at their own game of hide and seek.

A whistle broke the chatter and startled the LRRPS. The NVA used whistles to signal in battles, but this was to call the men from their meal. Several groups of twenty-five to thirty men moved from the first building toward the other two. It was not clear to Bensen what they were doing, but Chavez could see into one of the larger hooches. There was a man with a blackboard and easel, apparently lecturing the men. It was some sort of instruction; there were some weapons visible as well. The team watched for thirty minutes. Bensen had seen enough. He had been making notes on the condition of the men and their uniforms. He noted the numbers seen and guessed that his team was seeing less than half the camp.

He was ready to report to Zero. He thought he was seeing a political training camp or perhaps an R and R camp. He knew he had five hours of daylight left to fade away into the jungle and execute an extraction, leaving the NVA in the valley for another unit. A classic LRRP mission, "get in, do what you have to do and get out without any one ever knowing you were there." The team would climb the ridge and move back to the south. They would either hide near the primary LZ and extract in the morning, or extract later in the afternoon. Bensen requested an extraction, figuring that he had done all he could do. He also knew that he was playing with fire, being this close to this many NVA soldiers. His answer came quickly; Higher wanted another set of coordinates checked.

They all knew they were pushing their luck. Bensen asked again to be pulled, and was refused again. He knew they wanted to know if there was another trail in the bottom of the valley. Anderson unshackled the coordinates. It was only 150 meters away and at the tip of the ridgeline. If a trail existed, it would be there. The 150 meters was the short way, but it forced the team to move close to the hooches. Anderson suggested climbing to the top of the ridgeline and then moving north on the western side. This was longer, but it placed the terrain between the Rangers and the known NVA. It offered the best chance to get to the blue line undetected. Bensen also knew that they might be walking parallel to a trail on that side. His choice was between bad options. He seldom allowed himself to be talked into something by his team, but today they seemed to have the best of bad options.

The extra climb for Sigler was a concern, but the point man was not going to concede that he was unable to do the job. He clearly feared walking the east side of the ridge. Bensen agreed, and the team slipped up the hill.

The fifty-meter climb was not difficult for men full of adrenaline and they made it quickly to the top. Once on top, they stopped to rest and drink again. Bensen shacked the location, told Zero the route they would take and selected new pre-plots for the move to and from the objective. With 200 meters and a hill between the team and the NVA, the adrenaline inevitably gave way and the men started to get sleepy. Sleeping now meant less time to move away from the blue line, forcing them to spend the night close to the camp. They would move downhill now, saving the time for moving away later. The farther away from the camp they were, the safer they would probably be.

The route to the blue line was on a steep side slope and dropped rapidly toward the objective. The team was pulled down to their left and they had to fight to stay on course. Every step was a battle with gravity and the vegetation. The vines grabbed and cut at the men. It was easy to see that they would not be able to get out this way if they had to move fast. They all mentally plotted a route out if they had to go fast. It would be on the top of the ridge, in the open areas and perhaps exposed to the camp below. They stopped again.

They were close now and they prepared themselves for the final push. They filled their quart canteens again, using the last of the water they had carried in. As refreshed as they could be, they moved. A commo check was made on both radios. Anderson's radio was left on this time. Painstaking care to be quiet was required now. They were moving at a snail's pace. It took them several minutes to move a meter. Sigler was at his best here, he was good, and he had to be in this situation. At twenty meters, he stopped. Bensen was within arm's reach and soon saw why they had stopped. Not more than two meters in front of the team was a steep rock wall, dropping off into the creek below. Between the creek and rocks was a trail. The stream was narrow and fast running here. The far side of the creek was steep and heavily wooded. Bensen realized that the bunkers that they had expected to find were probably on the far slope. It would be impossible to see them from the air. It was now easy to see why the area was used as a camp. There was water and cover and even some space to train. If they moved uphill a few feet, they were concealed from the trail. Bensen's curiosity got the better of him and he moved the team a few more meters toward the camp. His curiosity was rewarded and they could see three more hooches in the trees below. They counted another thirty men. Both the point and the TL were making mental notes when they heard voices on the trail below.

This time Chavez got to see the men. He had seen another twenty men. It was time to leave! Romeo 5 was within 200 meters of no less of 120 NVA soldiers. They had good locations on the camp. They could do no more.

The team turned around. Drag was now point, and the order of march was reversed. Bensen had him back track as far as he could and then climbed to the top of the ridge. It took them an hour-and-a-half to go the 100 meters. They fell exhausted in the shade. They drank the water from the crater. They did not seem to notice the taste; only the need for water concerned them. They were faced with another decision. Try to stay in the cover on the side of the ridge or move out into the more open area. Bensen and Anderson knew they had pushed themselves and the team hard. They could not go too much longer in the thick stuff, but they were more concerned about the exposure on the upper part of the ridgeline. They had to try to stay in the cover as long as possible.

Sigler took point again and the team struggled for another twenty minutes in the thick undergrowth. Sigler could feel the ground get steeper and the vines were thicker. It was beginning to be impossible to move. Bensen could see that they were sliding down the side, away from the top. It was an insidious trap in the Highlands. A team could find itself at the bottom of a ridgeline very quickly. They could not risk that for many reasons. He turned to his ATL, who shook his head no, and pointed to the top of the hill. They had to go to the top.

At the top, the men again fell to the ground and drank heavily. Bensen reported to Zero that his team was nearly spent and they needed to be pulled out. To his relief, they agreed. He was still 200 meters from the extraction LZ. It would take the team two hours to get there. The birds would be ready. Sigler slipped out of the trees, hugging them as close as he could, hoping to use them as concealment. Bensen followed, Anderson, then Chavez, and they moved as quickly as possible. They had taken only a few steps when a whistle sounded and three signal shots fired. Chavez saw a muzzle flash on the far side of the valley. Someone had seen the team — or had they? Bensen moved to get the team into the trees again. A few seconds after the first three rounds were fired, another burst from an AK-47 removed all doubt as the rounds hit the trees behind them. The team was now compromised and had taken fire.

They were moving fast now, not as concerned about what might be in front of them as what they knew was behind them.

"Zero, Romeo 5, we are compromised and are moving to the LZ." Bensen did not hesitate; he was going to bring as much confusion and pain to the men in the valley as he could. He was buying time for the extraction.

He called for his active pre-plots. The first was on the coordinates of his first objective of the day. The second was on the coordinates that he had just checked. His third pre-plot, number 6, was in the valley floor. Three smoke rounds splashed and were safe to fire. Bensen called for a battery 5 on all three. Each of five guns would fire five rounds. The smoke rounds caused the camp below to come alive. Bensen again called for a battery 5 from all guns and shouted, "Fire for effect." The high explosive rounds were on the way. Romeo 5 was struggling toward the LZ when the first rounds ripped into the camp. Two batteries of 175 and one of 105 hammered the NVA. Bensen was pleasantly surprised at the location of the rounds. He could hear the screams of wounded men. The team kept moving.

Zero had scrambled the choppers and a FAC was on the way. Romeo 5 had climbed to the level of the insertion LZ. Bensen stopped the team and plotted their location. He sent it in the clear, no shack code now. He fired another battery on the same pre-plots and then shifted to one upstream from the rock ledge that they had just seen. Again the 175s slammed into the target. More 105 rounds walked down the valley floor. Bensen moved the team to the tree line and ordered a halt. They drank water as fast as they could and every man tried to regain his breath.

The pre-plots now became Bensen's best tool. He habitually added pre-plots on missions. By adding them at locations that the team had actually occupied, he had a much better idea of where the rounds would hit. One of these was the place where they had crossed the rock wall. Twenty-five of the smaller rounds hit that area. The 175 mm guns hit the team's back trail just above the blue line. Anderson was directing the team's defense on the ground. They had not been fired on again, but they were ready if it happened. They started to move again, still trying to maintain some degree of noise discipline. They would disappear into the jungle again if they could.

Chavez's sharp eyes caught the movement of pith helmets below the team. NVA soldiers were coming up the hill. It appeared that they had been trying to get between the team and the LZ. They were too close to use the artillery now. Anderson and Chavez waited a few seconds and fired on the two men closest to the front. Romeo 5 was now truly in contact.

"Romeo 5. Contact, contact, contact!" Bensen shouted into his handset and then at his team, "go, go, go!" The accuracy of the rounds fired by the team had stopped the pursuers for the moment, giving the Rangers a few precious minutes to put distance between themselves and the NVA.

Ten minutes of this pace was the limit and they stopped again. Artillery was placed in close behind the team. Anderson checked the back trail and saw nothing. He gave his TL the best information that he had. Both men were concerned with the aggressiveness of the troops following them. This was not a group of rookies, these guys appeared to be well trained and very aggressive. Anderson suggested that they "Leave Sigler's pack and claymore, we might slow them down again!"

"Okay, do it." Nothing more was said, Sigler slipped the ruck off his shoulders, grabbed what water was left and set the ruck on the ground. The claymore was facing down the back trail. He put the blasting cap in the mine and handed the clicker to Chavez. They were ready to move.

Quickly moving the length of the wire, they settled into the brush and waited. Zero was on the radio; Mallory and the gunships were about ten minutes out. The slicks were not far behind. Gambler 23, 24, and 33 were now on the frequency. Bensen now had to deal with at least three separate radio contacts and he would soon have a fourth when the slicks were close. Someone with the call sign "Green River 6" kept asking for information. Bensen did not know who it was, but decided to ignore the call sign. Someone else asked Green River 6 to stay off of the push. The FAC was now on station and flew over the area. He spotted enemy soldiers moving up the ridgeline, but had no idea where the team was. His warning was timely. It was time to move again.

The drag waited until the other three were moving and blew the claymore. Another battery of artillery hit at the same time. Chavez sprinted after the team, catching them in seconds.

The next pre- plot was the second NL. It was between the LZ and the trail. Bensen feared that this aggressive group of men would try to get between him and the LZ again. He called his smaller artillery in and knew quickly that his fear was well founded. A second and third volley followed. He walked the guns up the hill toward the LZ. Anderson yelled as he and Chavez engaged a group of four or five men, still following the team. Sigler was firing at something to the team's left. Anderson pulled the claymore from Chavez's pack, placing it on the team's trail.

Until Bensen felt his weapon knocked from his hand, he was not aware that the team was taking fire. The claymore behind him did its deadly work, but his Car-15 was now useless, an AK–47 round had destroyed the receiver. A third claymore exploded behind the men. The FAC saw the team from the air and could now help them move. More importantly, he could direct the gunships and help Bensen with the artillery.

Romeo 5 now made the final effort to get to the LZ. Firing as they moved, the tiny group of exhausted men made it to a point level with the LZ and ten meters or so from the edge of the tree line. They stopped and were quiet, listening, hoping that they had separated themselves from their tormentors. There were plenty of voices, cries and whistles, but they seemed to have stopped the pursuit for now. Quickly, Bensen's ammo was split up between the other three men. Anderson shoved his canteen at Bensen and said, "Drink!" He did, not noticing the water was warm and tasted awful. He was amazed at how thirsty he was. Back in stealth mode, they started to move toward the LZ.

Gamblers gunships were now on station and Bensen wasted no time in using them. His artillery was now unable to shoot, because the Cobras were in the air over the team, but the mini-guns were a far superior close support weapon. He had them make a run from the insertion LZ to the lower bomb crater, hoping to discourage anyone chasing them even further. Zero and the slicks wanted a location on the team, but Bensen was not going to risk giving his position away with smoke, not yet. As the team got to the tree line, Sigler's reactions told the team something was wrong!

All four men were close enough now to see the LZ and it was covered with Pungi sticks! After a few more seconds they could see several booby traps made with grenades. Anderson's premonition had been accurate. Had the team landed there it would have been a disaster for the team and for the choppers. It had to be cleared before they could use it. Bensen was on the radio, explaining that they would not be able to extract immediately. He crawled out of the trees and used his signal mirror to locate the team. Mallory was already letting everyone know where the team was. Anderson carried some C-4 plastic explosive and detonation cord. He quickly made a string of C-4 balls on the det cord. He tossed that onto the LZ and blew a path three meters wide and six meters long onto the LZ. The explosion covered the team with dirt. Bensen was now directing the guns in close to the team. The Cobras were working the area hard and had picked up several more small groups of men moving toward the LZ. They hit the hillside with mini guns and rockets, buying more time for the team to clear a spot to extract. Cobra gunships had a very discouraging effect on anyone on the receiving end of their weapons. They made another pass, this time firing the grenade launchers.

Both Anderson and the TL knew that there was no chance of clearing the LZ without using the artillery, and so the choppers had to pull out of the area. "Prepping" an LZ was usually something that line units did before they went in.

It involved firing artillery onto the LZ and into the surrounding area. The purpose was to clear out any enemy soldiers or weapons, but it could also remove bobby traps to some degree. Bensen had a pre-plot on the LZ and called a battery on it. His request was denied! It was too close to fire without a smoke round first. He had no time to argue, he moved the coordinates away from the team and south on the LZ. The round splashed onto the ground about 100 meters away. He adjusted them toward the team and fired again. Still safe, he adjusted and fired again. Still safe, close, but not close enough.

Anderson and the other three men now heard voices in front of them. The last two claymores were out and ready. Chavez was the first to see the men looking for Romeo 5. He fired and the other two were now fully engaged. They had some cover from a fallen log and fired from behind it. One of the claymores went off and the assault collapsed for a second. Bensen knew it would not last long and made his last red leg adjustment. He was denied!

"Romeo 5, that is too close!"

Bensen screamed into the radio, "Shoot it, if you don't we are going to get over run! Do it now!"

Mallory confirmed the situation and the rounds were on the way. He adjusted again and had the LZ hit as well as was possible. Anderson was fighting like a mad man behind him. All three men were engaging targets with careful and brutal efficiency. Quickly the last claymores were placed and the team moved a few meters along the tree line. Within seconds a group of ten NVA assaulted the team's last location and they were not there. The claymores again punished the soldiers' mistake.

Romeo 5 was locked in a battle for survival. Everyone was focused on his job. None of them felt fear now. They felt no pain, no thirst, no anger, and no emotion of any kind. Time seemed to slow. They were fighting for their lives, and they wasted nothing on anything else. Bensen was aware only of the things he needed to do to get his team out. It seemed to him that he was watching this contact from above. He did not hear anything except the radio. Chavez was coolly picking off targets, Sigler, unburdened with a ruck, could move quickly and used that to good advantage. Grenades were still available and the team used some of their supply. After the initial surge, the NVA stopped the assault on the team.

The silence was nearly as loud as the battle. Bensen knew it was likely their last chance to get out. They still had most of their grenades and two white phosphorous grenades. "Willie Pete" could be an effective weapon if you could use it. It was too dense here to throw one of them. They were low on ammo, but they had enough if they got out soon. Anderson filled all four canteens from his four-quart, punched a hole in it and left it on the ground. Everyone drank as much as they could. Bensen had less than two quarts left. After that the team was out of water. The only real advantage the Rangers had was that their exact location was still unknown to the NVA. It was no small thing.

The gunships were back on station and firing at anything they could see on the ground. They were beginning to run low on ammunition and fuel. There were more on the way. The slicks had fifteen minutes of fuel left. Bensen had very little time and he had to get the team out now! He moved the team a few meters into the trees away from the LZ and had the gunships work the extraction area with anything they had left. Mallory was now in a LOACH and could direct the slicks. The artillery was ready to pound the whole area as soon as the choppers cleared the LZ. Bensen and the aircrews knew that this was an ideal setup to shoot down a slick, but they had no choice.

The last gun runs were made and the team was ready to extract. The new guns were on station and ready to cover the slicks. The team moved just outside of the trees and Bensen threw purple smoke.

"Romeo 5 – Gambler 23, we have goofy grape."

"Gambler 23 — Romeo 5, I confirm."

Before he finished his transmission, green smoke popped on the far side of the LZ.

"Gambler 23, Romeo 5, I am not the green smoke!"

In seconds the gun ships were attacking the area around the green smoke grenade. Bensen had them work all around him now.

"Romeo 5 — Blackjack 32, we are about two minutes out, we will be approaching from the south."

"Blackjack 32, roger that, we will all board from the right side of the aircraft. Be advised we have bad guys on three sides. Expect small arms from the ridgeline, your 12 o'clock and the low side of the LZ." The team could now hear the chopper.

No one on the team would ever really know what happened next. Bensen saw a flash and felt himself being lifted into the air. It appeared to happen in slow motion. He was slammed into the ground and saw his team disappear in a cloud of dirt. They reappeared again in seconds. Anderson flashed the thumbs up sign and Chavez did the same. Sigler was stunned, but was checking his weapon. Bensen grabbed his handset and tried to speak. He could not. He could not breathe. He pointed to Anderson and his handset. Anderson was now the TL. Bensen was trying to get his breath back, but there was no time to waste. Anderson had the extraction. The slick was on final, when Bensen threw another smoke. This time his was the only one. Sigler and Chavez were throwing grenades into the trees behind the team. Anderson had the Cobras work the trees behind the team again. Sigler now turned to his TL and helped him to his feet.

Bensen was furious! He was sure he was not hurt, but he could not talk or hear a thing. His Car-15 was useless and now so was he. He was now nothing more than a spectator in the final moments of the extraction. Anderson was on lead now. The Huey came over the trees and the Blackjack on the nose was not yet visible. The nose was high now in the flare. The nose lowered and Bensen could see the pilot fighting to get the ship on the ground. The ace appeared as the pilot completed the controlled crash that was the final approach. The team was now firing their M-16s into the tree line and running to the bird.

Chavez was on first, then Bensen, Sigler and then Anderson. Anderson landed on top of the other LRRPs, and screamed, "Go!" It wasn't necessary; the door gunners had already counted the team and were screaming as well. The pilot pulled pitch and rotated the machine forward, climbing out of the LZ.

The turbine engine screamed as the pilots pulled maximum pitch and applied maximum power. The door gunners were firing their M-60s at the tree lines on either side of the LZ. The first thing a team leader did after he boarded the chopper was to count his men. Both the TL and ATL had already counted four men. Both men were checking to see that weapons were on safe and grenades were secure. Bensen saw a loose grenade on Sigler's web gear, and in frustration grabbed it, wishing he could throw it out of the machine onto the NVA below. Popping a spoon on a grenade inside a Huey was a no-no, so he had Sigler secure the grenade.

Lieutenant Mallory was still on board the LOACH, so Lieutenant Davidson had manned the extraction ship. He was now at the side of the TL, checking on both Sigler and the team leader. Sigler had started to gather himself and seemed to be only slightly the worse for his experience. He was drinking water from one of the door gunner's canteens. There was blood running down the side of his face. He had a cut in the hairline above his right eye.

The concern was more for Bensen than anyone else.

"Are you okay?" asked Davidson.

Bensen could read his lips, but could not hear him. He was breathing more normally now. "I think so, I need a drink."

Davidson handed him a canteen and he drank deeply. The water was clean, cool and had no halizone taste. He drank more. As quickly as he had taken the water in, it all came back out, covering the young officer's boots! The impact of the explosion, the lack of water, and the heat combined to humiliate the LRRP team leader. Andersen knew it was not really funny, but could not contain his laughter. The lieutenant was only a little kinder. All four of the men were filthy. They were soaked in sweat, covered with dirt and smoke from their weapons, and now their TL had puked on them. The Huey had leveled off now and was flying in a more normal manner when Andersen had the team clear weapons. It was the TL's responsibility, and he had been the TL since the explosion. He had not yet looked to his own needs.

A team leader was usually the last to remove his pack in an extraction. After checking on all of his team, the new TL relaxed and leaned back, slipping the straps off his shoulders. A bloody spot appeared on the right side of his chest. It was checked quickly. It did not appear to be a major wound, a small piece of shrapnel, perhaps from one of the team's own grenades. It was lodged in the muscle in his chest. It would be painful later, but now he felt nothing.

Sigler's wound seemed minor as well. Chavez was battered like the other men, but otherwise he was fine. Lt. was now on the radio, confirming that the team was out, accounted for and suffering only minor wounds. Lt. Mallory was now involved with Romeo 11. They had reported a large NVA unit in their AO, and were concerned about their extraction LZ being watched. Lt. Davidson had Romeo 5 for now.

As his ability to breath returned, Bensen regained his ability to focus on his team. He looked over the equipment and told each man to drink from his canteen. Only Bensen and Chavez had any water, and they had only a few swallows. The team had three fragmentation grenades and one white phosphorous. They had no more than eight full magazines of ammunition between them. Sigler was missing a white phosphorous grenade, apparently lost in the last moments of the contact. For the first time in several hours, the men felt fear. A Willie Pete was a fearful weapon, not one you wanted to be near when it went off. Only one radio was functional, Bensen's handset was shattered and the Car-15 that he carried was useless. Sigler's M-16 had jammed when he tried to clear it. The two men responsible for the team looked at each other and knew that they had come very close to losing everyone. Another two or three minutes and they might not have made it out.

The chopper banked to the left and started to lose altitude. It was far too soon for them to be at An Khe, they were going onto LZ Banister. Only after they had landed did the team realize that one of the door gunners and the pilot had been hit during the extraction. The ship's radio had been hit and several warning lights blinked on the instrument panel. Getting the ship on the ground was a necessity. Like the team, none of the crew had life-threatening injuries. The door gunner would be going home and the pilot would fly again, but not for another year. The Huey settled onto the makeshift pad, creating a cloud of dust.

The LRRPS tried to thank the crew, but the medics on Banister were treating everyone and were not interested in a lot of talking. Someone brought water to the men and they drank their fill. Line units had water in large rubber containers. It was very warm, and tasted of rubber, but it was pure refreshment for the dehydrated men. Anderson did a quick debriefing at the TOC on Banister. The LRRPs problem now became the problem of some line unit. The 1/10 Cav reactionary force was probably going to be catching hell very soon. Romeo 5 was done with the situation. A medivac Huey came to pick up the wounded gunner and pilot, and a second Huey brought in a repair crew to check out the broken extraction ship.

Anderson had taken control of the team and Chavez was working as ATL. The new TL was called to brief "Green River 6" on the area that they had just left. Chavez made sure weapons were safe and clean enough to function, several grunts took care of Bensen's and Sigler's equipment. Both men were improved, but needed more time to recover. Bensen was getting his hearing and voice back. Sigler was recovering from the beginnings of heat exhaustion. The aircrew was gone and the Rangers had collapsed in the shade of a poncho tent. They were the source of considerable interest among the line troops. Several made it a point to walk by the bedraggled men, staring. Davidson tried to discourage it, but to little effect. On any other day, the Rangers would have reveled in the fact that "line doggies" were so impressed. Today, they did not notice. Choppers were not available now while Romeo 11 was being extracted. Once they were safely out, Romeo 5 would be flown back to An Khe.

The adrenaline had started to wear off and the men were beginning to feel the effects of the day. They boarded the chopper on Banister for the forty-five-minute ride to the Golf Course. Within a few minutes, they were all sleeping. When the team landed, they were met by the First Sergeant and several LRRPs on stand down. The debriefing on Banister was enough for Higher, at least for now. The equipment and weapons were taken by the other LRRPS to be cleaned and turned in. The CO would meet them later. The team went to the shower area to clean up. The water was only warm, but they didn't notice. They put clean fatigues on and then went to the mess hall. They needed water and food, but none of them could eat much. There was a great deal of talk about the mission. To hear them tell it, it was a bit of a lark, a grand adventure. The bravado was thick, but the men were rapidly losing the battle with fatigue. They all needed to sleep now. They fell into their bunks and were asleep in minutes.

A K Company team at the Golf Course, possibly listening to a contact on the radio, L to R, unk, unk John Brashears and Mike Smith.

Ten hours later, Bensen was the first to awaken. He discovered that he could hardly move. He was not alone. The physical beating that they had taken would now be felt to its fullest. They ate again, more urgently this time. They poured tea, water, milk, or lemonade into their bodies. They returned to the cots and slept again. This pattern was repeated several times over the next twenty-four hours. Chavez, the strongest of the four men, was the first to regain the desire to do anything but sleep. Sigler was so beaten up from his fall and the explosion that he would forego his normal stand down routine and stay in the company area to sleep. He left only to see the medic. Bensen and Andersen spent most of the time talking. They critiqued the mission as they always did. There was plenty of opportunity to recount the events of the last day in the bush, but neither man had any enthusiasm for it. Romeo 5 was given an additional forty-eight hours of stand down. Bensen and Andersen sensed that they might have pulled their last mission together.

The two men were called to the 1st Sergeant's office after morning chow. They did not have to be told what it was about, there was really only one reason, and it meant only one thing. Romeo 5 as they knew it was no more. Bensen and Sigler would stay on Romeo 5 and two new men would join them. Sgt Stevens was the new ATL. He was a Ranger School graduate with three missions on another team. Yost was new to the company but had been to Recondo School for LRRP training. Anderson would get Romeo 9, replacing the TL who was scheduled to go home in a few weeks. He would have Chavez as his ATL. Romeo 9's point man would stay on and a new Recondo graduate named Taylor would fill out the team. Both teams would get another day of stand down to prepare themselves for a mission.

One day later, the two friends were in the Brigade TOC for a mission briefing. Both men saw the maps and smiled. K Company was giving them at least one mission to get to know the new teams. No mission was ever easy or safe, but these were better than many.

Bensen and Anderson left the briefing and shook hands. Bensen knew his friend was ready and he knew Chavez was as good as anyone in the company. He had no doubt that they would succeed. He thought his new team would be okay as well, but the nagging reality of the risk they took never left him. There was no longer any regret, there was not time for that now. They had a mission to prepare for. They would pull this mission and in five days both teams would be back in Base Area 266. The war and the Army waited for no one.

Anderson would have his first contact as a team leader on that mission and Bensen would have his last contact mission in the same area three weeks later. Forty years later, it would seem impossible to them, but for now it was just the way things were, normal life for a LRRP in the Highlands of Vietnam.

CHAPTER 52

There But for the Grace of God

A t every Ranger reunion, I look around and see men who could have been me. I could have been one of them. Every one of us wonders why we were spared and others were not. There seemed to be neither rhyme nor reason to the casualties. It is probably true that errors caused casualties, but it cannot be said that those mistakes always caused someone to get hurt or killed. Some of us made the same mistakes and paid no price!

After a particularly frustrating mission near the "hair pin" on QL 19, I boarded a chopper with my weapon loaded and the safety off. The weapon was pointed directly at the pilot! I got away with that, but others did not. Accidentally discharging a weapon could and did cause casualties. I was spared this pain, while others were not. "There but for the grace of God go I."

While trying to deliver a radio to a team on LZ Snipe, I was flat on my belly on the floor of the bird as it hovered over the tiny LZ. A fellow Ranger was sitting beside me, with his feet hanging out the door. I was forced to extend myself as far out of the door as possible to lower the radio to the team on the ground. My head and the other man's feet were just inches apart. LZ Snipe was named for the sniper who popped off rounds at anything on the LZ. He took this opportunity to shoot at us. Who he was shooting at remains a question, who he hit does not. The foot just a few inches from my head took a round. If my memory is correct, the career of a promising young baseball player ended that day. "There but for the grace of God go I."

Perhaps the most dangerous thing that a LRRP team could do was to use an LZ multiple times on the same mission. Particularly dangerous was the use of an insertion LZ as the extraction point on the same mission. It was not always possible to avoid this, and I was forced to do it several times. In each case, the team was pulled without incident. There were other teams who were not as fortunate. I know it happened to two other teams and both teams suffered casualties. "There but for the grace of God go I."

On a heavy ambush mission late in my tour, I was shown the capricious nature of war. Two teams made up the ambush unit. I was doing a check mission for one of the team leaders. We were stopped while one TL looked over a potential ambush site. The rest of us were the security element. I was prone, not more than ten feet from the other TL. A single VC suddenly appeared on the trail not more than thirty feet from us! He and the other Ranger fired at each other. Both men emptied a magazine at each other and missed. All of the rounds from the AK-47 hit between the TL and me, and missed us both. They were close enough to throw dirt and leaves onto my body. Clearly mistakes were made for the VC to get that close, but I paid no price. This kind of close contact was very often fatal. "There but for the grace of God go I."

Ranger teams and bunkers did not mix well. The teams were very good at personal camouflage and it was rare for the NVA or VC to see a team before the team saw them. The NVA, on the other hand was very good at camouflage of bunkers and detecting them was very difficult. A LRRP team that walked into a bunker complex was very likely to suffer badly. My team discovered bunkers three times that I can remember. The first time they were old and the camouflage gave them away before we got too close. In the second instance the bunkers were empty, and in the third case we were able to withdraw without being detected. Three of the most deadly situations we faced, and no price to be paid. Others paid dearly. "There but for the grace of God go I."

Survivor guilt is almost universal among the Vets I know. I think all of us know that when we see a name on the Wall, an artificial limb, a man with a limp, or just a sad face under a Ranger company hat, we know that it could have been us. I know with absolute certainty that "There but for the grace of God go I."

CHAPTER 53

Thoughts on War

———————✦———————

S omeone once wrote that in the last 2,000 years, we could only document eighty-eight years when there was not a war in the earth. War in some form of the other has been around since the beginning of recorded history. I would be willing to bet that if you included murder or fighting as war, you would be hard put to find eighty-eight hours without war. It is who we are, it seems. Scripture teaches that we have wars because we want and cannot have. The implication is that we take by force; kill out of jealousy or to gain revenge. That would seem to be a pretty difficult position to refute.

As humans, we will probably always have wars. I think it not at all surprising that it is so. In fact, I am surprised that it is not more so. There is in us something that keeps us from just going to war all the time. It may be that we can see the fearsome cost, or that we are not willing to face the fear, or our selfish nature keeps us from sacrificing our lives for someone else's desires. I believe that there is a Power that keeps us from destroying ourselves. In us is a spark of the perfect goodness that God put into mankind. It is not always there. It does not always stop the war in us. It does not always bring that better instinct to the fore, but it does sometimes.

We sometimes can make ourselves believe that the war we are in is a "just war," and perhaps that has been true of some of the wars. That might be true of some in the future. But if every war has two sides, and if my side is "just," then your side, by definition, cannot be. And there is the crux of the matter for me. Mankind can, has, and always will be able to rationalize the reasons for going to war, and as long as that is true, we will go to war, over and over and

245

over again. And, as long as someone can convince himself or herself that it is "just," they will be willing to fight.

While we may argue the justness of any war, what is not arguable to me is the cost of war. I read once that if the money spent fighting wars was made into a gold belt, it would be ninety-six feet wide, thirty feet thick and go around the earth one time. The cost in lives lost is unknowable. The cost in human suffering cannot be measured, and often cannot be seen by most people. Physical scars show the wounds to the body, but wounds to the soul and spirit are harder to see. Their cost cannot be measured or even described.

General Eisenhower said that war could reveal the very worst of mankind while revealing the very best of individual men. He understood the dichotomy of war. He understood that at its root and in its practice, war was evil. He knew also that when men are forced into war, some would be able to rise above the evil and do remarkable things. Men can and do place the welfare of fellow soldiers and human beings above their own. We call them heroes. We stand in awe of these selfless individuals who give all for others or for the cause. It is not always so. At times we have attacked the soldier as the evil. We have vilified whole races for the actions of a few. We have lost our way and forgotten our own reasons for "justification." Soldiers, placed in harm's way, sometimes do dreadful things. They sometimes lose all control and commit the most horrific crimes. Sometimes they know it is wrong, sometimes war so warps them that they are convinced it is right. In the end, everyone who is involved in war has to come to terms with what they did.

For some of us, forgiveness and grace is the key to moving on. Most of us find a way to put the experience into some perspective and to use it for some good. Some of us try to bury it, or drown it in some way. Some of us talk about it, many of us don't. Most of us find a way to build a life after our war. However we cope, the survivors of war all have to deal with what has happened to us. We are not allowed the luxury of unthinking rationalization to justify our actions while in our war. At best, the healing takes a very long time. At worst, it never happens. We may at some point see our war in a more civilized light, and it will not be pretty. We will struggle to make sense of it all and at some point we will make some peace with it.

For me that peace is this: War is evil, it is always evil, and it is always a great evil. Sometimes, it is not the greatest of the evils we face. If I did wrong in my war, I have been forgiven. Since I have been forgiven, I need to share that forgiveness. It is the people who shared my war with me who best know my pain, but it is those who love me best who can help heal my pain.

A QUIET MOMENT AT CAMP RADCLIFFE, JUST BEFORE I LEFT FOR HOME.

Books cited

Reflections: *True Vietnam Combat stories as shared by the Elite LRRPS, LRPS and Rangers of the 4th Infantry Division.* Compiled by Rueben H. Siverling. Copyright June 2008 [Kansas City Digital Press]

Achilles in Vietnam: *Combat Trauma and the Undoing of Character.* Jonathan Shay, MD, PH.D. Scribner, Copyright 1994 ISBN 0-689-12182-2

Inside the VC and NVA: *The Real Story of North Vietnam's Armed Forces.* Michael Lee Lanning. Ballantine Press, Copyright 1992 ISBN 0-449-90716-3

About the Author

———————❖———————

Dave Bristol is a retired high school math teacher, principal, and coach. He is married and has four children and four grandchildren. He committed his life to the Lord while in Advanced Infantry Training. He is a graduate of the U.S. Army Ranger School, Jump School and the NCO Academy. He served in the Central Highlands of Vietnam, from September 1969, to June of 1970, with K Company 75th Infantry Rangers as a Long Range Reconnaissance (LRRP) team leader. He lives with his wife, Janet, in the mountains of Colorado. This is his first effort at formally writing about his experiences in Vietnam.

Endorsements:

———————❖———————

I personally served with Dave on three teams and twenty missions as part of K/75th Airborne Rangers. Dave was a Ranger Qualified Staff Sergeant when he came in country and volunteered for the Rangers or LRRPs as we liked to be called. Even with all of his state side training he was a green as I was. We trained under SSgt Rick Williams, team leader of Romeo 2, who we thought was one of the best, if not the best team leader in the country. We made mistakes on our first missions, but it did not take long for us to form a bond that would last during our tour in Vietnam and for forty-five years after! He recalls that I saved his life twice, but I can't count the times he saved us with his leadership and knowledge. He was one of those team leaders who always got it done right and brought his men home. He is my friend, mentor and a brother until the day we die.

Bob White
K Company 75th Infantry Ranger

The first thing that comes to mind is "been there done that," because I was there on several of these missions with David. Historians tell us now that we carried out the most dangerous missions in Vietnam. Most of these missions were only four-man teams, deep in enemy territory, a price on our heads and sometimes up against hunter-killer teams specifically trained to find us. In a contact we were usually outnumbered. The fifty-two names on the K Company list of Killed In Action attest to the danger and the price that was paid. David captures the essence of the constant struggle of a team leader to carry out the mission, try to think of every possible move an enemy might make and if necessary give his all to protect his brothers.

Roger Crunk
K Company 75th Infantry Rangers

Glossary

❖

AO: Area of Operation, usually an area about 2,000 to 3,000 meters square for LRRP/Ranger teams.

APC: Armored Personnel Carrier, a tracked vehicle used to carry troops, supplies and light weapons

Arc light: A B-52 bombing attack.

Arty: Slang for artillery

ATL: Assistant Team Leader

Azimuth: A compass direction. North would be 0 degrees, south 180. These were reported as viewed from the team's location toward the target location.

Back azimuth: A compass direction 180 degrees different from the azimuth reading. These were reported as the direction from the target to the team.

Base Camp Commando: Anyone not out in the field fighting, but especially someone who talked like they were.

BDA: Bomb or battle damage assessment. Teams were assigned missions in an area after artillery or bombing attack to report on the effectiveness of the attacks. These were very unpopular and often dangerous missions.

Black Jack: This was the call sign of the transport helicopters commonly used by K Company teams. These were used to identify specific aircraft.

Blooper: M-79 grenade launcher.

Blue line: A stream or river on a map. They were always drawn in blue.

Break Squelch: the PRC-25 radio always broadcast a small amount of static called squelch. When the microphone was keyed, this sound stopped. This quirk in the radios was used to respond to simple questions, with one breaking of squelch meaning no, and two meaning yes. It was a completely silent way to respond if that was needed.

BUFF: Slang term for the B-52 bombers.

Bug Juice: Insect repellent, 100 percent DEET.

Bush: The slang term for any area outside of the larger bases.

Cammo: Slang for camouflage.

C-rations: Canned field rations know as C-rats or simply Cs.

C-4: Composition 4, a commonly used plastic explosive.

CAR-15: A folding stock model of the M-16 carried by team leaders. They were highly prized and often handed down to a new team leader when someone left the company.

Charley: The name for the Viet Cong derived from the phonetic alphabet—Victor Charley. Sometimes Charles or Sir Charles was used, adding a grudging note of respect.

CIB: Combat Infantryman's Badge, awarded only to infantrymen who had been in actual combat. It was often the most prized award LRRPs/Rangers received.

Clacker: The hand-held detonator for a claymore.

Claymore: Command detonated anti-personnel mines used mostly for ambush and night security by LRRPs.

Cobra: special attack helicopter gunships.

Commo: Short for communications, usually a PRC-25 radio for teams in the field.

Contact: The term meant that a team had engaged the enemy and was in an active fight with them.

CP: Command post, the location of the unit's leadership personnel, the location of a unit's command leadership. Usually used only in the field.

Deep penetration: A recon mission at long range and often beyond normal artillery or helicopter support.

Dinks: A somewhat derisive term used to identify any Vietnamese.

Drag: The last man in the line as the team moved in the field.

Duce and a half: A two-and-one-half-ton truck.

E and E: Escape and Evade.

Extraction: Pulling a team out of an area of operation.

FAC: A Forward Air Controller, usually a small Air Force or Army spotter plane.

Fast mover: Jet fighter/bomber. The term was used to differentiate them from other aircraft types.

Firebase: Usually a smaller compound located away from the larger bases with its own artillery and infantry security.

First light: The first time in the morning when the human eye could begin to see light. It was a critical time for teams because it was a common time for an attack to begin.

FNG: An F____ing New Guy, a term for anyone new to Vietnam.

Frag: Slang for fragmentation grenade.

Gambler: The call signs for the gun ships commonly used by K Company teams.

Golf Course: The commonly used name for the heli-port at An Khe. When the 1st Cavalry built the airfield, they did the clearing by hand to keep the grass in place for dust control. Orders were given that the place was to look like a " Golf Course."

Goofy Grape: Slang code for purple smoke grenades.

Green line: The name for the perimeter around Camp Radcliffe at An Khe.

Grunt: Slang term for an infantryman.

Gunship: Helicopters armed to attack rather than carry troops.

H and I: Harassment and Interdiction fire; random artillery fire at suspected areas of enemy movement.

Hawkeye: The term used to designate a planned ambush mission.

HE: Short for high explosive artillery rounds.

Higher: Slang for the next higher-ranking person or unit.

Hip shoot: A temporary firebase, often used for only a few hours.

Hooch: Almost any form of shelter, but especially a temporary shelter.

Hot LZ: Slang signifying that the LZ was being fired upon or the team was in contact on the LZ.

Hump: Slang for infantrymen walking in the field. It probably came from the humped over posture caused by the heavy packs.

Huey: The common name for the UH-1 helicopter. The 1 appeared to be an I to some when the aircraft was introduced and thus the name. It was officially the UH-1 Iroquois.

In country: The common expression for being in Vietnam.

Insertion: Putting a team into an LZ or AO.

Last light: The time in the evening when the human eye could no longer see light.

LAW: Light Anti-tank Weapon, a single shot anti-tank rocket fired from the shoulder.

Lifer: A somewhat derogatory term for anyone who had made or might make the Army a career.

Line Doggie: Infantryman in a line unit.

Line unit: Any infantry other than the LRRPS and Rangers.

LOACH: Light Observation Helicopters.

LRRP: Long-range reconnaissance patrol, the men who pulled these missions, or the freeze-dried rations carried by the teams.

LZ: A landing zone, any place a chopper could land. Sometimes a firebase, i.e., LZ Action.

M-60: The standard machine gun for the Army.

Marking round: A smoke round fired before any high explosive rounds to ensure the location of the team.

Med-Evac: Medical Evacuation helicopters, call sign "Dust Off".

November Lima: Slang for night location, from the Phonetic alphabet for NL.

NVA: North Vietnamese Army. This differentiated these regular troops from the VC.

OP Order: An Operation order, detailed information on a mission being assigned. This was usually a statement of the actual task to be accomplished, but at the team level it was very specific to the equipment, and other material to be carried, and other planning details.

PRC-25: The radio used by all infantry units at the company level or below.

Point: Short for point man, the first man in a formation of soldiers; a dangerous and difficult task, avoided by most. Due to the small numbers on a LRRP team, everyone usually walked point at some time.

QL-19: The regional highway that ran from the coast to the Cambodian border through An Khe and Pleiku. It was the only major east-west road in the 4th Division's area of operation, the main supply route and the focus of many attacks.

R and R: Rest and Recreation, usually about seven days away from the war. Hong Kong, Thailand, Australia and Hawaii were the places most commonly used. Married men went to Hawaii where wives could meet them.

Rally point: A designated location on the ground for team members to go to should they became separated during a mission.

Recondo School: An in country training course for LRRPs and Rangers.

Recon: Slang for reconnaissance.

Red Legs: artillerymen.

Repo depo: Replacement depot, the place where new replacement soldiers were processed into the Division and assigned their units.

Ruck: Slang for Rucksack or the packs that infantrymen carried.

Sapper: These were NVA or VC soldier trained to breach the wire around American installations. They crawled on ground with explosive charges to destroy any available target.

Shack codes: Short for Shackle codes, it was a small card with a system for encoding short messages. It functioned by randomly assigning a letter or number to another letter or number. Each card contained several such lists. A word like Dog might become 8tv, when sent. The receiving station could then un-code the message back to Dog.

Shunt: A safety device on the clacker to prevent accidental detonation of the claymore mines.

Sit Rep: Situation report, a short statement of the team's tactical situation. Negative and green meant "no contact and quiet."

Six: The call sign designation for the commanding officer of a unit. Romeo 6 would be the commander of K Company. It also was used as a short version of your "6 o'clock," meaning your backside or the area behind you.

Slack: Third man in the line of four LRRPS.

Slick: The transport Huey, armed only with two M-60 machine guns.

Smoke: A grenade generating smoke, or an artillery round used to mark the impact area.

Snakes: A term used to designate Cobra gunships from the UH-1 based gunships.

SOP: Standard Operating Procedure.

Spec 4: Specialist 4, the rank of most E-4s in K Company.

Splash: Artillery shells were fired and then a "splash" call given to tell the teams it was about to hit.

Strong point: A defensive position on Highway QL-19, usually occupied by a tank or other armor.

The World: The United States, home.

TL: Team Leader

TOC: Tactical Operations Center. This was where units planned and tracked operations.

Tracks: Slang term for any armored vehicle, but most specifically for armored personnel carriers.

VC: Viet Cong.

Ville: Slang for village.

VR: Visual Recon, the pre-mission flight over an AO to locate LZs and other pertinent information to guide the team after insertion. These were usually at high altitude and done only once to avoid attracting attention to the area.

Willie Pete: White Phosphorous grenade.

Yards: Short for the French term Montagnard, meaning mountain people, the indigenous people of the highlands.

Zero: The usual radio call sign for the team's command center or TOC.

CPSIA information can be obtained at www.ICGtesting.com
Printed in the USA
LVOW09s2237280515

440381LV00016B/322/P